Contemporary West Asia

Politics and Development

Contemporary West Asia

Politics and Development

Edited by

Anwar Alam
Director, Centre for West Asian Studies,
Jamia Millia Islamia, New Delhi

New Century Publications
New Delhi, India

NEW CENTURY PUBLICATIONS
4800/24, Bharat Ram Road,
Ansari Road, Daryaganj,
New Delhi – 110 002 (India)

Tel.: 011-2324 7798, 4358 7398, 6539 6605
Fax: 011-4101 7798
E-mail: indiatax@vsnl.com • info@newcenturypublications.com
www.newcenturypublications.com

Editorial office:
LG–7, Aakarshan Bhawan,
4754-57/23, Ansari Road, Daryaganj,
New Delhi – 110 002

Tel.: 011-4356 0919

First Published: **July 2010**

ISBN: **978-81-7708-247-0**

Published by New Century Publications and printed at Salasar Imaging Systems, New Delhi.

Designs: Patch Creative Unit, New Delhi.

PRINTED IN INDIA

Contents

About the Book

War, conflict and terrorism define the face of contemporary West Asia at popular level. However there are far more other important issues and challenges that are currently troubling the governments of West Asian nations. These include (a) political, economic and social challenges, (b) Islamic militancy, (c) growing unemployment, (d) democratic reforms, (e) human rights, (f) living conditions of expatriates, and (g) urbanization. Added to this list are environmental risks with such dimensions as overfishing, soil and water pollution by petroleum industry, scarcity of fresh water and desertification. This book—containing 11 contributions by scholars in the field—deals with these internal challenges of the region.

About the Editor

Anwar Alam is currently Professor and Director, Centre for West Asian Studies, Jamia Millia Işlamia, New Delhi. He has served as a Lecturer in the Department of Political Science, Aligarh Muslim University (AMU), and Assistant and Associate Professor at the Centre for West Asian and African Studies, School of International Studies, Jawaharlal Nehru University (JNU), New Delhi. He has been awarded the ICSSR Doctoral Fellowship (1991), International Visitor Programme (Islamic) Scholarship, USA, (2002), Indo-French Social Scientist Exchange Programme Fellowship (2003) and Alexandor Von Humboldt Post Doctoral Fellowship (2004-2006). He has been Visiting Fellow at Maison des Sciences de l'Homme (MSH), Paris, France (March-April 2005), Centre for Citizenship and Ethnicity, Department of Sociology, University of Bristol, Bristol, UK (May-June 2005) and at International Institute for the Study of Islam in the Modern World (ISIM), Leiden, Netherlands (July-August 2005). He has authored 3 books, *Religion and State: A Comparative Study of Contemporary Egypt, Iran and Saudi Arabia* (1998); *India and West Asia in the Era of Globalisation* (edited, 2008) and *Iran and Post- 9/11 World Order* (edited, 2009). Besides, he has contributed several articles in national and international referred journals and chapters in edited books. His areas of research interest include International Politics, Political Theory, Religion and Politics, Political Islam, Globalisation and Muslim Society.

Contributors

Jajati K Pattnaik	Associate Professor, Department of Political Science, Indira Gandhi Government College, Tezu, Arunachal Pradesh.
A. Kannan	Lecturer, Department of Public Administration and Development Management, Faculty of Business and Economics, Wollega University, Nekemte, Ethiopia.
Asif Suja	Doctoral Candidate, West Asian Studies Division, School of International Studies, Jawaharlal Nehru University (JNU), New Delhi.
M.V. Bijulal	Lecturer and Chairperson, Centre for West Asian Studies, School of International Relations and Politics, Mahatma Gandhi University, Kottayam, Kerala.
Gazzala Sabana	Doctoral Candidate, Department of West Asian Studies, Aligarh Muslim University, Aligarh.
Kumar Raka	Senior Research Officer, National Disaster Management Authority, Ministry of Home Affairs, Government of India.
Arshi Khan	Associate Professor, Department of Political Science, Aligarh Muslim University, Aligarh.
Vrushal Ghoble	M.Phil. and Ph.D. from Centre for West Asian Studies, Jawaharlal Nehru University (JNU), New Delhi.
Kundan Kumar	Doctoral Candidate, Centre for West Asian Studies, School of International Studies, Jawaharlal Nehru University (JNU), New Delhi.
Fazzur Rahman	M.Phil. and Ph.D. from Centre for West Asian Studies, School of International Studies, Jawaharlal Nehru University (JNU), New Delhi.
Rajeesh Kumar P.P.	Doctoral Candidate, Centre for International Politics, Organization and Disarmament, School of International Studies, Jawaharlal Nehru University (JNU), New Delhi.

Introduction

By Anwar Alam

The Region of West Asia continues to be fulcrum of world politics. Its significance in terms of its geo-strategic, geo-political and geo-economic richness primarily centred on hydrocarbon resources hardly requires any elaboration. It is for these reasons that the region has been hotbed for the global power politics since the beginning of nineteenth century. The discovery of oil in the region in the beginning of twentieth century further intensified the intervention of external powers at unprecedented level in the region. Though the region represents merely two percent of world surface and contains two percent of the world's population, it plays a key role in the world's economic structure on account of its vast hydrocarbon resources. The vast proven reserve of Oil and Natural Gas, the high level of income and consumption and market for investment has made this region a 'highly contested space'. The leading powers of the world seek to influence and control the region as it provides the critical leverage to the respective powers to assert its position in the global power politics. The political history of the region from the period of Pax Britannica to the present day Pax Americana of the region testifies this trend. Following the incident of 9/11 the region has attracted the global scholarship and media attention mainly in terms of rise of Islamic militancy, violation of human rights, Gulf War, institutionalized authoritarianism, atrocities of Israel and plight of Palestinians, Iranian nuclear programme, securitization of region etc. These developments mostly concern the external dimensions of the region. However the global pressure on the region over the years has deeply affected the process of change and development in the region. The collection of articles in this book seeks to highlight the changing internal dimensions of the region.

Contemporary West Asia is facing enormous political,

economic, social and environmental challenges. Islamic militancy, growing unemployment, democratic reform, human rights, living conditions of expatriate, urbanization, overfishing, ground and water pollution by the petroleum industry, the scarcity of freshwater, environmental degradation through warfare, and desertification are among the majors issues confronting the West Asian policymakers. The countries of West Asia witnessed major socio-economic transformation and demographic change including substantial agricultural expansion and industrial development owing to massive commercialization of petroleum products in the aftermath of Second World War period. Nowhere the impacts of oil-driven developments are more pronounced than in the Gulf region. It is probably for this reason that Gulf has attracted the major attention of this book.

Jajati K. Pattnaik in his piece on '*Neo-Liberalism and Development Debates: Contextualizing in Saudi Arabia*' examines the developmental models in the context of Saudi Arabia. Drawing from Foucauldian notion of development he criticizes neo liberal discourse of development as it provides only the macro indicator of evaluating the parameter of the development of the country. As against this the author utilized the framework of human development paradigm to address the question of development in Saudi Arabia. From this point of view the author concludes that while some progress in the field of human development has been made in the Saudi Society they are not sufficient to realize the goal of sustainable development. The author therefore advocates the need of policy shift in the Saudi Arabia that includes vigorous implementation of Saudization of work force, democratic political reform, institutionalization of human rights and gender equality.

A. Kannan in his article on '*The GCC Countries' Response to Desertification*' discusses the nature and impact of the process of desertification in the region and then examines the policy responses of GCC countries to the problem of desertification. In particular the author discusses the measures taken under the UNCCD in detail which include creation of Focal Points, setting up of National Coordination Bodies, formulation of National Action Programmes, establishment of Administrative Institutions and enactment of Legislations. However in view of bureaucratic dysfunctions, lack of centralised databases on desertification issues, inadequate monitoring and assessment, the nature of political process and other factors he concludes that "considering the nature and gravity of the problem, efforts made by the governments in the GCC Countries to combat the developmental problem related to desertification are inadequate and insufficient".

West Asia is notable among the many regions in the world facing increasing shortages of freshwater resources. As people adopt modern consumption patterns, most of West Asian nations find themselves without the soil or water resources that are necessary to approach even minimal self-sufficiency in regard to their food production needs. Governments in this region are wary of dependency on food imports because of the heavy financial burdens they entail and the potential for strategic vulnerability that they imply. Many Arab countries have experienced the 'nation-wide' violent "bread" or "urban riots" in recent years: Egypt, January 1977, 1984, 1986, 1989 ; Morocco, 1981, January 1984; Sudan, March 1985; Algeria, October 1988; Tunisia, 1984, 1986; Jordan, April 1989. In addition to these major events, localized, small scale food riots have been occurring throughout 1990s and even in 2000s in all these countries. They were provoked by austerity measures linked to one form or another of structural adjustments, stabilization, liberalization and privatization programmes resulting in sudden rises in food and fuel prices. National security among West Asian countries thus translates into food security, and food security translates into water security. The extreme scarcity of water in West Asia has caused major economic challenges for many nations and provokes major international conflict in this region. International conflict over water usage stems mainly from the use of riverine water. The Tigris, Euphrates, and Jordan Rivers cross or run along various international borders in this region. The Tigris and Euphrates Rivers both start in Turkey and then flow through Syria and into Iraq. The Jordan River serves as the border between Israel and Syria in the north and Israel and Jordan farther south. The diversion of water from the Jordan River has influenced political conflicts in the region. Israel first built a dam on the Jordan in 1964, retaliatory water projects were begun in Lebanon and Syria in 1965, and Israel attacked the projects, precipitating the 1967 Arab-Israeli War. The ongoing Israeli-Palestinian conflict is further exacerbated by the reliance of Israel on water from outside its original borders. Nearly two-thirds of the water Israel now uses originates in occupied territories such as the West Bank and the Golan Heights. Water is a great complication in the efforts to negotiate an end to Israeli occupation of Palestinian territories.

Asif Suja 's paper on *'Globalisation and Social Change: The Case of United Arab Emirates (UAE)* examines the impact of process of globalization on social and cultural changes in UAE. He analyzed the process of social and cultural change in UAE by examining the changing patterns of kinship and family structure, the role of education, influence of media and the contemporary behavioural norms of people of Emirates. According to him the impact of globalisation on the society of UAE brings forth three important trends. First, consumerism has become the dominant value and digital divide between the emirates, huge number of expatriates in the country and native population is increasing. Second, although the traditional cultural and ethical imperatives such as its religion (Islam) and language (Arabic) remain unchanged, much of the ways of life of the Emiratis have changed towards modernisation. Third, the overwhelming presence of expatriates in UAE has resulted in greater national identity on part of UAE nationals suppressing the traditional tribal strife to a great extent. He further concludes that if the present pace of globalisation continued, it might result in a violent conflict between forces of tradition and forces of modernity.

One of the developmental problems in the region relates to the ongoing process of desertification. Desertification continues to threaten the relatively few agriculturally productive regions of the Fertile Crescent. The largest unbroken expanse of desert sand on Earth, *the Empty Quarter Desert,* is the hottest region of the world. The Empty Quarter lies primarily in Saudi Arabia, at the heart of the Arabian Peninsula. Desert and semi-desert also cover much of the five smaller Gulf Cooperation Council countries (Oman, the United Arab Emirates, Kuwait, Qatar, and Bahrain). Rainfall is scarce in most of West Asia, which puts much of the region's farmland at risk for degradation. In the twentieth century, war and quickly rising human population levels have overstressed many lands, threatening the livelihood of both farmers and shepherds.

Writing from this perspective M.V. Bijulal in his paper on *'Migrant Work and Human Rights in the GCC Countries: Emerging Scenario after Migrant Labour Unrest'* explores the human right conditions in GCC countries in general and reflect upon the emerging trend in this direction particular in the context of migrant labour unrest that took place in 2004. The author concludes that while the governments in the GCC countries have initiated some measures they smack 'tokenism' than a genuine commitment to address the issue of human rights of migrants. In order to effectively improve the condition and status of immigrants in the region the author calls for the shift in the conceptualization of human rights. In the words of author, "From the interactions with the workers it was clear that productive employment, respect and dignity at work place and the security were matter of urgent concern. In general the workers experience showed a crucial non-states area that decided guarantee of rights in all these aspects. This area defines the internal world of the unseen, illegal and inhuman side of the labour arrangement, and which till now is not addressed as a matter of human rights violations. Negotiating this labour arrangement paradox, and bringing it to the location of governance is central concern for the collective state and non-state human rights actions". In addition to this the author calls upon the government of GCC countries to adhere to the norms concerning labour rights that have been laid down in the various international conventions on human rights.

Political changes in the region have been extremely controversial, e.g., the creation of the State of Israel. The development of State of Israel has fundamentally changed the nature of politics in the region. It not only introduced 'the permanent war condition' in the region but also acted as one of the major factors that strangulated the process of democratization in the Arab World and legitimizes the 'securitization of political processes in the region. The democratization deficiency and securitization of political process goes hand in hand in the region. On the other hand the 'collective Arab nation' serves the Israeli political leadership as 'the reason' to unify internally differentiated Israeli society and nation. Given this political scenario a just solution to Palestinians looks bleak in the near future. Notwithstanding this political impasse the discourse on development in contemporary West Asia would be incomplete without the reference to Israel. The state of Israel, while facing the political and economic isolation in the region and other obstacles, demonstrated its resilience not only to survive but managed to emerge as the strongest state in the region: political, economic and military.

It is in the above context that Gazzala Sabana's paper on '*Water Sharing in West Asia: A Case Study of the Euphrates River System*' becomes significant. In her paper she has discussed the nature of river system in the region of West Asia, particularly the Euphrates River System, with special reference to Iraq, Syria and Turkey. She has also highlighted how the issue of access to water resources of Euphrates River has strained the political relations between these three countries. Since economic prosperity of Turkey, Syria and Iraq revolve around the two rivers as they constitute the principal sources of hydropower and agricultural development, she calls for the coordinated effort among the nations of the Arab world to harness the water energy for the purpose of achieving the sustainable development in the region.

Expatriates are another dominant facet of Contemporary West Asia, particularly in the Gulf. They constitute 80 to 90 percent of total work force in the Gulf region. Over the years they have emerged as 'partner' in the development of the region. However despite their imminence contribution to the economic transformation of the region, their 'imagined partnership rights' in terms of access to basic human rights have not been translated into reality. The immigrants, particularly unskilled labourer, continue to suffer from 'brutality of life experiences' in the absence of grant of basic human rights in the Gulf. In fact the human rights violations are rampant in the region. This exposes the 'developmental paradox' in the region: a high level of economic development accompanied by profound lack of sensitivity to the issue of human dignity and rights, particularly related to the immigrants.

Kumar Raka's *'Aspects of Economy and Human Resource Development in Israel'* attempts to examine this dimension of Israeli state and society. According to him, the key to Israeli socio-economic development is the human resources. The human resource development through high economic growth in Israel was mainly facilitated by the three factors: exemplary role of education, better health care services and quality of immigrants. In part, the economic changes were brought about through the increase of population by way of immigration (the human capital and resources brought by the immigrants and their contribution to production and consumption) and the increased economic investments made in Israel from outside the country. He concludes that whether demographic changes generated the economic change or vice-versa, both population size and economic production have increased considerably over time.

As noted in the beginning of this paper every dominant power of the world has attempted to dominate this region for variety of reasons. The process of Americanization of the region that began in the aftermath of Second World War period finally culminated in the physical occupation of Iraq in 2003. The occupation and destruction of Iraq by the United States in post-decolonization period cannot be understood merely in terms of nature of international politics but also exposes the dark side of western liberal modernity. In terms of liberal political theory of state the preservation of sovereign states is considered as one of the major principles of maintaining security, peace and order in different regions of the world. This was clearly violated in the case of Iraq and thus plunged the country in the midst of anarchy, chaos and conflicts for long time to come.

Arshi Khan's paper on '*Situating the Hobbesian State of Iraq in Contemporary International Relations*' raises some of these theoretical implications of US occupation of Iraq. The paper exposes the *illiberality* of Western liberal paradigm of development and provides a detailed account of destruction of life and property of Iraqi society on the pretext of democracy. The author identifies three phases in the systematic destruction of Iraqi state and society. The first phase is the phase of genocidal sanctions of over 12 years which crippled Iraq. Simultaneously, the US-UK coalitions' military actions gradually demolished conventional defense capacity of Iraq. The second phase occurred at the time of brutal invasion of Iraq in March 2003 with the use of all the weapons of mass destruction in major cities with massive media operations resulting in the collapse of the Iraqi State. The third phase of destruction is now going on to germinate all sources of difficulties, despair and damages which could never build a united, lawful, progressive, democratic, manageable and viable state of Iraq.

The historical interaction between Islam and modernity has decisively shaped the ideological spectrum and moorings of the Muslim World, particularly the region of West Asia. The multifaceted interaction between the two has simultaneously given rise to many shades of Islamic movements in many of Muslim nations ranging from Islamic modernism and reformism to Islamic fundamentalism and terrorism, each acquiring the dominant edge vis-a vis others at different period depending upon the specific political, economic and social context. Today it is the Islamic political movements or Political Islam (or pejoratively Islamic fundamentalism and terrorism) that is defining the political face of much of Muslim world, particularly the region of West Asia. The reasons behind the emergence of Islamic political movements are many and complex, the elaboration of which is the outside the scope of this introductory piece. In general, the emergence of Islamic political movements in contemporary West Asia is symptomatic of crisis of modernization model of development that miserably failed to address the issue of material deprivation and social justice, political participation, the plight of Palestine and dominance of western powers in the region. There are four sets of the paper that have reflected on this aspect of contemporary West.

This includes Vrushal Ghoble's *'Oil, Democracy and Terrorism: An Inevitable Nexus in the Gulf'*, Kundan Kumar's *Islamic Responses to the Western Modernity Project: Within and Beyond,* Fazzur Rahman's '*Changing Dynamics of Muslim Brotherhood in Egyptian Politics*' and Rajeesh Kumar P.P.'s *Islamic Resurgence in the Age of Globalization and Democracy: Hamas' Changing Strategies in Palestinian National Movement'*.

Ghoble first highlights the significance of Gulf's oil for world energy security and maintenance of the US domination in the world and then demonstrates the linkage between Oil, Democracy and terrorism in the Gulf region. The linkage is sustained on the one hand by unprecedented level of undue interference of external powers, particularly the United States of America and other Multinational oil companies in the Gulf countries and Islamic oppositions, partly funded by oil driven economy, to the existing monarchical regimes and growing Americanization of the region on the other.

Kumar in his article provides an historical account of Islamic responses to Western modernity project. He does so by examining the responses and engagements of prominent Islamic scholars and leaders-both Arab and non- Arab- to the challenges of Western modernity. Highlighting the plural dimension of Islamic responses as against the monolithic one to the project of Western modernity the author concludes that "in the process of creating an alternate Islamic modernity by way of adapting, re-appropriating, negotiating, contradicting, and defying the Western modernity, Islam has, in consonance with all other faiths and religions, been in the constant struggle to reshape the concept of modernity which is already in crisis today".

Rahman focuses upon the changing dimensions of Muslim Brotherhood in the Egyptian Politics. Muslim Brotherhood founded by Hasan-al-Banna in 1928 in Egypt is the first prototype representative of political Islam in the Muslim world and continues to inspire many Muslims for creating 'Islamic order' in the world. The author has traced the evolution of Muslim Brotherhood and demonstrates how the organization has travelled far from its erstwhile radical thought and strategy to becoming of a moderate Islamic organization (in relative sense) in today's Egypt. As he noted, 'MBH since its participation in Egyptian politics in 1970s had adopted a strategy of adaptation with the existing circumstances and has always worked within the limit of the state institutional and never opted for unconstitutional means to capture the state apparatus'. While tracing this political trajectory of Muslim Brotherhood the author provides a detailed account of its cooperative and conflictual interaction depending upon the contexts with various Egyptian regimes including the current Mubarak regime. All regimes, even while utilizing the service of Muslim Brotherhood for various purposes, feared the oppositional potential of Brotherhood and therefore continue to deny the legal status of a political party. The author has rightly concluded that Muslim Brotherhood over the years has emerged as the principal oppositional forces in Egypt, carved out an independent and exclusive political space for its own and struggling very hard to capture the contested political zone of the state.

Finally, Rajeesh's paper explores the causes of Islamic resurgence in the age of globalization and examines the linkages and debates between Islam and democracy with reference to Hamas, a Palestinian nationalist organization. By analyzing changing political strategies of Hamas in the Palestinian politics which includes its participation in electoral politics the author demonstrates democratic and accommodative aspects of Islam and Islamic movements.

Taken together, the collection of these articles by young scholars provides a good thematic understanding of the various facets of Contemporary West Asia. This introduction would not be complete without acknowledging the contributions and supports that helped in making this book a reality. I am thankful to all individual authors who contributed their piece for this volume. Thanks also to the staff of New Century Publications, New Delhi, who undertook the tedious task of publishing this book.

June 2010 **Anwar Alam**
New Delhi

1

Neo-Liberalism and Development Debates: Contextualizing in Saudi Arabia

Jajati K. Pattnaik

Analyzing Neo-Liberalism and Development Debates

Neo-liberalism envisions free market as well as an open political system, which can effectively handle the crisis of development. This school emphasizes withdrawal of the state from the economic domain on line with the ideological foundations of free market capitalism to realize economic growth and development. The champions of this christen it as 'Development is freedom', while the opponents portray it in terms of 'trickle down theory'. [1] Globalization as the vehicle of this philosophy espouses liberal democracy and integration building policies through diffusion of knowledge and technology stretching de-territorialized economic growth. The driving forces behind this process are transnational corporations and international financial institutions which intended to create a new epoch in international relations with 'harmonious one world'. However, the global capitalism that vigorously shot up from eighties has not brought any significant change in the socio-economic conditions of the developing nations. During the end of the last century in accordance with the World Bank reports, approximately, one fifth of the global population, i.e., 1.2 billion lived in abject poverty with less than one US$ (dollar) per day. [2] The gap between the developed and developing one was widened in spite of the benefits of the global capitalism. Besides causing inequalities, the global capitalistic institutions with their financial supremacy also managed the political elites and served their interests often leading to bad governance and loss of accountability in the delivery system. Legitimate protest to correct the mistakes was viewed as hindrances to the process of development and freedom of people. [3] The neo-liberal development also brought its consumer culture often dominated by the U.S., Europe and Japanese allies. John Agnew and Stewart Corbridge marked that "a new de-territorialized geo-political order-the hegemony of transnational liberalism was emerging" and stated that "a new ideology of market being embedded in and reproduced by a powerful constituency of liberal states, international institutions, and what might be called circuits of capital themselves". [4] The global information infrastructures, a conglomerate of Bertelsmann, CNN, New Corporation, Poly Gram, Sony, Viacom and Universal promoted cultural industry of the west. The world market was gradually thronged with inexorable icons viz. Coca-Cola, McDonald's, Disney, Nike and landscape of Shopping Malls, Sports Stadiums and Branded Restaurants. [5] This new wave of McDonaldization created the thrust for cultural imperialism. [6] Neither the neo-liberal model attained prosperity nor it guaranteed security and stability. The critics are right in denouncing the western countries being hypocrite in their entire approach towards the poor countries. Even if one dissents with this, it is sure that the west seeks to follow its globalization agenda to grab the excessive share of benefits at the cost of the developing world. [7] It poses challenge to local cultures, augments global inequalities and aggravates the conditions of the destitute. In the process, it creates a 'world of winners and losers' a few blooming with prosperity and many sunk into a life of distress. [8]

Responding to the drawbacks of neo-liberal development, alternatives emerged in the discourse of development. The post-development theory, one of those alternatives, is an intellectual offshoot of the Focucauldian intellectual traditions. Drawing its principles from the works of French philosopher Michel Foucault, the post-development theory looks development in the mirror of a discourse. "This theory argues that development constitutes a specific way of thinking about the world, a particular form of knowledge. Development is, in the Foucauldian sense, a particular discourse which does not reflect but actually constructs reality. In doing so, it closes off alternative ways of thinking and so constitutes a form of power". [9] This theory holds that the objective of discourse is to legitimize and transpose the western model over the third world. The third world is not only predisposed to the economic power, but it is also constrained by the 'definitional power of the West'. [10] Development is a benchmark through which the west gauges the non-west. It disciplines differences and establishes the standard norms for the society. The measures of development become the devices for the exercise of power over others. [11] The post-development thinkers view that the third world is categorically objectified and the requirements of the people are externally decided. To find a solution, the post-development Scholar, A Escobar, advocates for defining the term underdevelopment to displace the discourse of development. [12] But a close analysis of the post development paradigm shows that it does not provide any specific framework for studying the problems of contemporary societies.

Realizing the deficiencies of the above paradigms, human development paradigm also surfaced as an alternative to the neo-liberal development. Amartya Sen's work provides a broader framework to Mahbub Ul Haq's human development paradigm which is defined as "enlarging peoples choices and enhancing their capabilities." [13] Amartya Sen interprets development in terms of capability approach and defines it 'as a process of expanding the real freedoms that people enjoy'. [14] He observes that growth of gross national product, technological progress and industrialization etc. may be the important denominators for realizing the freedom in a society, but they are not the end of development. The real development hinges upon the other determinants such as freedom for participation in public discussion, political and civil rights, provision for educational and health facilities, elimination of poverty, tyranny, social deprivation, intolerance and unrestrained power of the repressive states. [15] He holds that expansion of freedom is viewed as both the means and the end of development which can be called as constitutive as well as instrumental role of freedom in development. The constitutive role is the substantive freedom which is pertained to the enrichment of human life. The instrumental role is dealt with the presence of civil and political rights, economic and social opportunities and protective securities. [16] All of them contribute to the expansion of human freedom. Haq interprets development in the context of expanding people's choices. [17] He finds that the growth deals with the rise in individual income whereas development induces political, social and cultural aspects. He further observes that a link between the growth and human lives is to be established through public policy. This can be achieved by restructuring the economic as well as political power and having sweeping land reforms, progressive tax system, and provision of basic social services to the deprived sections, equality of opportunity and political and cultural freedom. [18] Haq says "In principle, these choices can be infinite and can change over time. People often value achievements that do not show up at all, or not immediately, in income or growth figures: greater access to knowledge, better nutrition and health services, more secure livelihoods, security against crime and physical violence, satisfying leisure hours, political and cultural freedoms and sense of participation in community activities. The objective of development is to create an enabling environment for people to enjoy long, healthy and creative lives." [19] So, this study indicates that the development is a holistic concept which is to be measured not only in terms of economic growth but also in the realization of political, social and cultural aspects for all round development.

The Arab Human Development Report (AHDR) began in 2002 on the basis of philosophical premises of human development paradigm. It viewed that development in the Arab world has undergone changes under the impact of globalization and one witnessed a structural framework characterized by capital market, foreign exchange reserve, information technology and civil society associations. [20] The authors found that the Arab world was confronted with the challenges of deficit in knowledge acquisition, democratic freedom and gender equality, and the redress of the same could lead to human development. They derived that "although Arab countries have made significant strides in more than one area of human development in the last three decades---the predominant characteristic of current Arab reality seem to be the existence of deeply rooted shortcomings in Arab institutional structure (which) are an obstacle to building human development." [21] Later, the successive Arab reports focused upon the hindrances and framed strategies to do away those deficits. Dwelling upon the AHDR (2003), the authors were quite dismayed by the state of acquisition, diffusion and production of knowledge in the Arab world. The report took serious note of the social, economic, political and institutional bottlenecks for the diffusion of knowledge in the Arab world. It concluded with 'strategic vision' for building up a knowledge society structured upon the five pillars. These are: i) provision for freedom of speech, opinion and assembly with good governance confining to the law of the land; ii) extension of high quality education for all; iii)promotion of science and augmentation of research; iv) move towards knowledge induced production in the Arab socio-economic structures; v) formation and sustenance of an 'Enlightened Arab Knowledge Model' that includes delivery of the true message of religion, promotion of Arabic language and protection of rich Arab cultural heritage; advancement and realization of cultural diversity as well as reciprocation with other cultures. [22] Similarly, the AHDR (2004) acknowledged freedom as key to good governance. It not only incorporated civil and political freedom, but also included freedom from oppression, hunger, disease, ignorance, poverty and fear for achieving development. The report suggested for safeguarding freedom through a set of structures and processes such as broadening people's choices, successful popular participation and representation, institutional reforms through separation of powers, free and fair election through regular or periodic mode, accountability to the people and independent judicial system for protecting the rule of law. [23] The AHDR (2005) dealt with the rise of women in the Arab world and viewed it as a key parameter of human development. The authors interpreted the empowerment in terms of providing equal opportunities between men and women for realizing human potentialities, safeguarding citizenship rights of women vis-à-vis their male counterparts, getting rid of gender discrimination for achieving equality. The strategic vision emerged out of this intellectual introspection sought to address the institutional challenges through two prong approach viz.; 'societal reforms' in the cultural milieu as well as 'societal movement' through the civil society groups for the rise of women in the Arab world. [24] The AHDR (2009) looked into the challenges of human security and defined it as "the liberation of human beings from those intense, extensive, prolonged, and comprehensive threats to which their lives and freedom are vulnerable." [25] The authors noted that the menace was to be restrained to attain human security whereas capability was to be expanded to achieve human development. Amartya Sen termed the former as "down turn with security and the latter as "expansion with equity". [26] The study indicates that the authors of the reports primarily sought to address the deficits of development in line with the thinkers like Amartya Sen and Mahbub Ul Haq. The basic principles of development thought viz.; increasing human capabilities, popular political participation, institutional reforms and societal changes through civil society associations remained the hallmark of this debate. No doubt, the economic growth, a major criterion of neo-liberal development supplements the theory in its comprehensive perspective.

The above indices put in the context of Saudi Arabia would certainly connote how far the kingdom is successful in materializing development in a neo-liberal order. Equally, the Vision 2020 evolved by the Saudi Ministry of Economy and Planning contemplated Saudi Arabia as "a diversified and prosperous economy that guarantees the existence of rewarding job opportunities and higher levels of economic welfare for the Saudi citizens, and provision of education and health care for the population to equip the labor force with adequate skills, in addition to preserving religious values and cultural heritage of the Kingdom." [27] It led stress upon five areas viz.; 'diversification of the economy;' 'development of human resources'; 'expansion of public services to carry out these objectives'; 'promotion of the private sector as a key partner in the implementation of Vision 2020' and 'streamline as well as modernization of the governance structures of the public sector to face the challenges of implementation.' [28] Thus, in the backdrop of this, demography and human resource development; rentier state and economic development; governance structures and political development are to be studied for an in-depth analysis of the subject.

Demography and Human Resource Development

Demography that deals with study of the population is an essential component of development. The population of Saudi Arabia which was 23.6 million in 2005 is estimated to reach 29.3 million in 2015. The average annual growth rate of population which was 3.9 percent during 1975-2005, is projected to come down about 2.1 percent during 2005-2015. [29] The life expectancy at birth, which was 71.6 years during 2000-2005, [30] is estimated to grow about 76.3 years in 2009. [31] The younger generation (0-14 years) that comprised 33 percent of the population in 2008 [32] is projected to reach 38 percent in 2009. [33] Besides this, the strength of the foreign work force also increased in the Kingdom and the international migrants constituted 27.8 percent of the total population in 2008. [34] The rank of Saudi Human Development Index (HDI) which was 75 in 2000 rose to 61 in 2007. Alike, the Gender Development Index (GDI) rank showed upward trend moving from 76 in 2000 to 70 in 2007. [35]

The considerable amount of Saudi dependency upon the foreign workforce exposed the Kingdom's ineffective strategies in the past to indigenize the human resources and its failure to render the Saudi nationals employable in the occupational sectors. Massive rural-urban migration also accentuated the problem. All of them gave rise to labor market contradictions in three sectors, viz. i) Change in the composition of rural-urban population; ii) gap between the tradable and non-tradable sectors and iii) divergence of skills in the labor force. [36]

The first type of contradiction occurred in the agricultural sector. The rapid migration of rural population adversely affected rural sector economy. The agricultural sector faced shortages of the labor because of large-scale migration from rural areas. This led to unemployment or under-employment in cities, and urban bias in the economic policy of the government. So, the government tried to absorb those challenges using government employment as an unemployment benefit substitute. The second type of contradiction occurred when the high proportion of the labor force did enter into manufacturing sector that faced international competition. This ultimately gave to the employment of large labor force in service sector and relatively low proportion in the manufacturing sector. The third type of market contradiction arose in the divergence of skill. This stage was found when in a society too many highly qualified candidates with PhD degrees became unsuitable for the modern industrial needs and led to a state of disguised unemployment. On the other, the society produced too few mechanics failing to satisfy the requirements of industrial sector. This gap between the two streams was responsible for the contradiction in the labor force. [37] The trend remained unabated in the subsequent period. The Saudi Human Development Report 2008 also found this difference between the productivity of education and the technical skill necessitated for the modern industrial concerns which gave rise to structural unemployment in the country. [38]

It is marked that the country is confronted with the dual crisis of external dependency upon the foreign workforce as well as structural unemployment owing to the skill mismatches. So, the Kingdom harped on two prong strategies to seek a detour out of this impasse. The Saudization drive that started during the second development plan got accentuated in the successive plans. Moreover, the Shura Council regulations in 2002 targeted to secure the jobs for the Saudis up to seventy percent by 2007. [39] Further, these policies were also governed by the factors such as expanding employment opportunities in all spheres of the Saudi economy; decreasing the dependency upon the foreign workforce and reinvesting the income to check the flow of the currency towards the expatriates. [40] Similarly, the new labor law announced by the Saudi Government in September 2005 also put limits up to seventy five percent of the jobs for the Saudis in the industrial enterprises. [41] It is anticipated that this increasing policy towards Saudization would reduce the crisis of external dependency upon the expatriates in the long term perspective. The knowledge revolution in the information age has called for structural reforms in the educational system to address the knowledge deficit witnessed in the contemporary societies. Comprehending the problems of human capital in the Kingdom, the Saudi Education Ministry evolved a ten year plan to steer the course of Saudi education for drawing a balance between the traditional and technical education. The plan was based on preserving Islamic values, selecting the flow of information, responding to the requirements of the labor market, preparing the students with knowledge for their future economic endeavor , stressing upon the primacy of skill-oriented learning, focusing education from social perspective and developing the will power of the citizens through awareness. [42] The vision of the Ministry of Education aims at achieving "Engendering of a new generation of male and female youth who embody the Islamic values in their persons, both theoretical as well as practical, are equipped with necessary knowledge, skills, and endowed with the right orientations, capable of responding positively to, and interact with the latest developments, and deal with the latest technological innovations with ease and comfort. They should be able to face international competition both at the scientific as well as technological levels to be able to meaningfully participate in overall growth and development. This is to be achieved through an effective and practical system of education which is capable of discovering the potentials and predispositions, and, create the spirit of action. All this, in an environment of education and training, charged with the spirit of instruction and edification." [43] Blending a balance between the tradition and modernism, the vision of the ministry seems to realize the mark of human resource development in the Kingdom.

It is to be observed in the above context how far the policies announced by the Saudi Government are being implemented for harnessing the human capital to resolve the challenges of knowledge deficit in the Kingdom. Here also the question arises whether the Saudis often motivated by patriarchy and strong Bedouin traditions are ready to accommodate themselves with the changes or not. In the background of this, the state, civil society and media are to be actively engaged in creating awareness about the dividends of two prong approaches for human resource development in the Kingdom.

Rentier State and Economic Development

Rentier economy of Saudi Arabia characterized by the principles of accumulation and legitimization is undergoing transformation in the contemporary era of globalization. The changes that transpire in the system would have tremendous impact upon the trajectory of development process in the economic sphere. The state prolonged its activities for capital accumulation gaining legitimacy from the people. But accumulation and legitimization are not always tantamount; rather they are incongruous to each other. [44] The state always strives to adopt the model that includes both the elements. James O' Conner says "the state needs to devise a fiscal regime which allows it to pursue either of the objectives because a state that openly uses its coercive force to help one class accumulate capital at the expanses of other classes loses its legitimacy and hence undermines support. But a state that ignores the necessity of assisting the process of capital accumulation risks drying up the source of its own power, the economics surplus production capacity and the taxes drawn from the surplus." [45] The nature of the sate expenditure is two fold in a rentier economy. It adds to the course of accumulation raising productivity in labor, adds to profit by funding industrial expansion and harnesses social consumption decreasing the cost of production. It also legitimizes through public investment to bring synchronization between labor and capital. State finance plays dominant role in rentier economy. The rent constitutes the main source of the revenue. The relationship between the state and society becomes very typical in the rentier economy. The policy of the state is governed by certain primary motives. These are: i) rendering welfare services. ii) Setting up new private sector and bureaucracy reliant on state support. iii) Strengthening state power. When the rentier state performs those functions, it involuntarily concedes legitimacy to the regime. The state sponsored welfare activities automatically create different type of political environment wherein the state authority assumes supremacy over social distribution. [46] And economic interest is served individually rather collectively. "The development of clan consciousness, profession for trade union organization is retarded – society atomized into individual rent and reward seekers and development of the autonomous institutions of civil society is severely stunted." [47] Consequently, the rentier state faces several fiscal crises. The volume of expenditure exceeds to the volume of revenue. The reduction of expenditure leads to the tapering of the economy. The rationalization of it gives rise to substantial reduction of welfare service, patronage and streamlining of the security sector. [48]

The economic boom in the seventies due to the steep hike of oil prices pushed the Saudi authorities to spend the 'oil rent' in the infrastructural developmental projects and subsidized services providing free education and health care in the Kingdom. Subsequently, the regime accorded 'functional' legitimacy to it drawing sustenance from the distributive–welfare nature of the state. [49] However, the swift fall of oil prices in the recent years has brought fresh challenges before the Kingdom. To seek a detour out of this, not only did the kingdom embark on the path of diversifying the economy but also it set the goal of achieving higher growth rate for sustainable development in future. The eighth development plan sought to augment the share of non-oil GDP from 24.9 in 2004 to 27.4 in 2024 with an annual average growth rate of 7.1 percent in the coming years. Correspondingly, the plan targeted to increase the share of industrial sector to GDP from 19.6 in 2004 to 20.4 in 2024 having an annual average growth of 7.8 percent during the same period. Alike, the service sector would raise its share to the GDP from 27.4 in 2004 to 41.9 in 2024 registering an average growth rate of 8.8 percent in the ensuing decades. [50] To facilitate the same, the Kingdom acceded to the World Trade Organization on December 11, 2005 with the obligations such as uniform application of WTO rules in the entire country; endorsement of trade documents bringing them at par with the WTO rules; removal of non-traffic measures possessing the right to limit the import and export of goods and services, execution of the agreements on intellectual property rights, technical obstacles to trade and implementation of sanitary initiatives; exclusion of export subsidies on the agricultural items; acquiescence to the foreign insurance companies and commercial banks to setup branches in the Kingdom and assent for seventy percent foreign equity in the telecommunication sector along with the other provisions to attain the necessary objectives. [51] Looking into the positive aspects of WTO accession, Fawaz Al-Alamy, Saudi Deputy Minister of Commerce and Industry for technical affairs observed that "WTO is an advantage to the Saudi economy because most of the world economic activities in all aspects take place within the economies of member countries." [52] He further said "Foreign direct investments (FDI) are a key source for increasing the Kingdom's GDP growth rate, and the WTO agreements will help to increase the flow of FDI into the Kingdom." [53] Much to the chagrin of Saudi policy makers, the global economic meltdown posed new challenges to the Kingdom. The economy that foresaw higher growth rate witnessed slow growth, reduced revenue, raising inflation and scant presence of domestic and foreign institutional investors. [54] It is also assumed that the crisis would further affect the flow of credit into the Kingdom and the prospect of major projects funded by the international financial institutions. [55] Unless the Kingdom is geared with effective policies, it would be tricky on the part of the Saudi authorities to carry forward the reform process. Here it is to be noticed how far the State becomes successful in thwarting the challenges and thereby upholds an equilibrium between economic growth, diversification and development in future.

Governance and Political Development

Structures of governance have vital role in enduring political development and guaranteeing peoples' empowerment. Saudi Arabia having a monarchical system has initiated reforms in the governance mechanisms to mark political development. The study of legislative, executive and judicial branches of the government along with the civil society and human rights conditions in this sense would indicate how far the Kingdom is successful in achieving governance reforms and development.

The role of the legislature is significant in a participatory political system. Coming to the structural form of the Saudi legislature, it was discerned that in the preliminary stage, Majlis served as informal legislative body in place of a formal law making institution. [56] However, it did not constitute an effective channel of communication whereby the policies of the state could be significantly oriented to address the needs of the people. The founder of Saudi Arabia, King Abdul Aziz and his successors Saud, Faisal and Khalid, could not institutionalize any formal legislative setup in the country. However, the growing Islamic opposition and demands for political reforms during the Gulf war (1990-1991) drove the King Fahd to announce Basic System of Rules on March 1, 1992 through which Majlis Al-Shura (Consultative Council) emerged as an appointed body in December 1993.The Basic System assigns the Consultative Council having the responsibility to debate the policies of the government and propose draft regulations to the King. The Consultative Council is to (i) 'express opinions on the general policy of the state (Article 15); (ii) 'propose amendment in an executive law' (Article 23); (iii) 'study international laws, charter treaties, agreements and make appropriate suggestions regarding them' (Article 15); (iv) 'interpret regulations' (Article 15); (v) 'discuss the annual reports submitted by the ministry and other government bodies and make appropriate suggestions regarding them' (Article 15); and (vi) 'question the ministers and other government officials' (Article 22). [57] At present, the Consultative Council is entrusted with the functions which were hitherto exercised by the Council of

Ministers. Generally, the Consultative Council does not by pass the Council of Ministers without the consent of the King .The actions of the Ministries are to be approved by the Consultative Council. Otherwise, they are to be 'referred back to the King'. [58] But its power to evaluate the functioning of the Council of Ministers is an important development in the matrix of Saudi political system.

It is derived from the above study that a nominated legislative body operates in place of a democratically elected institution that lacks the capacity of articulating as well as aggregating the genuine demands of the people in the process of convergence of interests. The instruments of political participation e.g. universal adult suffrage, competitive politics, multi party system, regular or periodic elections, and accountability to the people are absent in the system, and it brings authoritarianism in Saudi politics.

The role of the executive is highly important in the process of policy implementation. A synoptic look of the executive shows that Saudi Arabia is a Monarchical system which neither reflects the features of parliamentary Government nor the Presidential one. The Monarch as the Tribal Sheikh, Religious Imam and Temporal Malik rules the nation with the Council of Ministry. [59] He directs the execution of 'Shari'ah, general policies of the state and protection and defense of the country' (Article55).The King heads the Council of Ministers and the later assists him in discharging his functions according to the provisions of law. The Council of Ministers sets the privilege of the council with regard to 'internal and external affairs, organization and co-ordination between government bodies' (Article 56). The Monarch has the right to 'appoint and relieve the deputies of the Prime Minister and members of the Council of Ministers through Royal Decree' and they are collectively responsible to him for the execution of shari'ah and the policy of the country. The King also possesses the power to 'dissolve and reorganize the Council of Ministers.' (Article 57) [60]

It is derived that the Monarch is the final authority for the implementation of Shari'ah and the policy of the state being the Head of the Council of Ministers. No doubt, with the initiation of the Consultative Council in 1993, the role of the Council of Ministry got reduced on a number of matters. At present, the Consultative Council expresses opinion on the general policy of the state, proposes amendments in executive laws, treaties, question the ministers and thereby acts as a regulator over the executive. Nevertheless, the ultimate authority for the formation of Consultative Council as well as the Council of Ministry lies with the King and in the process he reins wielding considerable amount of authority in him.

The judiciary is imperative for delivering justice and implementing the rule of law. Generally, it is observed that in authoritarian political systems, it acts a pawn in the hands of the executive. The justice is either manipulated or delivered to retain the hegemony of the ruling clique. Constitutionally described, Saudi judiciary is quite independent and supposed to dispense justice in a neutral mode. The Saudi Basic Law defines the following provisions regarding the operational mechanism of judicial system. The judiciary is an independent organ of the government and the judges are subject to no one 'excepting in the case of Islamic Shari'ah' (Article 46); The citizens and residents are 'guaranteed the right to litigation on an equal basis' (Article 47); The courts shall apply the 'rules of the Islamic Shari'ah' mentioned in the Holy Quran and the Sunnah, and 'statutes decreed by the Ruler' in conformity with the Holy Quran and the Sunnah (Article 48). The courts shall 'arbitrate in all disputes and crimes' considering the provisions of Article 53(Article 49). The King or his deputized person is accountable for 'the implementation of judicial ruling' (Article 50); The authorities shall define the structure of the 'Higher Council of Justice, seniority of the courts and their prerogatives', (Article 51). The appointment and the termination of the judges are made by 'Royal Decree through a 'proposal from the Higher Council of Justice in accordance with the provisions of the law.' (Article 52) [61]

Albeit, a critical study denotes that neither does the Basic Law connote any major change in the organization of the courts nor does it ensure the independence of judges through adequate constitutional safeguards. Hence, the Saudi King Abdullah declared judicial reforms in 2007 for instituting new Supreme Court and Appeal courts substituting the old Judiciary council. [62] Hitherto, the reforms hang as enigma in Saudi politics. [63] So the crucial point is that the Saudi judiciary should implement necessary reforms to safeguard human rights, and guarantee its independence through the principle of separation of powers.

Civil society institutions seek to converge upon the interest of the public based on social interface and limit the coercive nature of the state paving the way for precision and conscientiousness in the system. [64] It is observed that with the appearance of global non-governmental organizations such as Friends of Earth, International Save the Children Alliance, Transparency International and World Faith Development Dialogues in Saudi Arabia, the space for civil society associations is gradually gaining ground at the grass root stage. The patterns of these institutions in the form of Every Saudi Stand Up; Million Votes for Reduced Prices; Saudi Debate Society; Jeddah, the Good, the Bad and the Ugly; Raise Jeddah; and Women Driving in Saudi Arabia are witnessed at the local level to address the needs of the neighborhoods. [65]

Likewise, national level civil society institutions such as Council of Saudi Chamber of Commerce and Industry, National Society for Human Rights and Independent Journalists Associations etc. operate in the system to represent their respective interests. [66] Besides, national dialogue sessions convened by the King Abdul Aziz Centre for National Dialogue (KACND) create positive environment in the Kingdom for public discourse on crucial issues confronted by the Saudi society. [67] On the other, the civil society institutions do not enjoy autonomy in the Kingdom, and are constantly monitored by the Saudi authorities. [68]

Unless the civil society associations are autonomous and delinked from close supervision, it would be quite difficult on the part of those organizations to direct the interest of the people in genuine ways. Nonetheless, the national dialogue sessions initiated by the Saudi authorities to have public discourse on vital topics is interpreted as a positive step towards expression of views on varied matters in the Saudi society. However, their success lies how effectively the dialogue processes are sustained and the outcomes are converted into policy alternatives in future.

Human rights are comprehensive issues, and they are to be addressed through a symbiotic relationship between the formal and the informal institutions of the state. The Kingdom enunciated certain constitutional provisions in the Basic Law for securing better human rights conditions. The articles that dealt with them are: The state secures 'human rights in accordance with the Shari'ah' (Article 23). The state gives security to all citizens and residents in the country and sees that no one is 'confined, arrested or imprisoned without reference to law' (Article 36). All citizens or any person having complaint or a grievance are free to participate in Councils organized by the King and the Crown Prince. He is allowed to 'address public authorities and discuss any matters of concern to him' (Article43). [69] No doubt, the above constitutional provisions, if implemented, would promote human rights conditions in Saudi Arabia. But the theory does not match with the practice since the Amnesty International and Human Rights Watch reported prolonged detention, unfair trials, flogging and practice of capital and corporeal punishment in Saudi Arabia. [70]

Similarly, Centre for Development Human Rights observed that women were not duly represented in the social, economic, political and scientific fields compared to other

Arab countries in the region. Neither they could drive the vehicles nor could they move without the consent of the male persons. They remained second fiddle to their male counterparts on the matters of marriage, divorce and recording of testimony in the court of law. [71] However, it is noticed, there are attempts at certain corners to prop up the women's rights in the kingdom. No doubt, the women were denied the right to vote in the first ever partial Municipal election held in 2005.But the election of two Saudi women into the twelve member Board of Jeddah Chamber of Commerce and Industry in November 2005 and one woman engineer into the ten member board of National Council of Engineers in December 2005 remained positive initiatives in the Kingdom. [72] The women are being gradually allowed to have business enterprises and the data suggests that near about 30.7 thousand women owned commercial houses till 16 April 2006. Out of this, Saudi women were found occupied in the business services with (46.2 percent) followed by the wholesale, retail, trade and commercial works (32.7 percent) and construction, building and contracting (18.3 percent). [73] Besides, the Saudis also looked for a new role of women in the changing scenario since the Gallup Poll conducted in 2007 indicated that around 75 percent men and 82 percent women preferred women's entry into the jobs on the basis of their qualifications. [74] Now it is to be observed how far the Saudi political establishment is prepared to bring such change in future for the promotion of women's rights in the country.

Governance reforms do not show any significant shift in the political system of Saudi Arabia rather they are piecemeal in character. The space for public discourse is constrained with checks and balances. The human rights situation is far from the constitutional obligations. So, in this context, it is to be ascertained to what extent the regime is set to bring further reforms for ushering a participatory political system in the country.

The study of neo-liberalism and development debates contextualized in Saudi Arabia exemplifies how development hinges upon the multiplicity of the factors for realizing its objectives. It also facilitated to derive certain parameters for analyzing the Saudi society from the standpoint of development discourse.

Neo-liberal reforms are to be tactically managed bridging the gap between the unbridled market forces and the state regulated economic enterprises for ensuring inclusive development in the Kingdom.

Saudization drive is to be vigoursly pursued to create indigenous Saudi work force to balance the large presence of expatriate workers in the country.

Professional and techno-managerial education is to be effectively induced for generating human resource to resolve the crisis of structural unemployment in the Kingdom.

Economic diversification is to be reinforced in Saudi Arabia to reduce its dependency upon the oil sector paving the way for sustainable development in future.

Symmetry between economic growth and development is to be maintained protecting the environment and cultural ethos of the Saudi society.

The political structures are to function on the principle of the separation of powers to check authoritarianism in the Saudi political system. Majlis Al Shura (Consultative Council) is to be an elected body to guarantee participatory political process in the system.

Civil society institutions through mutual trust and reciprocity are to create adequate space for public discourse on various issues confronting the nation. Subsequently, it would limit the authoritarian attitude of the state and address the deficit of democracy paving the way for transparency and accountability in the Saudi system.

Human rights are to be augmented through the rule of law and their capabilities are to be secured providing civil and political freedom as well as socio-economic opportunities in the different aspects of the Saudi society.

Gender equality is to be achieved in the country by providing equal opportunities to women in various spheres for gendering justice in the system.

To conclude here it may be added that the study of this subject deduces the above parameters for judging the dynamics of development in Saudi Arabia on a sustainable basis. The thrust for investigation is an endless chapter. So, there is need for uninterrupted intellectual introspection and critical inquiry of this debate to derive more theoretical inputs to examine the process of Saudi development in future.

Notes

1. NeoLiberalism,http://www.spiritustemporis.com/neoliberalism/theory.html Accessed on 18 November 2009.
2. Joachim Heidrich, "On Transnationalisation and the Strategy of Globalization, *The Indian Journal of Political Science*, vol. 62, no. 3, 2001, p. 378.
3. Atul Bharadwaj, "Understanding the Globalization Mind Game", Strategic *Analysis*, vol. 27, no. 3, July-September 2003, p. 321. For details see, Jajati K Pattnaik, "Revisiting Political Development: A Theoretical Construct", *Journal of Peace Studies*, vol. 13, no. 3, July-September 2006, p. 76.
4. Cited in Simon Murden, "Culture in world Affairs", in John Baylis and Steve Smith (ed.), *The Globalization of World Politics: An Introduction to International Relations*, (Oxford: Oxford University Press, 2007), p. 542.
5. *Ibid.*
6. Arie De Ruijter, "Globalization: A Challenge to the Social sciences", in Frans J. Schuurman (ed.), *Globalization and Development Studies: Challenges for the 21st Century*, (New Delhi: Vistaar Publications, 2001), p. 36.
7. Joseph E. Stiglitz, *Globalization and its Discontents*, (New Delhi: Penguin Books, 2003), p. 7.
8. Anthony Giddens, *Runaway world: How Globalization is Reshaping our Lives*, (London: Profile Books, 2004), p. 15. For details see, Jajati K. Pattnaik, "A Critique of Neo-Liberal

Development and Alternatives", *Mainstream*,vol.xlvi.no. 26, pp.15-17.

9. Cited in Andy storey, "Measuring Development" in *Gerard* McCann and Stephen McCloskey, *From the Local to the Global: Key Issues in Development Studies*, (London, Sterling, Virginia: Pluto Press, 2003), p.35.
10. *Ibid.*
11. *Ibid.*
12. *Ibid.*p.37. See, A. Escobar, "The Making and Unmaking of the Third World through Development', in M. Rahnema and V. Bawtree (ed.), *The Post-Development Reader*, (London and New Jersey: Zed Books, 1997), p. 92., See Pattnaik, n. 8, pp. 15-16.
13. The Human Development Concept, http://hdr.undp.org/en/humandev/ Accessed on 22 October 2009.
14. Amartya Sen, *Development as Freedom,* (Oxford: Oxford University press, 2004), p. 3.
15. *Ibid.*
16. *Ibid.* pp. 36-37.
17. Mahbub Ul Haq, "Human Development Paradigm in South Asia", *Mainstream,* February24, 1996, p. 7. See Des Gasper, *The Ethics of Development: From Economism to Human Development,* (New Delhi: Vistaar Publications), pp. 164-167.
18. *Ibid.*, p. 18.
19. See n.14.
20. Arab Human Development Report 2002, http://www.arab-hdr.org/publications/other/ahdr/ahdr2002e.pdf Accessed on 25 October 2009.
21. *Ibid.*
22. Arab Human Development Report 2003, http://www.arab-hdr.org/publications/other/ahdr/ahdr2003e.pdf Accessed on 27 October 2009.
23. Arab Human Development Report 2004, http://www.arab-hdr.org/publications/other/ahdr/ahdr2004e.pdf Accessed on 26 October 2009.
24. Arab Human Development Report 2005, http://www..arab-hdr.org/publications/other/ahdr/ahdr2005e.pdf Accessed on 26 October 2009.
25. Arab Human Development Report 2009, http://www..arab-hdr.org/publications/other/ahdr/ahdr2005e.pdf Accessed on 26 October 2009.

26. *Ibid.*
27. Strategic Positioning and Industrial Development Vision, http://www.commerce.gov.sa/industrial1.percent20report percent20on percent20vision percent2020.doc Accessed on 18 October 2009.
28. *Ibid.*
29. Human Development in Saudi Arabia, http://www.undp.org.sa/sa/index.php/human-development/human-development-in-saudi-arabia Accessed on 15 October 2009.
30. *Ibid.*
31. The World Fact Book, https://www.cia.gov/library/publications/the-world-factbook/geos/sa.html Accessed on 7 December 2009.
32. http://data.un.org/CountryProfileaspx?CrName=saudi percent20Arabia Accessed on 15 October 2009.
33. See n. 31.
34. See n. 32.
35. See n. 29.
36. Robert E. Looney, "Patterns of Human Resource Development in Saudi Arabia", *Middle Eastern Studies*, vol.27, 1991, pp. 670-671.
37. *Ibid.*
38. Saudi Arabia Human Development Report 2008, http://www.undp.org.sa/sa/index.php/en/human-development/human-development-in-saudi-arabia Accessed on 15 October 2009.
39. Grant F. Smith, "Saudization: Development and Expectations Management," http://www.saudi-american-forum.org/Newsletters/SAF_Essay_23.htm Accessed on 1 November 2009.
40. *Ibid.*
41. Saudization Quotas Eased for Some Job Categories, http://www.arabnews.com/?page=1&section=0&article=80127 Accessed on 1 November 2009.
42. The Executive Summary of the Ministry of Education Ten Year Plan (2004-14), http://www.moe.gov.sa/pdf/english/moe_e.pdf Accessed on 3 November 2009.
43. *Ibid.*

44. Girijesh Pant, *The Arab Gulf Economies: From Crisis to Reform*, (New Delhi: Har-Anand Publications, 1996), pp. 91-92.
45. Cited in *Ibid.*
46. *Ibid.*, pp. 93-97.
47. Cited in *Ibid.*, pp. 97-98.
48. *Ibid* ., p. 98.
49. Daryl Champion, *The Paradoxical Kingdom: Saudi Arabia and the Momentum of Reform*, (London: Hurst and Company, 2003), pp. 81-82.
50. Long Term Strategy for the Economy, http://www.mep.gov.sa/index.jsp;jsessionid=701EE9DDD22B9AEE1B2395E52F87EEF8.beta?event=ArticleView&Article.ObjectID=53 Accessed on 18 October 2009.
51. WTO General Council Successfully Adopts Saudi Arabia's Terms of Accession, http://www.wto.org/english/news_e/pres05_e/pr420_e.htm Accessed on 9 November 2009.
52. Saudi Economy and Culture can Withstand WTO Challenges, http://www.arabnews.com/?page=6&section=0&article=77736&d=13&m=2&y=2006 Accessed on 9 November 2009.
53. *Ibid.*
54. Brad Bourland, Saudi Arabia and the Global financial Crisis, http://www.saudi-us-relations.org/articles/2008/ioi/081216-jadwa-bulletin.html Accessed on 20 November 2009.
55. Saudi Arabia Feels the Effects of Global Financial Crisis, http://www.menafn.com/qn_news_story_s.asp?StoryId=1093217489 Accessed on 9 November 2009.
56. Tim Niblock, S*tate, Society and Economy in Saudi Arabia,* (London: Croomhelm, 1982), pp. 89-90.
57. Rashed Aba-Namay, "The Recent Constitutional Reforms in Saudi Arabia," *International and Comparative Law Quarterly, vol .42, April* 1993, p. 311.
58. Cited in *Ibid.*
59. Gulshan Dietl, *Through Two Wars and Beyond: A Study of Gulf Cooperation Council,* (New Delhi: Lancer Books, 1991), pp. 26-28.
60. Saudi Arabia: Basic Law of Government,http://www.mideastinfo.com/…/Saudi_Arabia_Basic_Law.htm Accessed on 17 November 2009.
61. *Ibid.*

62. Freedom in the World 2009 – Saudi Arabia, http://www.unhcr.org/refworld/type,ANNUALREPORT,FREEHOU,,4a64528723,0.html Accessed on 12 November 2009.
63. *Ibid.*
64. Civil Society, http://www.pogar.org/governance/participation.aspx Accessed on 15 November 2009.
65. Fatin Bundagji,The Future of Civil Society Association, ttp://www.arabnews.com/?page=7&section=0&article=108552&d=4&m=4&y=2008 Accessed on 20 November 2009.
66. Civil Society, :Saudi Arabia http://www.pogar.org/countries/theme.aspx?cid=16&t=2 Accessed on 15 November 2009.
67. King Abdul Aziz Centre for National Dialogue, http://www.kacnd.org/eng/ Accessed on 22 May, 2009.
68. Jafar Alshayeb, Civil Society and Human Rights in Saudi Arabia http://www.bridgingthegulf.org/menu-main/news0/gcc-civil-society-conference-october-2008/civil-society-and-human-rights-in-saudi-arabia-status-and-future-prospects Accessed on 11 November 2009.
69. The .Basic Law of Governance, http://www.mofa.gov.sa/detail.asp? Accessed on 23 May 2009.
70. http://www.amnesty.org/en/region/Saudi-arabia Accessed on 22 May 2009 see http://www.amnestyusa.org/all-countries/Saudi-arabia/page.do Accessed on 22 May 2009, see Gulshan Diet, *Saudi Arabia: People, Politics and Politics*, (New Delhi: NBT, India, 2006), p. 59.
71. Women's Rights in Saudi Arabia, http;//www.cdhr.info/Campaigns/Womens Rights Accessed on 11 November 2009.
72. Jane kinninmont, Saudi Arabia's Women Pioneers http://www.opendemocracy.net/conflict-middle_east_politics/saudi_women_3521.jsp Accessed on 19 November 2009.
73. Kingdom of Saudi Arabia: Millennium Development Goals, www.undp.org.sa/documents/mdg/mdgr_sa_2008_english.pdf Accessed 1 November 2009.
74. Magali Rheault, Saudi Arabia: Majorities Support Women's Rights,

http://www.gallup.com/poll/103441/saudi-arabia-majorities-support-womens-rights.aspx Accessed on 15November 2009.

2

The GCC Countries' Response to Desertification

A. Kannan

Land is a natural component of an ecosystem. Land resources are finite, fragile and non-renewable. Land serves many purposes of human kind, i.e., agriculture, forests and pastures, and infrastructure development. Besides these so-called economic uses, land also performs environmental (ecological) regulatory functions. These are related to controlling global warming and acting as a sink for many harmful chemicals. Desertification is land degradation in arid, semi-arid and dry sub humid areas resulting from various factors including climatic variations and human activities.

Desertification is a detrimental process that brings about a gradual and an unnoticed reduction in the productive capacity of land over a period of years. The end point of the process would be the formation of a complete wasteland incapable of producing anything useful. "Desertification is one of the greatest environmental and development problems of the 21st century. Some two billion people live in the world's drylands, whose biological productivity is under threat from the progressive degradation of soils and other natural resources. Desertification can trigger a vicious circle of environmental degradation, impoverishment, migration and conflicts, often also putting the political stability of the affected countries and regions at risk. It is estimated that about half of all armed conflicts present environmental causal factors characteristic of drylands." [1] Similarly "although it does occur all around the world, only developing countries in the world's arid and semi-arid regions are severely affected by its consequences." [2]

Standing at the intersection between domestic, international, and global pressures, the State is the preeminent institution with requisite political authority and steering capacity and institutional means to tackle ecological problems through multilateral environmental agreements and regulations of natural resources management. [3] Similarly it is the administrative system which translates the will of State. It plays the dynamic role of coordinating diverse actors in formulating and implementing the environmental policies and decisions.

Because management of highly interconnected and trans-boundary nature of environmental issues is one of the most difficult areas of public action, demanding inputs of scientific and technical knowledge and of skills in the organisation, planning, and coordination of complex programmes that are nowhere common attributes of government. [4]

Historically, the overall model of governance in the Gulf Cooperation Council (GCC) countries [5] is State-led, State-centered, and State-regulated. The rentier State [6] which emerged out of natural sources of wealth controlled by the State, "together with a political structure which took the form of traditional monarchies dominated by one family gave rise to public governance that minimises the role and participation of its civil society, magnifies the role of the state in the area of social welfare and distribution of rent." [7]

A critical analysis of the nature and character of administrative arrangements is essential to determine the role of the State in ensuring sustainable development in these countries. In this context, this paper analyzes measures and initiatives taken by the GCC countries to combat desertification - a major global threat.

Desertification

Desertification is a slow process by which the productivity of land is reduced over a period of time. It is also going through several stages before reaching the final one, which is an irreversible change. Natural threshold changes exist-historical events as well as current geo-socio-economic changes which constantly intensify the desertification process. [8] Desertification also differs from drought. Basically "drought is a temporary phenomenon occurring when precipitation falls below normal or when near normal precipitation is made less effective by other climate parameters such as high temperature, low humidity and strong winds." [9]

The word desertification has a Latin origin:*-fication*, which means the action of doing (or creating) comes from *fieri*, the passive form of the verb *facere*, to do, while desert is derived from both the adjective *desertus*, meaning uninhabitated, and the noun *desertum*, a desert area. In a wider sense, desertification can signify an environmental crisis which produces desert-like conditions or desert like landscapes in any ecosystem. [10] Therefore "desertification is not the natural expansion of existing deserts but the degradation of land in arid, semi-arid, and dry sub-humid areas." [11] It is a gradual process of soil productivity loss and the thinning out of the vegetative cover because of human activities and climatic variations. It occurs because dryland ecosystems, which cover over one third of the world's land area, are extremely vulnerable to over-exploitation and inappropriate land use.

The "term desertification was first coined in 1927 by the French scientist and explorer Louis Lavauden and first popularized in 1949 by the French forester Andre Aubreville. The latter (is) generally considered as the father of the term." [12] Early experts on desertification promoted the idea of the 'encroaching desert', 'moving desert' or 'advancing desert' to illustrate desertification. This "expansion of the desert" theory culminated in the assertion by Lamprey that the Sahara was marching at a rate of 5.5 km/year. [13]

"During the French occupations in West Africa, colonial foresters and administrators perceived clear signs of indigenous environmental mis-management and subsequent advance of desert. In 1907, a forestry mission lead by J.

Vuillet, chief of *Service de l' Agriculture* in the colony *Haut-Senegal et Niger*, stated: it is indeed true. The Sahara progresses toward the South; and that (is) because of Man's action." [14] This idea was later regularly supported by colonial administrative reports, research documents and findings and travel accounts. [15] Subsequent studies and extensive research proved conclusively that no threat from expanding deserts existed. [16]

Aubreville [17] was the first one to explain desertification as "not an extension of the existing desert. Desertification was not the result of the Sahara spreading outward but of localized activity that could begin anywhere." [18] He described desertification as the transformation of productive land into an ecological desert due to the ruinous act of erosion, often impelled by man-made deforestation. [19] "Aubreville was quite clear in his conclusion that desertification in tropical Africa was due to man's activity and that (there) had been no significant climatic change during the past thousand or more years. Most of that destructive activity has occurred within recent historic time by the action of agricultural populations." [20]

Almost 30 years after Aubreville published his treatise on desertification, the United Nations Conference on Desertification (UNCOD) [21] was held at Nairobi, in 1977 defined desertification as "the diminution or destruction of the biological potential of land, and can lead ultimately to desert-like conditions. It is an aspect of the widespread deterioration of ecosystems, and has diminished or destroyed the biological potential, i.e. plant and animal production, for multiple use purposes at a time when increased productivity is needed to support growing populations in quest of development." [22]

The UNCOD description did not clearly identify the target area of applicability of the term desertification. In other words, there was "no reference to the climatic zones in which desertification occurs." [23] This definition was found inadequate and not sufficiently operational to undertake the quantitative assessment of desertification. [24]

In February 1990 United Nations Environment Programme (UNEP), based on special studies and extensive discussions and aware of the danger of inflationary definitions of the term desertification, formed an Ad hoc Committee for the Global Evaluation of the Desertification: State and Methods of Investigation. [25] It "produced a new definition that equated desertification with land degradation and specified the climate zones to which the term applies." [26] It also suggested the following definition: "desertification is land degradation in arid, semi-arid and dry sub humid areas resulting from adverse human impact." [27]

Again this UNEP's new definition, which identified the human activities as the sole factor for desertification, was heavily criticised as being over simplistic and ignoring the role of climate factors. In this context, the Panel of Senior Consultants, convened by UNEP in Geneva from 25 to 27 April 1991, to discuss the first draft of a revised Plan of Action to Combat Desertification (PACD), considered the desertification concept as well. "It was pointed out that the new document should more clearly spell out the likely impacts of natural climatic conditions, particularly of recurrent drought, on desertification; it would be necessary to note that in certain instances desertification might not only be human-induced but climate-induced as well." [28]

Accordingly the UNEP in May 1991, considered this dimension. It underlined the need for further refinement of the definition of the concept of desertification, taking into account recent findings and new knowledge acquired in the course of detailed area-specific studies, surveys and assessments about the influence of climate changes and fluctuations and the resilience of soils. [29]

During preparations for the United Nations Conference on Environment and Development (UNCED) popularly known as the Earth Summit, held at Rio in June 1992, the definition of desertification was further disputed. After extensive consultations and diplomatic pressure from developing countries, an amended formulation developed for inclusion in *Agenda 21*- final Document of Earth Summit. The revised definition says desertification as "land degradation in arid, semi-arid and dry sub humid areas resulting from various factors including climatic variations and human activities." [30] This definition is now widely regarded to be the authoritative and reliable definition of desertification.

The United Nations Convention to Combat Desertification (UNCCD) 1994 also adopted the Earth Summit's definition on desertification. [31] The inclusion of climatic factors as a partial cause of desertification in the UNCCD's definition was "intended to soften the political consequences of a definition that places all responsibility on human activity." [32]

The main difference between the above two definitions lies in the latter's explicit and concrete inclusion of climatic factors as a major cause of desertification. There are several implications of accepting the latter definition. First, it reduces the emphasis in the first definition on human activities as being primarily responsible for causing and accelerating desertification. Secondly, it opens up the possibility of countries affected by desertification being able to claim that responsibility lies also with those countries, which have provoked climatic change at the global level, that is, those of the industrialized world. Accepting this could lead to claims for compensation to be paid to those affected by desertification in the form of financial resources and transfer of modern scientific and technological 'know-how'. [33]

Desertification in the GCC Countries

Historically, the Gulf region played a significant role in fostering a maritime trading culture, linking Arabia and Africa with Europe and Asia. It is bound on three sides by four water bodies: the Arabian Sea, the Gulf of Oman, the Red Sea and the Arabian Gulf, making it home to rich marine biodiversity and natural resources.

The Gulf Cooperation Council (GCC) countries are cemented by a number of common characteristics related to its distinct climate, ecology, history, language and customs and culture, which permeate its social fabric and frameworks, development aspirations, and quest for a meaningful future. These geographically contiguous States have similar political orientations and an economic system based on the rentier State.

The GCC countries are situated in extremely arid zones. The region is mostly a desert with the exception of narrow coastal areas and mountain ranges. The average annual rainfall ranges from 70 to 130 mm except in the coastal zone along the Red Sea in Southwestern Saudi Arabia and along the Gulf of Oman on the Eastern shore, where orographic rainfall reaches more than 500 mm. The total annual evaporation rate ranges from 2,500 mm in the coastal areas to more than 4,500 mm inland. With this harsh climatic conditions, the GCC countries have an extremely poor endowment of water resources. The amount of renewable aquifer volume is insignificant and shallow alluvial aquifers provide some renewable groundwater only in those limited coastal strips. Large deep aquifers are present in the region, which contain non-renewable supplies of fossil water, but have a finite life and quality limitations. Only Saudi Arabia possesses substantial amounts of non-renewable groundwater in deep aquifers. [34]

The GCC countries are endowed with abundant natural resources in the form of combined oil and natural gas reserves, but they are less fortunate in the critical resources of productive land and accessible renewable water resources. These countries witnessed major socio-economic transformation and demographic change including substantial agricultural expansion and industrial development, since oil was discovered at the beginning of the 20th century.

These countries are also facing a number of major environmental issues. The source, nature and intensity of environmental threats differentiate this region from the rest of the world. This is not because of the interaction between man-made and natural environmental problems but because of the magnitude, speed and extent with which this interaction takes place. The unprecedented levels of industrialization, inefficient use of limited resources, unplanned urbanization, large-scale consumption, higher population growth and lack of regulatory mechanisms produced a critical environmental situation in the GCC countries.

The scarcity of water and land resources is the most pressing. Deterioration of the marine and coastal environment, loss of biodiversity, increasing industrial pollution and poor management of hazardous wastes also threaten the sustainable development in these countries. Desertification has been a serious problem over the past decade, and the region's rangelands - important for food security - are deteriorating. Most land is either desertified or vulnerable to desertification.

Forms of Desertification in the GCC Countries

There are several forms of desertification prevalent in the GCC countries and it should be noted that two or more land degradation processes might interact in the same area. [35] These are wind erosion, water erosion, chemical degradation and physical degradation.

A. Wind Erosion: Soil erosion under the action of wind is the one of the major forms of land degradation which in turn leads to desertification. The area affected by wind erosion is gradually increasing because of the cultivation of marginal lands and the movement of sand dunes towards agricultural and rangelands and owing to the loss of precious vegetation cover, which binds together the soils particles. Similarly it leads to the loss of fertile top soils in arable lands which in turn accelerates desertification process. [36]

A study conducted by the Food and Agriculture Organisation (FAO) in 1992 shows that in Saudi Arabia alone, approximately 50 million ha was affected by wind erosion. [37] In Qatar, for example it was found that "the sand dunes encroach 8 meters / year towards the south and south east, which is in the dominant wind directions. In the eastern part of the country sand dunes movement varies from 7.9 to 20.7 m/year. This is due to the size of sand dune, sand dune slop, and moisture content especially along the coast. In addition to the sand dune movement, there are sand storms dust storms and clay storms. These lead to deposition of soil particles on plant leaves and on civil constructions." [38]

In comparison with other types of soil erosions, "all that is required for wind erosion to occur is a minimum wind shear stress that can detach and force the movement of naturally held soil particles from their place. Evidently, soils with smooth dry and loose surfaces offer the least resistance to blowing wind and are particularly vulnerable to wind erosion. Hence wind erosion is most pervasive in arid regions." [39] Wind erosion is the dominant form of land degradation in the GCC countries.

B. Water Erosion: Land degradation due to water erosion is very serious in mountainous areas particularly in Oman and Saudi Arabia. Although the rainfall is often higher, due to their inaccessibility mountainous areas tend to be the most isolated and marginalised areas. The complex landscape and topography of the mountainous region consists of steep slopes, terraced croplands, sloping rangelands, and scattered patches of shrubs and trees. The degradation of these areas includes severe soil erosion by water run-off on unprotected slopes, which in extreme cases can lead to silting of *wadis* and loss of agricultural land downstream, degradation of natural vegetation and depletion of biodiversity. [40]

Areas devoid of vegetation cover tend to have poor soil structure due to paucity of rooting systems and organic matter, resulting in poor permeability of water and increased runoff.

Runoff and erosion further results in leakages of nutrients to adjacent landscape components. [41] "The hydro-transmission characteristics of a soil profile or cloddiness of the soil and the slope of the surface determine the onset and subsequent intensity of erosion. Soils resisting the infiltration and percolation of water are more susceptible to water erosion, while soils with a non-cloddy, pulverized surface are vulnerable to wind erosion." [42]

Water harvesting plays a major role in combating desertification in mountainous areas suffering from water erosion and its subsequent adverse impact on soil resource and vegetation cover. [43] "Due to rising costs for maintaining past benching and terracing conservation and other runoff control structures on the slopes, vast areas have been completely degraded and abandoned, resulting in great loss in land and water resources." [44]

C. Chemical Degradation: The chemical degradation of land in the GCC countries involves salinisation [45] and alkalisation, the loss of soil nutrients and soil and water pollution. In drylands, irrigation is the key to overcome the adverse effects of arid conditions and recurrent droughts and it is also vital to ensure food security for a growing population. However poor management and inefficient use of water for irrigation resulted in salinisation, alkalinisation, water logging and nutrient depletion in large areas of these countries.

About 2 million ha of irrigated land area in Saudi Arabia and 33.6 percent of the cultivated land of Bahrain are moderately salinised. [46] For example in Qatar around 30 percent of irrigated agriculture land is salinised. [47] Similarly, "about 68 farms went out of production due to salinization (in Qatar). The yield in state farms decreased by 30 percent or about 1500 ha from irrigated soil degraded due to salinization." [48]

The extensive use of fertilizers and pesticides in irrigated agricultural areas cause soil and water pollution in the region. "The development of water logging and salinity/alkalinity is an outstanding example of man's role in inducing land degradation in areas that did not pose any problem earlier." [49] Despite today's understanding and the availability of preventive and remedial technologies, the problems of water logging and salinity continue to spread. As a result, the productivity of land and water resources is steadily declining and sustainability is at risk, if not already collapsed, as indicated by land abandonment and migration to nearby cities. [50]

D. Physical Degradation: The physical degradation of the land in the form of soil structure deterioration resulting from cementation, the accumulation of gypsum powder and the formation of soil crusts are also prevalent in these countries. The physical consequence of land degradation is the expansion of deserts and desert-like landscapes in areas where this did not occur previously, the generation of shifting sand dunes, expanding sand-seas and the crusting of bare soils. For instance, in northwestern Kuwait, the areas subjected to severe soil disruptions are invaded by mobile sand sheets, which support minimal natural vegetation. [51]

GCC Countries Response

Historically, States did not easily accept environmental responsibility. [52] In 1945 when the United Nations was created, the protection of environment was not an issue of global concern. [53] The UN Charter made no provision for ecological security. Thus even though the new organisation was given a significantly broader mission than that of the League of Nations, especially on economic, social and humanitarian matters, [54] the framers of the UN Charter never anticipated that environmental issues would accelerate in such a large scale and complexity.

"As globalization continues apace, environmental problems have become increasingly complex, in some cases threatening the sustainability of human livelihoods in both rich and poor countries." [55] Humanity in the twenty-first century faces a new generation of environmental challenges. These differ significantly from past environmental problems. These new environmental issues share several common features. They are global in scope, transcending national boundaries and affecting all, or substantial portions, of the world's population and natural resources. Their long-term consequences are irreversible and far reaching. The growing complexity of environmental problems makes it more difficult to get an overview of a specific problem in all its dimensions-ecological, economic, sociological and political. [56]

To effectively address "the integrated and interdependent nature of the new challenges and issues (which) contrasts sharply with the kind of institutions that exists today," [57] an unprecedented level of international coordination and collaboration involving governments, intergovernmental bodies, the private sector and civil society is urgently required. Significantly, the complex nature of environmental problems are characterised by considerable degree of scientific uncertainties concerning their causes, impacts, feedbacks, and the interrelationships among complex natural and social parameters.

The GCC Countries undertook several measures to address desertification under the Plan of Action of Nairobi Conference, 1977 and the United Nations Convention to combat desertification (UNCCD), 1994.

Response under Plan of Action (PoA) of Nairobi Conference (1977)

A severe drought in the Sahel region of Africa from 1969-1973 did catastrophic damage to grazing land vegetation, livestock, and eventually, refugees from the devasted land. The deterioration of productive ecosystem is an obvious and serious threat to human progress. Because of the global magnitude of desertification and its potential effects on populations and sustainable development, the United Nations has taken a leading role in providing an international framework for studying and resolving this problem.

In 1974, the UN General Assembly through Resolution 3202 asked the international community to undertake speedy and effective measures to address desertification and to plan for economic development of the affected areas. In view of the intensity of the problem, the UN General Assembly then decided to convene a Conference on desertification.

Accordingly, the UN Conference on Desertification (UNCOD) was held in Nairobi in 1977. Approximately 100 countries participated enthusiastically in a Conference that convened to address one of the most important environmental threats to the well –being of humanity. Out of Nairobi came a Plan of Action (PoA) to combat desertification, which recommended 28 measures that national, regional and international institutions could take to combat desertification. The UN General Assembly subsequently approved the report of the UNCOD and called upon the governments to consider, on a priority basis, the recommendations for national action and establish a national authority to co-ordinate and implement national action programmes. [58]

The governments in the GCC countries however, showed lack of interest in implementing the PoA. It was the UN specialized agencies and progammes that made substantial efforts to implement the PoA. In the West Asian region, the UN Economic and Social Commission for West Asia (ESCWA) made tremendous efforts to implement the recommendations of the Nairobi conference in this region.

As a follow-up to the UNCOD, the ESCWA considered the issue of desertification at its sixth session in 1979 and adopted Resolution 71(VI) on combating desertification in the region. Accordingly an Expert Meeting on Management, Conservation and Development of Agricultural Resources held in Damascus in 1981 in cooperation with the Food and Agriculture Organisation (FAO) and the Arab Centre for the Study of Arid Zones and Dry Lands (ACSAD). This meeting proposed a set of concrete recommendations to protect natural resources in this region, which formed the basis of ESCWA work in the area of desertification control. [59]

Since the convening of Nairobi Conference, the Agriculture Division of the ESCWA served as a Focal Point for the activities related with combating desertification in this region. It mostly focused its attention in undertaking studies and research on the assessment and integrated development of areas prone to desertification, preparing national action plans to combat desertification, formulating specific desertification control projects, and conducting training programmes in resource conservation and management. [60] These activities were undertaken by ESCWA either unilaterally or multilaterally in cooperation with concerned governments and other United Nations specialised agencies or regional and international organisations. [61]

The most important component of PoA was the formulation and implementation of National Action programme by the governments. "Although these national plans differ markebly in their details owing to the different socio-economic conditions in each member country, as well as resources potential, land-use practices and policies and other major factors influencing the phenomenon of desertification, the plans are in conformity with regard to the principal topics addressed." [62] By 1993 only three GCC countries prepared their national Action programmes. These were Bahrain, Oman and UAE.

Response under United Nations Convention to Combat Desertification (UNCCD)

After series of assessments on the implementation of PoA, in 1991, the UNEP concluded that the problem of land degradation in arid, semi-arid and dry sub-humid areas had intensified, although there were a few local examples of success.

African Environment Ministers met in November 1991 in Abidjan in order to prepare a common position to the 1992 Earth Summit. The Ministers were in unanimous in requesting a new convention to combating desertification. They also enjoyed the support of many other countries facing similar problems of desertification. [63]

The Earth Summit held in Rio (Brazil) in 1992 reviewed the progress in this regard and supported a new, integrated approach to the problem. The Conference asked the UN to adopt a Convention, an action framework designed to establish programmes to counter the threat of land degradation throughout the world, particularly in arid, semiarid and dry sub humid regions. The General Assembly acted swiftly and established the Intergovernmental Negotiating Committee on Desertification (INCD) through Resolution 47/188. The United Nations Convention to Combating Desertification (UNCCD) was adopted in Paris on 17 June 1994 and opened for signature there on 14 to 15 October 1994. A notable implication pertaining to the post-Rio emergence of the UNCCD is that it was framed as a sustainable development treaty rather than as an environmental treaty in the narrow sense. [64]

The UNCCD is "the newest link in the evolving international system for environmental governance. In linking a serious environmental concern with development issues, this convention can be viewed as an important step towards building a multilateral framework for sustainable development." [65] This Convention recognises desertification "primarily (as) a problem of sustainable development, poverty and human well-being, and environmental preservation. Social, and economic issues, including food security, migrations and political instability are closely linked to land degradation." [66] The UNCCD is "more strongly based on upon socio-economic criteria than the Convention on Biological Diversity." [67] Therefore it is "a much more comprehensive treaty than earlier efforts" [68] to combat desertification. Similarly "the perceived failure of the plan of action to combat desertification contributed significantly to the distinctive character of the convention." [69]

Under UNCCD, the GCC countries implemented the Convention at the national level through establishing Focal Points and National Coordination Committees, enacting legislations, creating administrative arrangements and formulating National Action Programmes.

Creation of Focal Points: A representative from each country serves as the Focal Point for the Convention to liaise with the convention Secretariat and to assist in inter-sessional work. National Focal Point "may be responsible to report information from the Convention secretariat to governmental bodies and report back to the Conference of Parties (COPs) on national implementation efforts." [70]

Parties to a Multilateral Environmental Agreement (MEA) often designate one or more Focal Points responsible for a MEA. There are two types of Focal Points: political and technical. The political Focal Point is usually responsible for the international processes, such as negotiating MEAs and participating in the COPs. Most States designate their Ministry of Foreign Affairs or a similar body as the political Focal Point. The technical Focal Point often bears the responsibility for implementing the MEA at the national level. [71]

Most governments generally designate the Chief Officer of the nation's Environment Agency as their technical Focal Point. In the GCC countries the Focal Points are mostly technical. Data on political Focal Points in the GCC countries are not available. Except in Bahrain where there are two persons acting as Focal Points for the UNCCD, all the other GCC countries have one person as a Focal Point.

The growing number of agreements to which states are becoming parties significantly increased the number of Focal Points and these are often spread across government ministries. This dispersion creates administrative and coordination challenges for most governments, particularly for the developing countries which lack the necessary institutional capacity to respond to and comply with environmental treaty obligations.

Table 2.1: The UNCCD Focal Points in the GCC Countries

S.N	Country	Focal Points
1	Bahrain	1.Undersecretary for Agriculture Ministry of Municipalities Affairs and Agriculture 2. Director of Agricultural Engineering Ministry of Municipalities Affairs and Agriculture
2	Kuwait	Chairman and Director General Environment Public Authority
3	Oman	Director of Coordination and Follow-up Ministry of Regional Municipalities, Environment and Water Resources
4	Qatar	Member Supreme Council for the Environment and Natural Reserves
5	Saudi Arabia	Director General Range and Forestry Department Ministry of Agriculture
6	United Arab Emirates	Director General Federal Environmental Agency

Source: UNCCD Secretariat, "Focal Points", [Online: web] Accessed on June 28, 2008 URL: http://www.unccd.int/focalpoints/focalpoints.php.

The Joint Inspection Unit (JIU) of UN also noted that UNCCD Focal Points are often located in weak ministries and appointed at a junior level. Moreover, many developing country Parties' Focal Points lack the financial and human capacities to effectively participate in COPs and associated Convention processes. This led to unequal participation among Parties and to a disconnect between Conference of Parties (CoPs) decisions and implementation at the national level. [72]

In order to discharge their functions effectively, the national institutions responsible for implementation of and reporting on MEAs need to be given high status in the government organisation with a clear mandate. [73]

Setting up National Coordination Bodies (NCBs): Environmental protection and natural resources management entail new responsibilities for most governments and require effective coordination in bringing together a number of functions and duties which are not previously related. Coordination, therefore, becomes one of the key instrument in achieving environmental objectives and tasks. [74]

Since the UNCCD is a comprehensive global treaty touching upon every aspect of the sustainable development process, effective implementation of this Convention mainly depends on constructive cooperation and coordination of all concerned stakeholders. In this regard the role of National Coordination Bodies [75] is crucial in achieving this objective. The GCC countries generally nominated particular Ministries as NCBs. These Ministries are expected to set up a National Coordination Committee comprising various ministries, research institutes and civil society representatives. This committee will in turn coordinate all the activities related with UNCCD implementation including the formulation of National Action Programmes and other policies.

Accordingly in Bahrain the "Ministry of Works and Agriculture-the responsible authority for combating desertification- is prepared to form a National Committee from the relevant organizations for combating desertification and to help organizing their activities. The Ministry will work on this subject to put it in action." [76]

The Environment Public Authority (EPA) in Kuwait "established the National Committee to Combat Desertification which was assigned to study the Convention, follow-up all subjects related to it, evaluate Desertification activities, prepare national action programs and a strategy according to the Convention's articles and the Asian Annex." [77]

Table 2.2: National Coordination Bodies (NCBs) in the GCC Countries

S. N	Country	National Coordination Bodies (NCBs) for UNCCD
1	Bahrain	Ministry of Municipalities Affairs and Agriculture
2	Kuwait	Environment Public Authority
3	Oman	Ministry of Regional Municipalities, Environment and Water Resources
4	Qatar	Supreme Council for the Environment and Natural Reserves
5	Saudi Arabia	Ministry of Agriculture and Water
6	United Arab Emirates	Ministry of Environment

Source: GRC, *Green Gulf Report* (Dubai: GRC, 2006), p.17.

In Oman "a committee to follow up the implementation was established by Ministerial Decisions in 2002. The committee has undertaken several activities on rehabilitation of degraded lands. These activities were used in the sustainable management of natural resources and helping to reduce the number of animals to 1970' level." [78] In 1997, Saudi Arabia "established a National Committee. The Committee consists of representatives from all government ministries and agencies pertinent to desertification and renewable natural resources and was mandated to prepare the Kingdom's national action programme to combat desertification. The members of this committee include: The Ministries of Agriculture and Water, Interior, Finance and National Economy, Higher Education, Planning, Municipality and Rural Affairs, Communication and ministry of Information. Specialized institutions such as King Abdulaziz City for Science and Technology, General Council for Meteorology and Environmental Protection, National Commission for Wildlife Conservation and Development and Prince Sultan Center for Environment, Water and Desert

Research (King Saud University) are also members of the national committee." [79] In UAE the Federal Environmental Agency (FEA) established the National Committee for the Follow up of the UNCCD on 17 June 2001. The committee consists of 25 members representing 17 bodies working in the fields related to the UNCCD. [80]

There is no such committee in Qatar. According to its report to UNCCD Secretariat "the national coordination activity of desertification is still in its very infant stages. It has no financial autonomy, separate human resources and logistic or independent entity organization. Even though, most activities could successfully be carried through the very powerful cooperation and harmonic element existing within the Ministry and with other bodies such as the university and its research centres" [81]

Even though all the GCC countries, except Qatar established National Coordination Committees, the composition shows a lack of people's participation, especially NGOs. Only a few research institutes are included in these committees. Lack of people's participation in the UNCCD related activities is in contrast with the very spirit of UNCCD principles and objectives.

Formulation of National Action Programmes: A central element within the text is "the commitment by the affected countries to devise national action programmes to combat desertification, which are intended to map out a set of priorities to include policy change, training needs, economic incentives, drought preparedness and clarification of tenure rules." [82]

Under Article 10 (1) of UNCCD the "purpose of national action programmes is to identify the factors contributing to desertification and practical measures necessary to combat desertification." [83] Since the issue of desertification is very closely linked to the development process itself, the UNCCD mandates the government to formulate comprehensive and detailed policies and programmes for sustainable development at national, sub regional and regional levels. [84]

Table 2.3: The GCC Countries' National Action Programme under the UNCCD

S.N	Country	Status	Year of Submission
1	Bahrain	Under preparation	---
2	Kuwait	Under preparation	---
3	Oman	Submitted	2005
4	Qatar	Under preparation	----
5	Saudi Arabia	Submitted	2005
6	U.A.E	Submitted	2003

Source: UNCCD Secretariat, "National Action Programmes of the Asian Countries" [Online: web] Accessed on 21 June 2008 URL: http://www.unccd.int/actionprogrammes/asia/asia.php.

Most importantly, NAP preparation should be preceded by a survey of the state of the environment in the affected countries to assess the causes and consequences of desertification and to determine priority areas for action. [85] The NAP is also expected to spell out its linkages with resource-users, grassroots level organisations working at community level, policy and decision makers at various levels, programmes of co-operation with other governments, international organisations and donor agencies, synergies amongst the various Rio Conventions (United Nations Framework Convention on Climate Change and the Convention on Biological Diversity) and recommend a plan of action for addressing the problems of land degradation in the dryland regions of the country. [86]

Among the GCC countries, Oman, Saudi Arabia and UAE completed the preparation of their NAPs and submitted them to the UNCCD Secretariat. During this authour's meeting with Experts at Arabian Gulf University, Manama, it was learned that the NAP of Bahrain was finalised and submitted to the government for final approval. The preparation of NAPs in other GCC countries is at the various stages. The reason for the delay was as follows:

... *Due to the severity of desertification experienced in the subregion, all countries had undertaken measures to alleviate the problem prior to the entry into force of the Convention in 1994. It was amply expressed in the reports that environmental strategies and programmes related to desertification are integrated into overall development strategies of Governments at a fairly early stage. Perhaps because countries of this Asian subregion are so used to dealing with an arid environment, it might have been difficult at first to identify additional efforts that could have been undertaken under the UNCCD. Due to these circumstances the preparation/review of National Action Programmes under the UNCCD was generally delayed in West Asia. This situation was compounded by still another aspect. Given the fact that some countries faced and still face an acute lack of financial resources, the implementation of a comprehensive NAP structure had to be postponed [87] (Emphasis added).*

Establishment of Administrative Institutions: The process for implementation of MEAs normally depend upon the provisions of the treaty but in most cases the actions range from adopting policies, developing and strengthening national legislation and institutions to implement MEAs. [88]

Environmental issues in the GCC Countries are gradually coming to the forefront of national concerns. There are also encouraging signs of an emerging awareness among the public of the need to protect the natural resources. The past few decades witnessed the emergence of environmental NGOs that are beginning to promote popular support for national efforts and initiatives to protect the environment. The industries also started to take its environmental responsibilities more seriously. [89]

In the GCC countries, governments established or designated the national institutions for formulating and implementing desertification related programmes under the UNCCD.

A. Bahrain: The national institutions involved to combat desertification include the Ministries of Housing and Agriculture, Municipalities and Environment, the Institute of Wild Life Production, University of Bahrain, Arabian Gulf University, and Non Governmental Organisations such as Technology Association, Association of Youth and Environment. [90] Besides these, the Bahrain Centre for Studies and Research and the Water Science & Technology Association are also playing important role in implementing desertification related programmes. [91]

B. Kuwait: In Kuwait, a number of institutions at the national level involve directly or indirectly in activities related to desertification. The Kuwait Institute of Scientific Research undertakes research activities. The Environment Public Authority (EPA) focuses on implementation of desertification related programmes. Kuwait University, Public Authority for Applied Education and Training (PAAET) and EPA engage in training. PAAET also involves in formulating policies and plans under UNCCD. [92] "A database was established for each authority involved in combat of Desertification, and they will be connected among a complete information network in the future." [93]

C. Oman: The important national institution concerned with desertification in Oman is the Ministry of Regional Municipalities, Environment and Water Resources, which has prime responsibility for desertification control and carries out planning and research activities in the field of desertification monitoring and control. [94]

Other institutions related with the implementation of the UNCCD in Oman include "Ministry of Agriculture and Fisheries, the Ministry of National Economy, the Ministry of Communication and Transportation, the Ministry of Information and the Sultan Qaboos University are all involved in one Way or another in desertification control. The role of each one in desertification control, however is not always spelled out in their establishment decrees or order." [95] Besides, there are other national level institutions in Oman that carry out activities related to combating desertification. These are the Council for the Conservation of the Environment and Prevention of Pollution, the Office of the Advisor for Conservation of the Environment and the Planning Committee for Development and Environment in the Governorate of Zufar. [96]

D. Qatar: The Department of Agriculture and Water Research and the Department of Agricultural Development are the important institutions involved in desertification related activities. University of Qatar engages in teaching, research. It also provides consultation to the government on issues related with desertification. [97] "An information centre had been formulated which started and still (is) in process of acquiring all information necessary for agricultural development in some sorts of databases." [98]

E. Saudi Arabia: The prominent national institutions concerned with desertification in Saudi Arabia are the Ministry of Agriculture and the Prince Sultan Centre for Environmental, Water and Desert Studies in King Saudi University. The first one involves different activities related to desertification such as research, implementation, planning and training. The second one undertakes researches on important areas related with desertification. The research areas include desertification monitoring, desert natural resources and their development and the use of modern technologies. Besides these institutions there are a number of other national organisations concerned with desertification such as the National Authority for Wild Life Protection and Development, the Saudi National Remote Sensing Centre in the city of King Abdul Aziz for Sciences and Technology, Centre of Rangeland Development in Al Jouf, natural resources and environment research institutions in Saudi Universities. [99]

Recently Saudi Arabia established a number of institutions and committees crucial for conservation of renewable natural resources and the environment. These include the Ministry for Water, the Supreme Tourism Authority, the Saudi Agency for Geologic Survey, the Supreme Council for Investment and the National Committee for the preparation of concrete action programme for preparedness to natural disasters. [100]

F. United Arab Emirates (U.A.E): A number of institutions are involved in protecting the environment, combating desertification [101] and the rehabilitation of the degraded lands and the vegetations cover in UAE. These are the Federal Agency for Environment, the Ministry of Agriculture and Fishery, the Ministry of Transportation, Forest Management in Al Ain, the Faculty of Agricultural Science at the University of UAE and many other institutes in each Emirate. [102] Besides these, UAE established the National Facility which consists of the main Centre for Metrological Predictions, Center for Metrological Communication, Center of Measuring Metrology Methods, Workshop for Metrological Systems Maintenance and General Library for Metrology. [103]

Enactment of Legislations: The GCC countries passed numerous laws dealing with the environment. In Kuwait, as early as 1964, the first law was passed to protect navigable water from oil pollution. Articles 15, 16, and 21 of the constitution of Kuwait were subsequently amended in 1976 and in 1980 to incorporate environmental protection principles and to establish mechanisms to enforce the implementation of environmental laws. [104] "Despite the often fragmented nature of organisational responsibilities for the environment, legislation in the region has been fairly cross-sectoral and all-encompassing since the 1980s. These laws, sometimes known as framework laws, facilitate to restructure the fragmented approaches to environmental management." [105]

With respect to legislation on combating desertification, the GCC Countries in their report to the UNCCD Secretariat claimed that

...appropriate laws relating to natural resources and land management are in place. The majority of these laws and legislative frameworks (which dealt with land tenure and land use, agriculture and grazing, forestry, water use and conservation, environmental protection, environmental management, environmental impact assessments, mining and mineral resources, zoning, urban development, etc.) were enacted prior to the entry into force of the Convention. They are in the process of reviewing their current legislative frameworks with a view to making them more consistent with the current situation. Many Parties have identified gaps in their present legislation and acknowledge the need for revision to strengthen its force. (Emphasis added). [106]

The followings are the country specific legislations related with desertification.

A. Bahrain: In Bahrain there are eleven legislations concerned with environment, wildlife, fisheries, veterinary medicine, palm trees production, environmental standard and groundwater. [107] In Bahrain the " laws, in the face of alarming water and land situation, have been formulated and made more stringent in 1997 to control and to monitor the abstraction and use of water for agriculture and landscape, beside domestic and industrial uses." [108] Besides, "the Amiri Decrees in respect of organizing date palm protection and land drainage system are effective to protect the state infrastructure to combat the menace of shrinking agricultural land." [109]

B. Kuwait: Kuwait makes efforts to combat desertification in a number of ways including enacting appropriate environmental legislations. The important legislations are rangeland law, camping control in rangelands, agriculture protection and quarrying exploration control. [110] In Kuwait "through analysis of available information, data and the past laws and decisions, it was noticed that there is a need to improve and reformulate laws and decisions by determining standards and environmental stipulations to protect and promote the environment and natural resources." [11] Accordingly some important legislations were enacted recently including constructing Natural Reserves Law and Environmental Impact Assessment Law. [112]

C. Oman: The Arab Center for the Studies of Arid Zones and Dry Lands (ACSAD carried a detailed survey on the existing administrative and legislative mechanism available in the GCC Countries to combat desertification. However this report did not include any legislative frameworks available in Oman to address the issues related with desertification. On the other hand the Oman national action programme to combat desertification proposes a project to be completed within a year with the following objectives: [133]

- Revise relevant existing laws and legislation
- Identify gaps in existing legislation
- Compare the existing legislation with the obligations under the environmental Conventions and treaties.
- Identify the necessary steps to ensure the ratification of the Conventions
- Prepare a comprehensive legislative framework to address environmental issues

Even in the report submitted to the UNCCD Secretariat Oman did not give specific legislations related with desertification. On the other hand it simply says that "Oman has realized the importance of the conservation of the environment, natural resources and their optimum utilization for the benefit of the present and future generations in a sustainable manner through the following:

- Formulation of environmental legislation;
- Provision of administrative and technical bodies to ensure enforcement of the laws…" [114]

D. Qatar: There are about 82 legislations in Qatar which are related to different environmental activities such as water resources , well drilling , use of waste water , control of grazing afforestation , urbanisation over agricultural land, etc. Violation of these legislations is common in Qatar. [115]

E. Saudi Arabia: Through its efforts to combat desertification, Saudi Arabia enacted a number of legislation such as: rangeland and forest legislation which deals with the protection of range and forest lands. Land legislation regulates land allocation and exploitation. Legislation on water resources conservation rationalises the use of water resources. Saudi Arabia promulgated some other legislations related to the protected areas and environmental protection. Keeping in view of emerging challenges, Saudi Arabia is in the process of reviewing and updating some of the legislations. [116] The updated legislation for forest and range and the strategy and the national forest programme was approved. [117]

F. UAE: UAE enacted a number of laws to protect the environment and the natural resources. These legislations are the Federal Law on Environmental Protection and Development (FLED) (24/1999), the Federal Law on the Establishment of the Department of Water Resources (21/1981), the Federal Law on Regulating the Hunting of Birds and Wild Animals (9/1983). Besides these some other important federal laws were also passed to regulate the handling of the production and importation of seedlings, fertilizers, pesticides, and seeds. [118]

Recent Response

Recently, the GCC countries undertook a number of measures individually as well as collectively. These initiatives have either a direct or an indirect impact on the efforts to combat desertification and to ensure sustainable resource management in this region. However theses are at the early stage which makes it difficult to draw conclusion. The following are some of the important individual efforts by the GCC Countries. Saudi Arabia decided to abandon wheat cultivation to protect depleting ground water. It planned to increase the plan allocation for R & D as part of its 20-year National Science and Technology Plan and also the number of bio reserves to protect the environment.

Qatar is in the process of introducing an environment-friendly public transport system of solar cars and battery-powered buses to reduce pollution and save energy. It also approved to set up camel farms to combat desertification. It also signed an MoU with the UNEP to enhance understanding, co-ordination and technical assistance for implementing the Qatar National Environment Plan (QNEP).

Oman adopted a master plan to regulate water management. Bahrain enacted legislation to strictly monitor the use of groundwater and drilling of wells and improving irrigation techniques including sprinkler irrigation system. Bahrain initiated a programme to replace Alfalfa with other suitable crops, like Rhodes grass, Barley, Oats, Rye grass, Sudan grass, and others, requiring not only less volumes and frequency of irrigation but also those which could withstand higher salinity and adverse drainage situation. By replacing alfalfa with other forage crops, a saving of 15 million cubic meters per year is anticipated.

UAE unveiled a strategic plan to save ground water and solar energy. These are the few examples of the GCC countries' individual efforts to protect natural resources in their countries.

Similarly the GCC countries took several measures collectively which will go a long way in ensuring the sustainable development of this region. These significant measures include adoption of the Gulf Green Initiative 2007 which focuses on unifying all environmental legislations among the GCC countries and the formulation of three integrated development projects-GCC rail network, GCC power grid and GCC water link. These three integrated development projects have huge potential to conserve energy and natural resources in this region. For example the rail network is expected to reduce the GCC countries' heavy reliance on road transportation which resulted in a major negative side-effect: the growing problem of road accidents and air-pollution.

Analysis of Response

Considering the nature and gravity of the problem, efforts made by the governments in the GCC Countries to combat are inadequate and insufficient. Administrative system in the GCC countries "although simple until recently, is being steadily inflated due to an unclear vision of future objectives and the abundance of financial resources. It is suffering from structural and behavioural defects of both external and internal origin." [119]

Bureaucratic dysfunctions are rampant in the midst of the GCC countries' political systems with excessive powers and unrestrained habits of intervention in every aspect of society. "During the past four decades public administration has been saddled with socio-economic development that has not served the cause of equity and social justice in the society." [120] The "list of bureaucratic deficiencies incorporates adjectives such as lethargic, apathetic, arrogant, corrupt, insensitive to the masses, non- innovative, venal and incompetent." [121]

The major problems before the GCC countries are "that their governments have found themselves obliged to act in several fields and expand their own activities and tasks. In addition, they have dominated the economy by establishing public institutions and firms. These agencies often fail to perform even their traditional tasks satisfactorily, and to be under an obligation to perform new development tasks, in addition to the traditional means lowering the standard of performance even further." [122]

Instead of managing the transition, muddled political processes failed "to provide meaningful institutionalised participation. Incumbent regimes have not developed clear, consistent national objectives with worthy strategies to achieve them." [123] In the GCC countries "although national development is undermined by the poor performance of the bureaucracy, any reforms that affect the power relationships of the dominant elite are unlikely to be entertained." [124]

Lack of centralised databases on desertification issues, inadequate monitoring and assessment, poor capacity-building for focal points and NGOs affect the sustainable development in these countries. Furthermore, in the GCC Countries, there is no comprehensive assessment of the degradation of irrigated land, rain-fed cropland or rangeland. Given the economic potential of these countries and the threatening extent to which desertification is impeding sustainable growth, more extensive cooperative and participatory efforts are necessary.

Adequate and reliable financial resources are necessary to address these shortcomings. The information base on the current magnitude of and trends in desertification at the national level needs substantial improvement. New technologies, techniques, methods, approaches, skills, ideas and systems will facilitate the efficient and effective use of limited and scarce natural resources in these countries.

Notes

1. Federal Foreign Office (Government of Germany), *Desertification: A Security Threat?-Analysis of Risks and Challenges* (Berlin: Technische Zusammenarbeit (GTZ), 2007), p. 3.
2. Bauer, Steffen, Per-Olof Busch and Bernd Siebenhüner, "Administering International Governance: What Role for Treaty Secretariats?", Global Governance Working Paper No. 29, (Amsterdam: Vrije Universiteit, Global Governance Project, 2006), p. 17.
3. Barry, John and Robyn Eckersley. eds., *The State and the Global Ecological Crisis*, (Cambridge: MIT Press, 2005), p. ix.
4. Caldwell, Lynton K. "Management of Resources and the Environment: A Problem in Administrative Coordination," *International Review of Administrative Sciences*, (Sage Publications Ltd), vol. 38, 1972, p. 119.
5. Bahrain, Kuwait, Oman, Qatar, Saudi Arabia and the United Arab Emirates (U.A.E).

6. The rentier State is the one in which the government relies for the lion's share of its revenue (certainly over 50 percent, in the Gulf Monarchies usually over 75 percent) on direct transfers from international economy, in the form of oil revenues, investment income , foreign aid, or other kinds of foreign direct payments.
7. Ashour, Ahmed Sakr, "Development-Driven Public Governance Reform in the Arab Countries", Conceptual Paper (Draft), 2005, [Online: web] Accessed on 23 June 2008 URL: http://www.arabgov-initiative.org/publications/egov/admin-reform-e.pdf, p. 9.
8. Odingo, R. S., "Review of UNEP's Definition of Desertification and its Programmatic Implications", in Odingo R., ed., *Desertification Revisited: Proceeding of an Ad-Hoc Consultative Meeting on the Assessment of Desertification*, (Nairobi: UNEP, 1990), p. 24.
9. El-Tantawi, Attia Mahmoud Mohamed., *Climate Change in Libya and Desertification of Jifara Plain: Using Geographical Information System and Remote Sensing Techniques*, Dissertation submitted in der Johannes Gutenberg-Universität in Mainz (Germany), 2005, p. 3.
10. Alexander, David, E and Rhodes W. Fairbridge, eds. *Encyclopedia of Environmental Science*, (Dordrexche: The Netherlands): Kluwer Academic Publishers, 2001, p. 125.

    The word desert originated as an Egyptian hieroglyph pronounced, *tesert,* meaning a place that was forsaken or left behind. From this came the Latin verb *desere,* to abandon. From the latter came *desertum,* waste place or wilderness, and *desertus,* meaning abandoned or relinquished. This in itself implies that desert had once been a better place. In it there was life- in some places teeming life. There was much vegetation, grasses and trees, many animals and human beings. Then something happened, and the place became a wasteland; it was deserted.
11. UNCCD Secretariat, "Frequently Asked Questions," [Online: web] Accessed on 23 June 2008 URL http://www.unccd.int/knowledge/faq.php#answer0.
12. Darkoh, M.B.K., "The Nature, Causes and Consequences of Desertification in the Drylands of Africa" in Darkoh, Michael and Apollo Rwomire, *Human Impact on Environment and*

Sustainable Development in Africa (Aldershot: Ashgate Publishers, 2003), p. 199.

13. Lamprey H F, "Report on the Desert Encroachment Reconnaissance in Northern Sudan, 21 October to 10 November 1975" *Desertification Control Bulletin*, vol. 17, 1975, pp. 1-7.
14. Adger, W. Neil., et.al "Advancing Political Ecology of Global Environmental Discourses", *Development and Change,* (Oxford), vol. 32, 2001, p. 689.
15. Ibid.
16. Katyal, Jagdish C. and Paul L.G. Vlek, "Desertification-Concept, Causes and Amelioration", Discussion Papers on Development Policy, Centre for Development Research, Bonn, October 2000, p. 7.
17. Aubreville, a perceptive and well informed Botanist and Ecologist, published a book on *Climate, Forests, et Desertificatiom de l Afrique Tropicale* in 1949.
18. Dregne, H.E., *Desertification of Arid Lands,* (London: Harwood Academic Publishers, 1983), p. 4.
19. Katyal , n. 16, p. 7.
20. Dregne, n. 18, p. 4.
21. Extensive preparations were made for this Conference through a number of technical studies, surveys and workshops.
22. Dregne, H.E., "Desertification: Problems and Challenges", *Annals of Arid Zone* (Jodhpur), vol. 34, no. 3, 2000, p. 365.
23. Rechkemmer, Andreas, *Global Environmental Governance: the United Nations Convention to Combat Desertification,* (Berlin: Wissenschaftszentrum Berlin für Sozialforschung (WZB), 2004), p. 55.
24. UNEP, *The Status of Desertification and Implementation of the United Nations Plan of Action to Combat Desertification,* (Nairobi : UNEP, 1992) p. 13.
25. ibid , p. 13.
26. Dregne, et.al, "A New Assessment of the World Status of Desertification", *Desertification Control Bulletin,* vol. 19, 1991, p. 12.
27. Mainguet, Monique, *Aridity: Droughts and Human Development*, (New York: Springer, 1999), p. 252.
28. UNEP, n. 24, p. 13.
29. ibid, p. 14.
30. Mainguet, n. 27, p. 252.

31. Martello, Marybeth Long, "Expert Advice and Desertification Policy: Past Experience and Current Challenges," *Global Environmental Politics,* (MIT Press), vol. 4, no. 3, 2004, p. 86.
32. Corell, Elisabeth., " Drylands Degradation- Africa's Main Environmental Challenge" in Chaytor, Beatrice and Kevin R. Gray, eds., *International Environmental Law and Policy in Africa,* (London: Kluwer Academic Publishers, 2003), p. 4.
33. Toulmin, Camilla, "Combating Desertification: Encouraging Local Action within a Global Framework", in Helge Ole Bergesen and Georg Parmann, eds, *Green Globe Yearbook of International Co-operation on Environment and Development,* (Oxford: Oxford University Press, 1994), p. 79.
34. World Bank, *A Water Sector Assessment Report on the Countries of the Cooperation Council of the Arab States of the Gulf,* (Washington D.C: World Bank, 2005), p. 3.
35. Gulf Research Centre (GRC) *Green Gulf Report* (Dubai: GRC, 2007),, p. 15.
36. Ali Abahussain, Asma, et.al, "Desertification in the Arab Region: Analysis of Current Status and Trends" *Journal of Arid Environments* (Amsterdam), vol. 51, 2002, p. 523.
37. GRC, n. 35, p. 15.
38. Arab Center for the Studies of Arid Zones and Dry Lands (ACSAD), *Inventory Study and Regional Database on Sustainable Vegetation Cover Management in West Asia (TN2),* Prepared for the Sub-Regional Action Program (SRAP) to Combat Desertification and Drought in West Asia, (Damascus: ACSAD, 2003), p. 69.
39. Katyal, n. 16, p. 28.
40. ROWA (Regional Office for West Asia) /UNEP, *Integrated Natural Resource Management for Combating Desertification in West Asia: UNCCD/SRAP Pilot Projects in Jordan, Lebanon, Syria and Yemen 2003-2006, Final Report*, (Manama: ROWA, 2006, p. 2.
41. GRC, n. 35, p. 15.
42. Katyal, n. 16, p. 29.
43. International Center for Agricultural Research in the Dry Areas and Arab Center for the Study of Arid Zones and Dry Lands, (ICARDA) *Integrated Natural Resource Management for Combating Desertification in West Asia, Pilot Projects Proposal*, Prepared for the Sub-Regional Action Programme

(SRAP) for West Asia of the UN Convention to Combat Desertification (UNCCD), (Manama : ROWA/UNEP, 2003), p. 19.

44. Ibid.
45. Salinisation is the main desertification problem in irrigated agriculture. Salinisation involves a number of interrelated processes occuring in the soil, for example waterlogging, increasing salt content, and alkalinisation, in which some nutrients can no longer be absorbed due to the increasing pH-value of the soil. This problem is caused by the overuse of water through unsuitable irrigation techniques, accompanied by inefficient drainage systems. See Nasr, M., "Assessing Desertification and Water Harvesting in the Middle East and North Africa: Policy Implications", Policy Paper no. 10, Center for Development Research, Bonn University, Germany, 1999, p. 9.
46. GRC, n. 35, p. 15.
47. ACSAD, n. 38, p. 69.
48. Ibid.
49. Katyal, n. 16, p. 31.
50. ICARDA, n. 43, p. 26.
51. GRC, n. 35, p. 15.
52. Marauhn, Thilo, "The Changing Role of State" in Bodansky, Daniel, et.al, eds, *The Oxford Handbook of International Environmental Law* (Oxford: Oxford University Press, 2007), p. 729.
53. Rechkemmer, n. 23, p. 31.
54. Soroos, Marvin S., "Global Institutions and the Environment: An Evolutionary Perspective", in Vig, Norman J., and Regina S. Axelrod, eds., *The Global Environment: Institutions, Law and Policy* (London: Earthscan, 1999), p. 29.
55. Paehlke, Robert and Douglas Torgerson, eds., *Managing Leviathan: Environmental Politics and the Administrative State* (Ontario: Broadview Press, 2005), p. 271.
56. Ryding, Sven-Olof, *Environmental Management Handbook*, (Amsterdam: IOS Press, 1998), p. 5.
57. Vogler, John and Andrew Jordan, "Governance and Environment" in Berkhout, Frans, et al, eds, *Negotiating Environmental Change: New Perspectives from Social Science*, (Cheltenham, JK: Edward Elger, 2003), p. 310.

58. UN, *UN General Assembly Resolution 172*, adopted its 32nd Session on 19 December 1977
59. ESCWA, *The Role of ESCWA in Resources Conservation and Management and the Combat of Desertification*, [Online: web] Accessed on 23 June 2008 URL: http://www.fao.org/docrep/x5322e/x5322e00.HTM.
60. Ibid.
61. Ibid.
62. Ibid.
63. Chasek, Pamela, "The Convention to Combat Desertification: Lessons Learned for Sustainable Development", *Journal of Environment and Development*, vol. 6, no. 2, 1997, p. 150.
64. Bauer, n. 2, p. 17.
65. Kjellen, Bo. "The Desertification Convention: Towards creating a multilateral Framework for Coping with Global Threats" in Rolen, Mats, et.al, eds, *International Governance on Environmental Issues*, (London: Kluwer Academic Publishers, 1997), p. 71.
66. Onchere, Naftali Maddy, "The United Nations Convention to Combat Desertification in Easten Africa" Arnalds, Olafur and Steve Archer, eds, *Rangeland Desertification* (London: Springer, 1999), p. 198.
67. Wolfrum, Rudiger, and Nele Matz., *Conflicts in International Environmental Law* (London: Springer, 2003), p. 96.
68. Kemp, David D., *The Environment Dictionary,* (London: Routledge, 1998), p. 99.
69. Humphreys, David and Susan Carr, " Land Degradation and Sustainable Resource management in an African Context" in Thomas, Alan, et.al, eds., *Environmental Policies and NGO Influence: Land Degradation and Sustainable Resource Management in Sub-Saharan Africa* (London: Routledge, 2001), p. 33.
70. Martin-Mehers, Gillian., et.al., eds., *Achieving Environmental Objectives,* (Cambridge(UK): IUCN (World Conservation Union), 2004), p. 121.
71. UNEP*, Manual on Compliance with and Enforcement of Multilateral Environment Agreement* (Nairobi: UNEP, 2006), p. 179.
72. UNCCD Secretariat, *Situational Analysis of UNCCD*, (Bonn: UNCCD Secretariat, 2007), p. 8.

73. Persson, Linn, et.al, "Multilateral Environmental Agreements on the Ground – Lessons from Supporting Implementation of the Montreal Protocol" Policy and Institutions Programme - Working Paper, Stockholm Environment Institute, Stockholm, 2007, p. 1.
74. Caldwell, n. 4, p. 116.
75. The National Coordinating Body (NCB) is the government Ministry or Agency designated to coordinate the work of the UNCCD at the national level and the national focal point (NFP) is the contact person for the UNCCD within the NCB. For further details refer UNCCD Secretariat, *Regional Implementation Annex for Asia National Reports on the UNCCD Implementation: Help Guide*, (Bonn: UNCCD secretariat, 1999).
76. Ministry of Works & Agriculture (MWA), Government of Bahrain, *National Report on the Implementation of the United Nations Convention to Combat Desertification* (Manama, April 2000), p. 21.
77. UNCCD Secretariat, *Report of the Conference of Parties, Fourth Session, 2000*, [Online: web] Accessed on 23 June 2008 URL: http://www.unccd.int/cop/officialdocs/cop4/pdf/3add1(d)eng.pdf p. 42.
78. Ministry of Regional Municipalities, Environment and Water Resources, Government of Oman, *National Action Programme to Combat Desertification in the Sultanate of Oman*, (Muscat, 2005), p. 77.
79. UNCCD Secretariat, *Summary of the Second National Report of the Kingdom of Saudi Arabia on the Implementation of the United Nation's Convention to Combat Desertification* (Bonn, 2002), p. 3.
80. UNCCD Secretariat, *Summary of the Second United Arab Emirates National Report to the UNCCD* (Bonn, 2002) , p. 4.
81. UNCCD Secretariat, *The National Report of the State of Qatar on the UNCCD Implementation*, (Bonn, 2000), p. 12.
82. Toulmin, Camilla, "The Desertification Convention" in Dodds, Felix, ed, *The Way Forward: Beyond Agenda 21* (London: Earthscan, 1997), p. 58.
83. Article 10 of UNCCD, n. 15,
84. Ministry of Forest and Environment (MoFE), Government of India, *National Action Programme to Combat Desertification,* (New Delhi: 1998), p. 43.

85. Ibid, p. 43.
86. Ibid, p. 7.
87. UNCCD Secretariat, n. 77, p. 7.
88. UNEP, *Training Manual on International Environmental Law*, (Nairobi: UNEP, 2006), p.39.
89. UNEP, *Global Environmental Outlook, 2000*, (Nairobi: UNEP, 2000), p. 159.
90. ACSAD, n. 38, p. 38.
91. MWA, n. 76, pp. 21-22
92. ACSAD, n. 38, p. 61.
93. UNCCD Secretariat, n. 77, p. 43.
94. ACSAD, n. 38, p. 72.
95. Ministry of Regional Municipalities, Environment and Water Resources, Government of Oman, *National Action Programme to Combat Desertification in the Sultanate of Oman*, (Muscat, 2005), p. 96.
96. ACSAD, n. 38, p. 72.
97. Ibid , p. 70.
98. UNCCD Secretariat, n. 81, p. 12.
99. ACSAD, n. 38, p. 57.
100. UNCCD Secretariat, Summary of the Second National Report of the Kingdom of Saudi Arabia on the Implementation of the United Nation's Convention to Combat Desertification (Bonn, 2002), p. 3.
101. UAE opposes the term 'combating desertification' and it uses the term 'Greening the Desert', for further see UNCCD Secretariat , *Summary of the Second United Arab Emirates National Report to the UNCCD* (Bonn, 2002), p.1. and GRC, n. 35, p. 16.
102. ACSAD, n. 38, p. 94.
103. UNCCD Secretariat, *Summary of the Second United Arab Emirates National Report to the UNCCD* (Bonn, 2002), p. 4.
104. UNEP, *Global Environmental Outlook 1997* (Nairobi: UNEP, 1997), p. 202.
105. Ibid, p. 203.
106. UNCCD Secretariat, *Report of the Committee to Review the Implementation of Convention, First Session, 2003*, [Online: web] Accessed on 28 June 2008 URL:http://www.unccd.int/cop/officialdocs/cric5/pdf/2add1eng.pdf.

107. ACSAD, n. 38, p. 38.
108. MWA, n. 76, p. 14.
109. UNCCD Secretariat, n. 77, p. 3.
110. ACSAD, n. 38, pp. 61-62.
111. UNCCD Secretariat, n.77, p. 42.
112. Ibid.
113. MRM, n. 95, p. 103.
114. UNCCD Secretariat, n. 77, p. 17.
115. ACSAD, n. 38, p. 70.
116. Ibid, p. 57.
117. UNCCD Secretariat, *The Third National Report for the Kingdom of Saudi Arabia about the Implementation of the United Nations Convention to Combat Desertification (UNCCD): Executive Summary*, (Bonn, 2006), p. 3.
118. ACSAD, n. 38, p. 94.
119. Ansari, Shahid Jamal., *Political Modernization in the Gulf*, (New Delhi: Northern Book Centre, 1998) p. 143.
120. Jreisat, Jamil E., "The Predicament of Administrative Reform in the Arab States" in Farazmand, Ali., *Administrative Reform in Developing Nations*, (London: Praeger, 2002), p. 168.
121. Jreisat, Jamil E., Bureaucratization of Arab World: Incomplete Influence" in Farazmand, Ali ed, *Handbook of Comparative and Development Public Administration"* (New York: Marcel, Dekker, 2001), p. 1008.
122. Ansari, n. 120, pp. 137-38.
123. Jreisat, n. 122, p. 1014.
124. Common, Richard, "Administrative Change in the Gulf: Modernization in Bahrain and Oman", *International Review of Administrative Sciences*, vol. 74, no. 2, 2008, pp. 182-83.

3

Globalisation and Social Change: The Case of United Arab Emirates (UAE)

Asif Suja

With a population of over four million [1], the United Arab Emirates (UAE) assumes importance in the West Asian regional and world at large due to its rapidly growing economy and changing social conditions. Formed as an independent state in 1971, UAE is the only functioning federation in the Arab world (Weiner 2007: 144). Its constituting emirates are the two wealthy oil-producing emirates of Abu Dhabi and Dubai apart from the smaller emirates of Sharjah and the four "village states (ibid.)" of Ras al-Khaimah [2], Umm al-Qaiwain, Ajman, and Fujairah. Abu Dhabi and Dubai are the two main commercial regions where most of the population of UAE is concentrated. While Abu Dhabi, which is the largest emirate, is the capital of UAE, Dubai has earned the reputation of being "the most important part (Europa Regional Survey 2006: 1181)" of the country because of its high volume of transit trade.

This study attempts at a theoretical treatment to the empirical findings of the social change in UAE resulted by the process of globalisation. Without getting into the contemporary debate on the meaning of globalisation, a workable definition of the term 'globalisation' is furnished that serves as a tool of investigation in the context of changing imperatives of society and culture of the region that is now known as the United Arab Emirates (UAE). [3] A brief note on the meaning of 'social change' and the approach to measure such change is subsequently furnished.

In the context of UAE the most important point is to trace

the point of departure from a 'rentier economy' to a 'globalised' economy. The dominance of oil-wealth in most of its history as independent nation makes it difficult to trace when the process of globalisation started in UAE leaving behind the oil-based economy. These issues are discussed in detail in a subtopic that covers the economic condition of UAE in the context of globalisation.

Social change in UAE is analysed by observing the changing patterns of kinship and family structure, the role of education, influence of media and the contemporary behavioural norms of the emiratis. The overwhelming presence of expatriates in UAE leaves any analysis of social and cultural change in UAE incomplete. Therefore, for a comprehensive treatment to the subject, the condition of the expatriate labour force and the resultant cultural proliferation has been studied in detail. Finally, the challenges posed by these social and cultural changes along with the measures of the UAE government to strike a balance between modernism and traditionalism have also been presented.

Contextualising Globalisation

A clear understanding of the term 'globalisation' is predicated for a meaningful study of social change in UAE. Although, the advent of globalisation as an era has been much contested, a sense was developed during the 1980s and 1990s that gave prominence to a "collective wisdom (Bisley 2007: 1)" that "globalization was everywhere and changing everything (ibid.)." We will talk about globalisation in the "context (ibid.)" in which the domestic economies of states were fully integrated to the world economy and this event started the process of cultural proliferation.

How much this cultural proliferation has penetrated the society of UAE and what is the nature of the resultant social transformation, would be our subject of inquiry. Globalisation has been "reorganizing the patterns of social life (ibid.)" and a careful analysis of UAE makes evident such changes in the life of its people. Therefore, globalisation may be treated as the "transformation (Mittelman 2004: 28)" of society and politics, involving "a series of continuities and discontinuities with the past (ibid.)."

Although it has been established that "no single universally accepted definition of globalization exists (Held and McGrew 2000: 3 in Modelski 2008: 2)," a workable definition of the term would serve as the investigating tool. Globalisation, therefore, may be understood as "a process of emergence that is multi-dimensional, and historically significant, and a term obviously basic to understanding global change (Modelski 2008: 3)." The "globalizing process (Mittelman 2004: 28)" is, therefore constituted by the global integration of financial markets and the accompanied "intercultural contact (ibid.)," a process that is evident in the contemporary period. This process is equally evident in UAE, manifested in the social and economic spectrum of the state.

It is also argued that "modernity is inherently globalizing (Held and McGrew 2000: 92in Modelski 2008: 3) or "modernization causes globalization (ibid.)." Although, UAE has transformed itself from semi-feudalism to advanced capitalism in the last four decades, it has a long tradition of business. Due to its geographic location, it was famous for pearling and fishing industry. Islam as a dominant religion and the traditional tribal structure have also supported the region in its business activities. Although, the economic development and social transformation of the region can be explained with the help of Marxist ideas, 'semi-peripheral development' concept of World systems theory, 'Cultural lag' hypothesis of Ogburn and Nimkoff and 'theory of multiple modernity', "most of these theories can come under the rubric of globalisation (Khondker 2008)" when we attempt to study and explain the contemporary phenomenon of modernisation and its economic, social and cultural challenges to the region.

Measuring Social Change

The subject of this paper is the social change in UAE in

the context of globalisation. "Social change is usually described in terms of modernization, revolution, cultural breakdown, and social movements (Moghadam 1993: xiii)." Technological advancements, political actions or class conflict are recognised by the scholars (ibid: 3) as instruments of social change. However, in case of UAE, principal instrument of social change has been the unprecedented wealth due to oil production and its export and subsequently, due to the process of globalisation. The process of social change was given impetus due to the diversification of economy and foreign direct investment. This is particularly so for the two wealthy emirates of Dubai and Abu Dhabi.

While conceptualising social change, we can benefit from Parsons' views on the subject. According to Parsons (Harlambos 1994: 527-29), the basis for order in society can only be the commitment to common values. He conceptualises social change as a 'social evolution' and believes that society moves from a simple to complex form and therefore he gives high prominence to cultural changes. He believes that initial impetus might be due to the economic factors but what is more crucial to social change is the change in culture. This conception of social change is more pertinent to our analysis of the society of UAE in the era of globalisation.

Further, this "understanding of the social change in the region can benefit from Daniel Lerner's study *Passing of a Traditional Society* (1958) (Khondker 2008)" which was a "comprehensive study of changes in society and culture (ibid.)." This study was carried out with the help of a set of questionnaire for the purpose of measuring the modernisation process. Applying the study in case of UAE, we observe that in terms of its high rate of literacy, media exposure and Internet usage, UAE seems to follow the "modernization model of Daniel Lerner (ibid.)." Further, on the cultural front, it appears that UAE has been following "cosmopolitanism from both above and below (ibid.)."

For a true assessment, it should be noted that social change is a multidimensional process which may be understood in terms of changes in politics, economy, culture and technology. Additionally, the consequences of such changes also form an integral part of such study. Our inquiry would include how UAE society is coping with the social changes in everyday life and what is the implication of social transformation on the social and cultural identity of the emiratis.

Globalisation of the UAE Economy

At the outset it should be noted that "the process of change in the UAE cannot be adequately understood outside the dynamics generated by the oil economy and the larger forces of globalization (Khalaf 1999: 273)." Due to the commercial production of oil in 1962 Abu Dhabi acquired immense wealth. This gave it an opportunity for economic development and its society was "suddenly transformed (Europa Regional Survey 2006: 1182)." Petroleum was discovered in Dubai in 1966.

While benefiting from oil-wealth, Dubai developed a "trading and transshipment economy (ibid.)." Consequently, the territory assumed unprecedented importance due to oil. After its independence from British, UAE set itself on the path of economic and social development despite "a set of disadvantageous determinants and imposed structural frameworks (Taryam 1987: 254)." It never looked back since then and boldly faced the challenges posed by the adverse movement in oil revenue.

Riding on the Wave of Globalisation

UAE made attempts to go on fast track economic movement by capitalising on the wave of globalisation. Graduating from an oil-based 'rentier-economy', it went on diversifying its economy to a great extent. It has made attempts at developing a sound manufacturing sector and has developed many free trade and industrial zones (United Nations Conference on Trade and Development 2007: 51). Such free trade zones provide high potential to industrial growth since investors here are provided special facilities and incentives for establishing their industries. In such zones the government of UAE has allowed 100 percent participation to the foreign investors. There are 15 free trade zones in UAE with Dubai's Jebel Ali Free Zone (JAFZ) as the largest (ibid.) and over 100 countries have participated in such free trade zones with more than 5000 business entities.

Globalisation or "the integration of the world economy (World Bank 2007: 313)" has been in continuous discourse since the last quarter century. Political and social organisations of countries definitely get altered due to the cross-border economic activities. It is not possible to measure all effects of globalisation directly. However, the pace of change due to globalisation can be monitored by measuring the economic indicators such as trade in goods and services, financial flows, the movement of people, and diffusion of technology and knowledge (World Bank 2007: 313). UAE's integration with the world economy and its march towards globalisation can be measured by the high growth of merchandise trade of this country. As a percentage of its GDP, this trade was 151.3 percent in 2005 against 103.2 percent in 1990 (ibid: 318). This was a considerable growth for a traditionally oil-based economy.

A Departure from Rentier Economy

The political economy of UAE is changed to such an extent that it would not be appropriate to describe it as a "Rentier State (Khondker 2008)." The substantially diversified economy of UAE, resulting in a huge construction sector, a sound industrial sector and a rapidly growing tourism sector give credence to this argument (ibid.). The UAE economy has done well in recent years due to its diversification efforts. According to the UNDP Human Development Report 2007-2008, out of a total 177 countries UAE ranked 39 in the Human Development Index (HDI) for the year 2005 (United Nations Development Program 2007: 229). Also, the report gives its GDP per capita (ppp US$) for the year 2005 as 25,514 which is substantially high.

UAE is now known worldwide due to its ambitious development projects. In particular, Dubai has launched a massive development drive diversifying its economy in the face of decreasing oil wealth (Heard-Bey 2005: 358). With its towering skyscrapers and amazing architecture Dubai has become a truly "global city (Khondker 2008)" with tourists thronging from all over world and giving a picture of cosmopolitanism. "Now the desert, which in the past was common tribal grazing land, but for which the current generation has no use any more, is being turned into a source of instant wealth in the form of marketable real estate (Heard-Bey 2005: 358)." Other emirates are similarly trying to market their respective assets (ibid.).

The Process of Modernisation

"As far as UAE ruling elites are concerned, their goal is modernisation (Khondker 2008)." The ruling elite is also aware of the challenges that has been posed by the rapid pace of modernisation. "It may be instructive to examine the modernisation process of the UAE as an instance of her being caught up in the process of globalization (ibid.)." UAE economy is now completely integrated to the world economy. In fact, there is a pressing need to replicate the globalisation experiences of UAE in other oil-rich states. Due to oil revenues, the oil rich states managed to move easily to the new millennium without much structural problems. However, the "harsh new economic realities" of the present time leaves the region no other option "but to adjust, adapt, confront and meet the challenges of the new globalized economy." [4]

While these developments are much cherished by the people of UAE, "estimating the price in terms of social cost proves an enduring source of much debate among national politicians (Heard-Bey 2005: 359)." For one these developments require massive inflow of expatriate manpower changing the shape of demography of the land. While globalization has completely changed the landscape of UAE, particularly the two rich emirates, Abu Dhabi and Dubai, it has also posed some challenges in terms of social changes taking place due to the development initiatives. The regime of UAE is struggling to cope with such challenges. These issues are covered in the following section.

Social Change in UAE

Since the time oil replaced pearls, the face of UAE and life of its people "has changed beyond recognition (UAE Ministry of Information and Culture 2004: 43)." It would not be far-fetched to say that for most of the inhabitants of the region now known as UAE, "a traditional lifestyle is but a distant memory (ibid.)." It may be observed, however, that despite the changes taking place due to fast paced modernisation and the impact of globalisation, "the very essence of traditional society, religion, language, family and tribal affiliations, remain constants (ibid.)." Nevertheless, a careful look at the patterns of kinship, ethics and education system reveals the underlying currents of discernible changes which, although at a micro level at present, may magnify disproportionately in the future if the present pace of change is continued.

The Changing Demographic Profile

A careful look at the demographic data of the region now known as UAE reveals that the population of this region has steadily increased over the last six decades. The period of oil-boom explains, in part, the sharp increase in the decade of 1970-1980. Table 3.1 represents the population growth of UAE since the middle of the twentieth century.

A similar growth is evidenced in the population density of the region (Table 3.2), with striking growth since the early 1990s. The gender differential is also increasingly adverse to the female population with the sex ratio more than doubling over the period 1950-2005.

Table 3.1: Population Growth Rate of UAE (in percent)

1950-1955	2.51
1955-1960	2.69
1960-1965	9.38
1965-1970	8.86
1970-1975	17.17
1975-1980	13.00
1980-1985	6.58
1985-1990	5.61
1990-1995	5.28
1995-2000	5.79
2000-2005	4.69

Source: United Nations (2007), *World Population Prospects – The 2006 Revision (Vol. I: Comparative Tables)*, New York: United Nations, Department of Economic and Social Affairs, Population Division, p. 470.

Table 3.2: Population, Density and Sex Ratio of UAE

Year	Population (thousands)	Density (Per sq. km.)	Sex Ratio (males per 100 female)
1950	70	1	102.8
1955	79	1	102.6
1960	90	1	102.4
1965	144	2	138.4
1970	225	3	167.4
1975	530	6	225.5
1980	1015	12	223.2
1985	1410	17	184.9
1990	1867	22	189.3
1995	2432	29	194.9
2000	3247	39	207.2
2005	4104	49	212.1

Source: United Nations (2007), World Population Prospects – The 2006 Revision (Vol. I: Comparative Tables), New York: United Nations, Department of Economic and Social Affairs, Population Division, p. 470.

Kinship and Family Structure

In the West Asian societies, kinship is more prominent than citizenship. Typically, for government services, it is of utmost importance to have 'connections' (*wasta*) (King-Irani 2000: 268) with the influential people. Traditionally, same has been the case with UAE. Chronicling the traditional society of UAE region before its preeminence as a wealthy oil state, Heard-Bey (1982) comments:

"Traditionally, social differentiation in the Trucial States [Now UAE] stemmed from the tribal structure rather than from class distinction and material well-being. The various levels of identification – family, sub-tribe and tribe – allocated a person his particular place in society; thus even the poorest member of a powerful tribe could have more social prestige than a prosperous trader without tribal connections in the sheikhdom." (Heard-Bey 1982: 162)

Thus, like other Arabian territories, in the UAE region too, tribes were the primary political units. Now the territorial boundaries of the modern nation-state have replaced the traditional '*dirah*' (the area of influence of a particular tribe) and the nomad culture is virtually disappeared. However, despite the political authority of the ruling families in the respective emirates, "the loyalty of the tribes (Perk 1986: 62)" was still considered important and was "actively sought by emiral rulers (ibid.)." However, with the onset of globalisation, the situation has changed to a great extent despite the remaining essence of tribalism. In particular, with the growing population of expatriates there has been a reactionary trend among the tribes towards feeling as a unitary whole – as the citizen of one nation.

While the essence of tribal structure remains despite perceptible changes, the rapid social changes brought about by the process of globalisation has posed new challenges to the Arab family, particularly in UAE. Muna Al Bahr [5] (Khaleej Times Online, 29 December 2005), Professor of Social Works at Zayed University observes these changes in the following words:

"Today, the Arab family is expected to carry out tasks which are radically different from the traditional ones carried out until recently ... The Arab family is now required to do what may be called 'empowerment for the future' which consists of developing the general competence of the individual as a whole and which goes beyond simply receiving good grades in class or just passing from one grade to another. These changes have affected every aspect of our lives." (Khaleej Times Online, December 29, 2005)

The family of contemporary Arab society is therefore more concerned with making their children well-equipped to successfully cope with the fast-paced global world. The greatest impact of globalisation, however, is witnessed on the younger generation of the Arab society. In Al Bahr's words:

"Being the prime focus of globalisation, the youth are the most affected by these fast changes coming in culturally, socially, politically and economically. In other words, the youth are globalisation's human capital. Globalisation is the youth's civilisation and is based mainly on their enthusiasm, energy, love for adventure and yearning for the future ..." (Khaleej Times Online, December 29, 2005)

Such concerns notwithstanding, due to the rapid pace of modernisation and development, there has been witnessed an increasing rate of female participation in the labour force. In 1990, the labour force participation rate for female (for ages 15-64) was 25.9 percent which increased to 39.0 percent in 2005 (World Bank 2007: 46). Further, there has been a shift away from the traditional patriarchal system with the young girls increasingly choosing their own husband and denying arranged marriages. This is further enhanced due to carrier-oriented education of women which provides them economic independence. The government policy is also supportive of such changes.

Role of Education System

The education system of the UAE is a point of serious attention when we talk of the changing social structure of the country. The traditional education system has been replaced by more career-oriented and technical universities with the Western universities proliferating the student community immensely. The cultural baggage of 'westernisation' that comes with such education system has to be coped with the emiratis if they have to conserve their traditional norms.

According to the UNDP Human Development Report 2007-2008 (United Nations Development Program 2007: 229), adult literacy rate (percent aged 15 and above), for the period 1995-2005 was as high as 88.7 percent. However, the combined gross enrolment ratio for primary, secondary and tertiary education for 2005 was 59.9 percent which was a cause of concern since it was much lower than the neighbouring Bahrain (86.1 percent), Qatar (77.7 percent) or Kuwait (74.9 percent) for the same year. With the onset of globalisation, there has been a great influence of Western education on the native students of UAE.

A partial change has also been observed in the emirati female students due to the social changes brought about by the globalisation. Although the core cultural imperatives such as religious beliefs and language have not been affected, the perceptible changes "signal a Western value orientation (Khaleej Times Online, December 29, 2005)." Without conflicting with Islamic values, such changes have reflected the "new realities of the country (ibid.)" and "go along with modernisation (ibid.)." For instance, although one can still see women wearing *abayah* (long drapery), the *burqa* (the traditional Arab veil) is increasingly becoming unfashionable. The main challenge of such changes, therefore, is to educate the female students the ways to strike a balance between going on the path of modernisation while at the same time adhering to the local culture.

Patterns of Ethics, Values and Behaviour

The prevalent ethics and values of any society determine the character of the particular civilisation at any given point of time. The behaviour of people of the society and their reaction to the external environment work as the mirror of their values and norms. Therefore, any meaningful study of the social change in UAE should include the patterns of ethics, values and behaviour of its people. In case of UAE, we witness deep impact of globalisation on these variables.

With the introduction of modern facilities such as air conditioned houses, cars and sprawling malls, the consumerism in the UAE society is on a very high. The lifestyle of the people has become highly westernised with the youth going to films, disco and fast-food joints. Increasing habit among the youth to go to the fast-food joints has impacted the values of traditional extended family system. There has been an increasing trend towards individuality among the youth.

There has been a widespread influence of media and communication technologies on the people of UAE, specially the youth. There has been a proliferation of external opinions and information through English and Arabic newspapers, Internet, and satellite television. Such influences definitely alter the culture of the people and therefore, attempts have been made by the UAE government to preserve the heritage of the traditional society. It has been observed that process of modernisation and accompanied crisis of national identity has resulted in the "invented tradition (Khalaf 2000: 243)" such as camel racing. In the modern democratic states such efforts are usually made by the civil society. However, in case of undemocratic and highly welfare state of UAE such responsibilities lie with the government. How far such revivalist techniques are successful is yet to be seen.

In this context it would not be out of place to mention that although UAE "is technically a republic, in reality it is a federation of emirates with no suffrage and no political parties

(Gerner 2000: 115)." Notably, over the years, despite the development of the nation, the individual emirates have retained their individual identity and "over the decades each of the ruling families has been able to consolidate greatly their leadership, while their respective emirate has developed its distinctive economic and social role (Heard-Bey 2005: 362)." Such a unique character of the country also has bearing on the patterns of behaviour of its people.

A major consequence of massive development has been an overwhelming inflow of migrant workers to UAE. The situation today is such that the emiratis are reduced to minority in their own country. While nationals are 20 percent, an overwhelming 80 percent of the total population of UAE is constituted by the expatriates, majority of whom are from south Asia and south-east Asia. Interestingly, non-Arab immigrant workers have outnumbered the Arabs in UAE (Europa Regional Survey 2006: 1181). This is mainly because "migrants from other Arab countries are most feared as constituting a political threat (Perk 1986: 69)." Further, the "fear of compromising economic privileges and of diluting their identity has led natives of the UAE ... to reject the option of absorbing immigrants as citizens (ibid.)." Such behaviour pattern has resulted in the protectionist tendencies, popularly known as 'emiratisation.'

Consequences and Challenges

There has been widespread consequences and accompanied challenges of the social change due to globalisation. Most prominent among them are the economic divide between the emirates, huge number of expatriates in the country and highly consumerist native population.

Economic Divide between the Emirates

At the time of formation of UAE, the option of a federation seemed the "only logical solution (Zahlan 1978: 197)." However, due to the great economic divide, there have been periods of tension among the emirates. The dominance of the two wealthiest emirates – Abu Dhabi and Dubai – creates ripples among the emirates. Still, their "criticism is constrained (Gerner 2000: 115)" because without these two emirates the federation would not have existed.

When the region was known as the Trucial States, its society was homogeneous. The poor economic condition did not give much chance to any section of population to be substantively different from the others (Heard-Bey 2005: 360). The moral guidance even at that time was derived from Islam. However, at that time, this common understanding was "free of sophisticated differences of interpretation (ibid.)." This homogeneous character was initially eroded due to the immense wealth of oil, particularly in the two emirates of Abu Dhabi and Dubai, and subsequently due to the impact of gloablisation.

"Over the last three decades these inequalities have grown rather than diminished (ibid: 361)." Therefore, despite their good effects, the rapid development of the country has also been criticised due to its social costs. There is also huge pressure on the government for improvements in health services, education and the condition of employment of the natives, particularly in the five poorer emirates.

Huge Number of Expatriates

The greatest challenge perhaps is the number of growing expatriates in UAE. Massive infrastructural and developmental projects and high level of foreign direct investments together with the lack of native's participation in the unskilled jobs have put tremendous pressure on the country for foreign labour. This has changed the demographic profile of the country to an extent where only 20 percent of the population is nationals. This percentage of the nationals in the labour market is even lower – with only 9.3 percent (Khondker 2008). Further, with the UAE destined to be transformed into a knowledge-based economy, even the highly educated and skilled professionals are likely to increase.

Weiner (2007) portrays a quite grim picture of the migrant labours of the oil-rich countries of the Persian Gulf. His account of their condition gives us a clue of the condition of the migrants in UAE. He observes:

"... although migrants have become an inextricable part of the economy, they are pressed to live in their own social enclaves, cannot obtain citizenship, own property or join trade unions, have restricted access to social benefits, and are excluded from participation in the political system. The result is a sharply divided political and social order in which less than half of the population are citizens with full rights while the remainder, constituting two third of the labor force, are migrants living in a subordinate position and subject at any time to expulsion." (Weiner 2007: 131)

The "humanistic paradox in the migrant's life" is "that migration is their 'exile' and 'refuge' at one and the same time. This is a philosophical irony which depicts in dialectical terms the human condition in which migrants live (Khalaf 1999: 296)." The overwhelming population of expatriates in UAE poses many cultural problems. Most important of them include the influence of foreign language speaking people on the children of nationals, the youth attitude, the threat of democratization.

According to Heard-Bey (2005: 361), main implications of this population difference are:

- The minority position of the nationals have brought them together to form a privileged class.
- Despite old rivalries on tribal and hierarchical discrimination, all natives consider themselves first as UAE Citizens and later anything else.
- A particular national solidarity has been created.
- In the absence of the need of taking up unskilled job, the UAE nationals can be categorised as coming under 'middle class' or above.

A Highly Consumerist Native Population

Although, there have been attempts at preserving the traditional norms and values, the impact of globalisation, particularly the inflow of expatriates have posed serious challenges to such attempts. A government estimate (UAE Ministry of Information and Culture 2004: 226) puts the UAE nationals accounting for a meager 2 percent of the total workforce in the private sector of the economy. The gravity of the problem can be judged by the fact that private sector accounts for a whopping 52.1 percent of the overall jobs in UAE. This is in sharp contrast to the period just 14 years ago in 1995 when the share of nationals to the total workforce was 9 percent.

Although the oil-producing states such as the United Arab Emirates, Kuwait, Qatar, Bahrain and Oman all have about two-third of the labour force that is imported, they have a common strategy of not allowing the migrants to become citizens (Weiner 2007: 127-28). Additionally, the welfare nature of the state allows them to keep the people away from political participation.

So, while at one end, these states share their wealth with their citizens and facilitate their life style by erecting modern infrastructure such as roads, airports and state of the art communication networks, at the other end labour is imported from other lesser developed countries to develop and maintain such facilities (ibid: 128). Such a strategy is "producing a social order divided between a consumer-oriented native population and a productivity-oriented migrant population, with the result that economic growth is occurring without the local population acquiring the values with the modern productive life (ibid: 130)."

Conclusion

A careful observation of the impact of globalisation on the society of UAE brings forth three important points. First, UAE has set itself on a seemingly irreversible path of gloablisation.

Second, although the traditional cultural and ethical imperatives such as its religion (Islam) and language (Arabic) remain unchanged, much of the ways of life of the emiratis have changed towards modernisation. Third, the overwhelming presence of expatriates in UAE has resulted in greater national identity on part of UAE nationals suppressing the traditional tribal strife to a great extent.

As far as the challenges posed by the globalisation are concerned, the most pressing issue is to come to terms with the increasing modernisation, which to a great extent is what is called 'westernisation' of the society and culture of emiratis. How far the attempts of the government to conserve the traditional culture with the help of official cultural and heritage organisations help is yet to be seen. As far as the presence of expatriates and 'emiratisation' are concerned, the goal of turning UAE into a knowledge-based economy indicates that the number of expatriates are likely to increase with the result of greater challenges of cultural assimilation with the inflow of people with diverse cultural background.

Notes

1. Census of December 2005 (Europa Regional Survey 2006: 1181).
2. Ras al-Khaimah joined the Federation in 1972.
3. This region was formerly known as the Trucial States.
4. Forward by Mervat Tallawy, Executive Secretary, ESCWA (Economic and Social Commission for West Asia 2003: p. v).
5. Muna Al Bahr said these words while addressing a seminar that was organised by Zayed University Media Centre and Research at Dubai Media city in December 2005 (Khaleej Times Online, December 29, 2005).

References

Bisley, Nick (2007), *Rethinking Globalization*, New York: Palgrave Macmillan.

Economic and Social Commission for West Asia (2003), *Survey of Economic and Social Developments in the ESCWA Region 2002-2003*, New York: United Nations.

Europa Regional Survey (2006), *The Middle East and North Africa 2007: Europa Regional Survey of the World* (53rd edition) (2006), London: Routledge.

Gerner, Deborah J. and Philip A. Schrodt (2000), "Middle Eastern Politics", pp. 81-128, in Deborah J. Gerner (ed.) (2000), *Understanding the Contemporary Middle East*, Boulder, Colorado: Lynne Rienner Publishers.

Haralambos, Michael (1994), *Sociology: Themes and Perspectives*, Oxford: Oxford University Press.

Heard-Bey, Frauke (1982), *From Trucial States to United Arab Emirates – A Society in Transition*, London: Longman.

Heard-Bey, Frauke (2005), "The United Arab Emirates: Statehood and Nation-Building in a Traditional Society", *Middle East Journal*, Summer, 2005, Vol. 59, No. 3, pp. 357-375.

Held, D. and A. McGrew (2000), *The Global Transformations Reader: An introduction to the globalization debate*, Cambridge: Polity Press, in George Modelski, Tessaleno Devezas and William R. Thomson (eds.) (2008), *Globalization as Evolutionary Process: Modeling global change*, London: Routledge.

Khalaf, Sulayman (2000), "Poetics and Politics of Newly Invented Traditions in the Gulf: Camel Racing in the United Arab Emirates", *Ethnology*, Vol. 39, No. 3, Summer 2000, pp. 243-261.

Khalaf, Sulayman and Saad Alkobaisi (1999), "Migrants' Strategies of Coping and Patterns of Accommodation in the Oil-Rich Gulf Societies: Evidence from the UAE", *British Journal of Middle Eastern Studies*, Vol. 26, No. 2, November 1999, pp. 271-298.

Khaleej Times Online (20 August 2009), Online Newspaper of UAE, "Rapid social changes pose new challenges to Arab families", 29 December 2005, Accessed on 20 August 2009, URL: http://www.khaleejtimes.com/Displayarticle.asp?section=theuae &xfile=data/theuae/2005/december/theuae_december852.xml.

Khondker, Dr. Habibul Haque (2008), "Social Change in the United Arab Emirates: Challenges of Migration and 'Emitatisation'", A Lecture delivered at the Middle East Institute on 11 July 2008, Published by Middle East Institute, Singapore, Middle East Institute Website: www.mei.nus.edu.sg.

King-Irani, Laurie, "Kinship, Class, and Ethnicity", pp. 263-292, in Deborah J. Gerner (ed.) (2000), *Understanding the*

Contemporary Middle East, Boulder, Colorado: Lynne Rienner Publishers.

Mittelman, James H. (2004), *Whither Globalization? The vortex of knowledge and ideology*, London: Routledge.

Modelski, George, Tessaleno Devezas and William R. Thomson (eds.) (2008), *Globalization as Evolutionary Process: Modeling global change*, London: Routledge.

Moghadam, Valentine M. (1993), *Modernizing Women: Gender and Social Change in the Middle East*, Boulder: Lynn Rienner Publishers.

Perk, Malcolm C. (1986), *The United Arab Emirates – A venture in Unity*, Boulder, Colorado: Westview Press.

Taryam, Abdullah Omran (1987), *The Establishment of the United Arab Emirates 1950-85*, London: Croom Helm.

UAE Ministry of Information and Culture (2004), *United Arab Emirates Year Book 2004*, London: Trident Press.

United Nations (2007), *World Population Prospects – The 2006 Revision (Vol. I: Comparative Tables)*, New York: United Nations, Department of Economic and Social Affairs, Population Division.

United Nations Conference on Trade and Development (2007), *World Investment Report – Transnational Corporations, Extractive Industries and Development*, New York: United Nations.

United Nations Development Program (UNDP) (2007), *Human Development Report 2007/2008 – Fighting climate change: Human solidarity in a divided world,* New York: Palgrave Macmillan.

Weiner, Myron (2007), "International Migration and Development: Indians in the Persian Gulf", pp.128-176, in Prakash C. Jain (ed.), *Indian Diaspora in West Asia: A Reader*, New Delhi: Manohar Publisher and Distributors.

World Bank (2007), *World Development Indicators 2007*, Washington: The World Bank.

Zahlan, Rosemarie Said (1978), *The Origins of the United Arab Emirates – A Political and Social History of the Trucial State*, London: The Macmillan Press Ltd.

4

Migrant Work and Human Rights in the GCC Countries: Emerging Scenario after Migrant Labour Unrest

M.V. Bijulal

Background

After the importance of the GCC countries in terms of their strategic control on Oil resources, it was the large scale urban development initiatives that attracted the world attention to the GCC countries. The booming construction industry was one of the worst hit sectors due to the strikes in 2008. The widespread labour unrest in the Arab countries in 2008 was quite unexpected to a larger global audience. The physical landscape of the Gulf countries was preparing for a large make over to suit the large scale development processes, which had already attracted global attention. The workers, mainly in the construction sector took to street demanding fair wages as well as better working conditions. Demonstrations acquired violent turn, as in many places street protests ended up damaging public and private property leading to frequent street fights between the protestors and the police. Popular media reports on the crisis anchored the discussion on the severe wage reduction as the primary reason for the strikes. Strong indications existed on the deplorable conditions in which the workers were living and working. It is also important to consider that the living and working conditions of the informal, unskilled workers who were protesting, was already a matter of discussion at the governmental level as the later parts of our discussion will show. The 2008 labour strikes almost repeated the same demands of similar strikes in many Gulf countries since 2004. [1]

The proportion of foreign labour compared to the whole workforce in Saudi Arabia, is 88 percent. It is 84 percent in Kuwait, 95 percent in the UAE. As per 2006 figures, the proportion of expatriate workers and employees in the private sector compared to the employed nationals in Kuwait amounted to 90 percent, in the UAE to 98.7 percent, and in Qatar to 96 percent. Strikes in the present decade in the GCC countries raised the issue of poor wages along with dignity and security at work. The workers were mainly complaining of the poor wages and raised the issue that rate of inflation and living cost was not considered for revising minimum wages. Together with this they also raised the issue of poor working situations, issues of security at wok, irregular payment of wages, non payment of wages, non-payment of overtime and lack of fair treatment. Anomalies engrained in the transit and stay of labourers warranted immediate attention in many cases, and there exists a strong lack in documentation at both the ends. Economic exploitation and rights denials continue to occur since many of the workers do not have access to information related to their conditions of work, contract etc and in many cases those who have adopted illegal means dare not question excesses for the fear or punishment, once their illegality is exposed. Since 2004, better wages and better working and living situations were the major demands. Strikes had different dimensions, and the responses to the strikes were also quite varying. While in Kuwait, Bangladeshi workers were at the frontline of strike, in other countries Indian workers and others were in the forefront. The issue of strike was quite seriously taken by the Kuwait Government, which held a parliament emergency session on September 10, 2008 to discuss the problems of foreign workers. In UAE the government's responses and measures to address labour issues is still continuing. Issues relating the strikes are quite diverse and needs special attention in different locations. There are strong indications regarding the Gulf Cooperation Council (GCC) countries plan for a common plan to address the situation after the labour strike through a dialogue involving both public and grass-root authorities and associations. GCC is giving special importance to the problem in light of the unemployment among nationals in the GCC countries. The following section is an analysis based on the human rights issues surfaced in the recent mass labour unrests, based on International human rights instruments. The relevant ILO Conventions and other United Nations Conventions pertaining to migrant work and the rights questions of the migrant worker will be referred here.

This paper is an attempt to explore the reasons leading to the struggle, looking at the dynamics of labour contracting, domestic laws, employer's responsibilities and violation of labour rights. Responses from various interested agencies is discussed, considering the struggle as a means in communicating the need for immediate redressal of the human rights violations at work and other related spaces.

Historical construction of these lapses is attempted here, with study on the roles of various actors. The struggle, and the responses to it and the initiatives taken by the governments, civil society and employers are the broad topics selected for analysis. This paper is also exploring the possibility in part, by making reference to human rights discourse as a platform in combining inferences from multiple locations, an attempt shared with previous studies on construction of migration in south Asia (Jeevan Raj Sharma, 2008). The general body of academic literature concerning labour flows was in part helpful in identifying the issues of labour rights, in field research for this paper. Direct testimonies from workers who worked in the Gulf hailing from Kerala are also used to construct the observations. It also documents the contributions of civil society organizations and human rights bodies, in influencing the state making or making interventions through public pressure and informed advocacy.

Nature of Migrants in the Gulf

Gulf Arab countries account to the first three positions in the list of countries all over the world in terms of percentage of migrant population in the total population according to the 2002 estimates.

In the Gulf countries, unskilled labour force for building and marinating of infrastructural projects is historically coming from the South Asian or South East Asian countries. This labour flow also reveals a dependence on labour power especially after 1991 as we saw earlier, the impact of such dominance is viewed as a threat to national security by some countries, while the negative economic implication in the event of deportations makes other countries to seek a more cautious position. Catering to the needs of migrants is also looked upon as an opportunity to have a positive image in the international arena, to have the status as an employment provider for people coming from lower income countries.

Table 4.1

Country	Percent of total population	Number of migrants (thousands)
United Arab Emirates	73,8	1.922
Kuwait	57,9	1.108
Jordan	39,6	1.945
Israel	37,4	2.256
Singapore	33,6	1.352
Oman	26,9	682
Estonia	26,2	365
Saudi Arabia	25,8	5.255
Latvia	25,3	613
Switzerland	25,1	1.801

Source: International Migration Report 2002, United Nations (Department of Economic and Social Affairs, Population Division).

Large scale migrations, usually refereed to as voluntary human movement across national spaces and international boundaries is on the increase and some estimates suggest that one person in thirty-five are a migrant in one way or the other. Disaggregated data on reasons of migration notwithstanding, research is still needed on the factors under which the worker opts to migrate (whether volition was a free choice) as well as the factors influencing on workers decision stay. Analysis of situations leading to the labour strikes in the GCC countries also opens up a possibility for investigations on this matter. Wage factor was one of the major concern of the strikes as it appeared in the media where the weekly payment of workers was quoted as US$160, for six-or seven day week where as the payment for a citizen of the host country was seven times more than the amount. [2] Direct testimonies from workers returned from the Gulf in Kerala indicate that they got a pay, if calculated annually, a sum of Rs. 8000- 12,000. Any increase from a standard rate of Rs. 8-10 thousand is achieved through extreme hardships including working under hazardous conditions without adequate security gear. As one testimony reads.

My life was really good, though salary was quite low, the facilities given were excellent. Imagine I had a chauffer driven Toyota Corolla car. My work was to supervise 150 workers. Most of them from India had come there paying many lakh of rupees as commission to agents. Including the overtime allowances they could get a monthly income of Rs. 11,000. They were treated like slaves by the employer, since they had no options left they were silent to the most inhuman forms of ill treatments. Most often I had differences of opinion with the employer, who in the end of the week asked me to cut certain part of the weekly payment, without any reason. When I challenged I was asked to keep quiet. I raised the question of poor basic facilities like 150 of them having just 8 toilets and all of them were supposed to report to work at 06.15 am every day, all the days. It was the height, you can imagine how stressed they would be after a days work to complete all the chorus including cooking and to leave for work. I have nothing else to call this system but slavery. I had all the facilities amidst this suffering, I couldn't stand this, I left still I get calls to join back I will not join again. [3]

As per some responses the workers pay exorbitant rates to get visa to GCC countries and are forced to pay at intervals to ensure their stay and work. Workers are assigned a main job, which requires them to be either six days a week or many cases seven days a week varying from eight to ten hours. Many of the workers are not paid overtime wages or not even get time compensation as leisure. In most cases the workers, mostly in minor supervisory positions are supposed to do many other works.

Human Rights Instruments Relating to Migrant Rights

This analysis is structured on the conceptualization of workers rights codified in the International Instruments relating to human rights of migrant workers, viz., the Convention on the rights of all migrant workers and their families 1990, the UN general assembly Palermo Protocols regarding forced work. Human rights of migrants 2004, the ILO Convention No. 97 on Migration for Employment, 1949, and the ILO Convention No. 143 on Migrant Workers (Supplementary Provisions), 1975. [4] Policy changes and the governmental, civil initiatives in the donor and recipient countries are also discussed.

The International Labour Organisation (ILO) has a chequered history in formulating labour rights instruments for migrant workers. ILO Convention of 1949 was a watershed in this regard, an improvement of the Migration for Employment Convention, 1939, adopted by the Conference at its Twenty-Fifth Session of the ILO in 1937. The Convention, 1949 advocated for unrestricted exchange of migration related state data, as well as policies among parties of the Convention (Article1). It also called for "an adequate and free service to assist migrants for employment, and in particular to provide them with accurate information" (Art 2). Article 4 of the Convention talks about appropriate mechanism for employment related travel, stay and departure of the migrant to be dealt with appropriate state interventions, while the Article 5 emphasize the responsibility of the receiving state to provide appropriate health care and to ensure hygienic conditions of living to the migrants. Conceptualisation of right to equality as per the Article 6 of the convention would be one of the earliest instruments of International order on the issues of rights of migrant workers. [5]

It is relevant here to refer to international declarations on prevention of oppressive forms of labour including trafficking and the concept of modern slavery are also referred to widen the scope of situation. ILO Convention No. 143 on Migrant Workers (Supplementary Provisions), 1975, "undertakes to respect the basic human rights of the migrant workers" (Art.1). It remained more specific on the illegal acts of transfer of persons under the cover of migration and stressed the need for more frequent and effective sharing of data between countries on the matter of migration. Articles 2 to 7 of the Convention, explicitly mention to prevention of trafficking.

The ILO Convention on Rights of All Migrants and Families 1990 identifies the need "to make further efforts to improve the situation and ensure the human rights and dignity of all migrant" in addition to the existence of an already established body of principles and standards". The coordinated effort to formulate an international convention on rights of all migrant workers was an extended processes starting from 1979 to 1989. The 1990 Convention was made with specific reference to "instruments within the framework of the International Labour Organisation" like the Convention concerning Migration for Employment (No. 97), the Convention concerning Migrations in Abusive Conditions and the Promotion of Equality of Opportunity and Treatment of Migrant Workers (No. 143), the Recommendation concerning

Migration for Employment (No. 86), the Recommendation concerning Migrant Workers (No. 151), the Convention concerning Forced or Compulsory Labour (No. 29) and the Convention concerning Abolition of Forced Labour (No. 105). Article 7 of the 1990 convention refers to the cross cutting themes in Human Rights as per the international human rights instruments followed by part II that deals with the Human Rights of all migrant workers and their families. These include freedom of movement right to "at any time to enter and remain in their State of origin". Legal protection to the right to life of migrant workers and members of their families (Article 9) protection from torture, cruel, inhuman or degrading treatment or punishment. (Article 10) protection from slavery or servitude, protection from performing forced or compulsory labour. (Article 10 and 11) Social and cultural rights are referred in Article 12 to regarding matter of freedom of religion (observance, practice and teaching) freedom of expression; including freedom to seek, receive and impart information and ideas of all kinds, regardless of frontiers, either orally, in writing or in print, in the form of art or through any other media of their choice.

Other important provisions of the Convention are Right to access to legal proceedings in matter of verification by law enforcement officials of the identity of migrant workers (Art 16, immediate communication to consular or diplomatic authorities of the migrant concerned in the event of arrest or detention and to avail legal protection while being in custody from abuse, etc (Article 17) right to equality with nationals before law at the host country, Right to protection from collective expulsion (Article 18) equal status in remuneration, and other work related conditions and benefits with nationals (Article 25), right to form unions (Article 26) and take part in meetings and activities of trade unions and of any other associations established in accordance with law, with a view to protecting their economic, social, cultural and other interests, right to medical care (Article 28), right to personal liberty and right to education of the children of the migrants right to transfer earnings and savings personal effects and belongings (Article 32).

Protocol to prevent, suppress and punish trafficking in persons, especially women and children, supplementing the United Nations convention against transnational organized crime 2003 was the most recent International human rights instrument that extended the debate on Human rights of migrant workers.

The definition of trafficking in persons as per the Protocol, Article 3, reads "For the purposes of this Protocol: (a) "Trafficking in persons" shall mean the recruitment, transportation, transfer, harboring or receipt of persons, by means of the threat or use of force or other forms of coercion, of abduction, of fraud, of deception, of the abuse of power or of a position of vulnerability or of the giving or receiving of payments or benefits to achieve the consent of a person having control over another person, for the purpose of exploitation. Exploitation shall include, at a minimum, the exploitation of the prostitution of others or other forms of sexual exploitation, forced labour or services, slavery or practices similar to slavery, servitude or the removal of organs.

The protocol was a reification of the right to protection of human rights as listed in the protocol. The prominent contribution to the discourse regarding forced work in the protocol is the most mentionable aspect, which has immediate applications to all situations where question of forced work as well as denial of dignified work are concerned. In the context of universal human rights documents the rights experience in GCC countries could be looked at, considering that the legal rights regime for the migrant workers may not encode the rights as prescribed by the ILO conventions or other relevant International Bodies. However, the country reporting in select case, as the response to the Committee on International Convention on Elimination of All forms of Racial

Discriminations (ICERD) indicate to commitments to United Nations Human Rights Mechanism. [6]

Debates in Migration and Citizenship

One of the important universal questions regarding the status of workers in the host country is the legally sanctioned discrimination against the workers as non-citizen connected to social, economic and political and cultural rights. However the recent initiatives followed by large scale labour unrest demand an enquiry into, addressing the question from a new vision on citizenship; a citizenship of residency in place of citizenship by national membership. Seyla Benhabib speaks about moving away from the conceptualization of citizenship as national membership and more towards citizenship of residency with civil and social rights, and in some cases political participation rights, extended to non-citizens (Benhabib, 2007). What occurs could be, as Aihwa Ong (2006) identifies, that "the various components of citizenship, such as rights, membership in a state, and territory, are becoming disarticulated from each other, and becoming re-articulated with universal principles of neoliberalism and human rights as diverse mobile populations claim rights" Delineating the human rights component of this argument (while the neoliberal part it connects with the human rights component is a matter of another discussion) is relevant in this context, since the United Nations International Convention on the Protection of the Rights of All Migrant Workers and Members of Their Families has vexed on the universality of rights against all forms of discriminations as well as safety and secure livelihoods to migrant workers as the Article 1 of the Convention reads. [7]

Civil Initiatives in India

Statistics given by Kapiszewski, Andrezej (2006) indicate a large share of workers from India in the GCC countries. While academic and public discussions highlight the strategic economic importance of migrants to the national wealth, it was only in recent years that the Indian media started focusing on issue of the rights of the workers. This trend was also visible in academic literature as well which broadly restricted the discussion of workers to the realm of economic significance of the remittances of the workers. On the other hand there was a rights campaign that focused on the issues since 2008 [8]. This has led to wide discussion of the rights issues as well as formulation of a document through civil society initiatives for the protection of the rights of workers.

Status of Migrant Labour in the Gulf

Studies on migrants' remittances and their implications to host economies, as well as relations between migration and trade (Sajitha Beevi Karayil 2007) still continue to be a major stream of interest in academic research. Some studies in this stream have cited the importance of migrant remittances in clear terms [9] indicating a strong national interest orientation. [10] Some studies have also dealt with migration as a modernising experience as well as empowering experience of migrants at the receiving country. Katy Gardner and Filippo Osella (2003) talks about the experience of the Sri Lankan women in the Arab Gulf countries, citing the meaningful changes occurring to them by frequenting with task demanded by the new work situations. At the broader social readings on the experience of migration in totality has emerged stronger in recent times, focusing on the aspects of how modernity (upscale urbanization) impacted on the civil, political and cultural aspects of migrants across the world. This paper follows the discursive realm set by a new genre of research which broaden the scope in research on understanding the dynamics of development in the Arab gulf, and the rights of migrants in that larger context. This is also contributing to the understanding on how new dynamics in urbanization have determined the parameters for rights as a human person. Some of these researches have chosen to locate the migratory experiences outside the realm of conventional discussions based on official data. A specific crisis in this regard related to the Gulf countries is explained in Edward J. Malecki and Michael C. Ewers *Prog Hum Geogr* 2007. There is apprehension about accuracy of data among the recipient states in the Gulf about the foreign migrants suggesting that the data from sending countries, must be relied as true proof. (Winckler, 2005)

The temporal specificity of the data, as well as the major lapse in the official data due to non-representation of undocumented migration was the major challenges/ lapses in the official data. Undocumented migration is a major issue in transnational migration, which is applicable to all continents. In the case of Europe, thousands of illegal migrants from Asian countries and erstwhile socialist block countries of the Eastern Europe pay heavy commission to agents, who take them across through risky routs. [11] For those who juxtaposed the experience of workers with the popular media representations of the Global city/World class city etc., the main critique was the lack of dialogue between the experience the social and economic well being of the migrant workers and the human and citizenship rights of the migrants. [12] Such a trade off is well detailed in the commentaries of the experience of workers, while traveling though various documentations on migrant life in Arab countries. One of the factors that came out strongly in the interactions with workers was their observations regarding the conflict between the moral principles of Islam, the state religion in the Arab countries influencing in all ethical, social political and economic matters, and the system of exploitation surviving in the countries in the labour sector. To many of the workers such conflict explained the strengthening of the new exploitative orders in work related arrangements and the lack of formal legal/governmental systems in addressing this ethical and moral crisis in the Arab societies and cultures.

From the interactions with the workers it was clear that productive employment, respect and dignity at work place and the security were matter of urgent concern. In general the workers experience showed a crucial non-states area that decided guarantee of rights in all these aspects. This area defines the internal world of the unseen, illegal and inhuman side of the labour arrangement, and which till now is not addressed as a matter of human rights violations. Negotiating this labour arrangement paradox, and bringing it to the location of governance is central concern for the collective state and non-state human rights actions. The workers feel that as long as this gray area is unattended by law or human rights principles the crisis is to remain. Since the matter is connected to individual status as migrants, at some point the rights connected to institutional citizenship face a challenge. Here the post-citizenship advocate's arguments need to be considered, for uniform acceptance of respect to rights when rights are restricted for a person as a citizen of a country. [13] Benhabib recognizes that changes in the patterns of political belonging have been accompanied by forms of exclusions and that some groups (e.g. asylum seekers and refugees) have not benefited from the spread of cosmopolitan norms (2007). And Ong (2006) similarly acknowledges that citizenship rights have been extended to some migrants but not others when she observes: 'instead of all citizens enjoying a unified bundle of citizenship rights. These readings constitute a counter-hegemonic discourses because they question particular elements of state sovereignty and would, if accepted, undermine those facets of the global political economy that require the labor of underpaid and insecure migrants. (Abella, 2006; Pécoud and de Guchteneire, 2006)

Considering the activities engaged by the workers as direct acts of development this institutional model becomes more applicable with nuanced adaptations in various countries. Another important model in civil engagement is the effort to bring in inputs in revising rights situations, with application of non-codified human rights principles. Some prominent examples in using a mixed model of hegemonic and counter hegemonic human rights for advocating human rights of migrants in the US and Canada connects the advancements in application of human rights norms in securing human rights for migrants. Such initiatives communicate the present day civil society human rights advocacy on migrant has reached a stage where the international community has taken the task of socializing the dissenting states to institutionalizing accepted principles, with an emphasis on implementing norms. (As Tanya Basok says while exploring the contributions of civil initiatives on advocating for non-hegemonic rights in the case of migrants in the U.S. and Canada "hegemonic human rights norms are congruent with liberal notions of formal equality between individuals and individual freedom from coercion, as well as principles of national sovereignty while counter-hegemonic human rights values are the ones that in one way or another challenge the status quo, either by undermining the political economic foundations of liberal democracies and/or the principles of national sovereignty. The need for open non-state perceptions on rights is furthered in Benhabib, 2007 through an argument for "delinking citizenship rights, from mandatory membership in a nation-state, a core to the new human rights debate on migrants, opting for a the conceptualization of citizenship as national membership and more towards citizenship of residency with civil and social rights, and in some cases political participation rights, extended to non-citizens". (Benhabib, 2007)

In the case of GCC countries, reminiscences of low skilled, underpaid workers demonstrate a working and living situation akin to forced labour, where denial of all human rights are used as means to control, discipline and exploit. In the last few years this private narrative find a legitimate expression in the visual and print media, which are abuzz with large-scale violations across the Arabian Gulf against informal workers from South and East Asian origins. In many cases practices of control and exclusion clearly indicate to violation of universal human rights principles, inalienable and nonnegotiable for the dignified and safe human existence in any situation. [14]

Response from GCC Countries

The GCC countries, it is argued that, generally turn a blind eye to their poor wage structure, non-payment of salaries, lack of medical care and sub-standard housing. Further, the GCC states promulgated legislations that not only offered restricted participation of workers but also laid down stringent measures for organizing or participating in strikes. [15]

However, there were efforts from the state, as in the case of Saudi Arabia, where the government decided to initiate a representative system of workers in those units where one hundred or more workers were enrolled in. Though this development in 2002 was hailed as an important step in the history of social and labour rights by the ILO in 2009, critiques mark this development as symbolic and nominal, with no real power vested in the committee of workers. The ILO did not publicize the fact that the committees will lack real independence. Employees at each company may form only one committee, with three to nine members. The minister of labor and social affairs must approve committee members; the minister and companies' management have the right to send representatives to committee meetings; and the minutes of all meetings must be provided to management.

At the outset, there is a range of responses among GCC states on the large scale use of expatriate workers. Some countries see it as threat to the countries' national cultures, traditions and values, while few others see the use of migrant work essential to benefit from globalisation. At the same time there is a thinking to continue the status quo in workforce for promoting the image of GCC reducing the gap between the wealthy and poor nations. There is an opinion that most of problem of the workers arise from their countries of origin and then worsen in the host countries of this region, and main reason is that workers come to one of the Gulf countries after taking large debts to pay recruiting agents to find work in the region. There is an agreement in principle that "recurring strikes and violent acts by expatriate workers reflect some dimensions of their ordeals and suffering". [16]

Over the years, however, the responses from GCC on the labour unrest showed a change from use of law and order and punitive actions that were on the higher side at least till 2008. The state policy towards demands of the striking workers was today more of a dialogue and concern for human rights than in 2008 where the approach was more of using law to repress the struggles. [17]

According to credible sources, in a response to the strikes in 2006 and 2007 UAE Labour Minister Ali al-Kaabi had announced some measures concerning basic protection of life for the workers. One of the measures was the introduction of mid-day work breaks during the hot summer months. In another instance the Minister had ordered a well-known company to pay about US$2m in fines for failing to pay its workers. However these labour friendly measures ended up as, Mr. Kaabi was replaced in 2008 invoking doubts about the extent of acceptability of his measures. On the other hand Bahrain is reported to have taken a consultative course to deal with situations arising from the labour unrest.

Another measure following the 2008 unrest is the setting up a commission to arbitrate in the dispute. Further the GCC countries are taking initiatives to change the ethnic composition of the workforce by opening up more areas of work for the nationals. [18]

The following description (Box 1) deals with an ILO initiated multi-stake holder imitative that gave an inventory for collective action for ensuring rights at all stages of activities relating to migrant labour, from recruitment. This will help improving transparency at recruitment and fairness in terms of wages. The initiative has wider implications by invoking rights of the migrant at the policy level, for constant institutional supervision of processes and leading to reduction of illegal and exploitative processes.

Box 1

The Colombo Agreement: Feizal Samath, SRI LANKA: Unions strike landmark deal to protect migrant workers, May 11, 2009

The historic agreement between trade unions from West Asian countries (Bahrain, Jordan and Kuwait) with Srilankan trade unions, on the welfare of migrant workers is a major step. The Colombo agreement as it is referred; stands for guaranteeing all internationally recognized labour rights to Sri Lankan workers, with unions in receiving countries ensuring implementation. This agreement was facilitated by the Bureau for Workers' Activities (ACTRAV) of the International Labour Organization (ILO). ACTRAV is active in Strengthening the labour movement, Promoting fundamental rights and principles at work, Collective bargaining and social dialogue, Combating the exploitation of child labour.

Improving working conditions and the environment, fighting unemployment and underemployment and workers training.

Of the 1.6 million Sri Lankan migrant workers in the Middle East, Asia and Europe, there are over 300,000 workers in Kuwait, over 75,000 in Jordan, and 45,000 in Bahrain. The unions will now step in and help workers having problems in the workplace in terms of disputes over wages, harassment or any other issue, free of cost.

A key clause in the agreements is that, in line with ILO conventions, labourers will not be treated as a 'commodity.' Other sections in the agreement deal with equality for migrant workers, access to healthcare and protection from dangerous work. The important point is that the General Union of Air Transport and Tourism in Jordan, said his union separately reached an agreement with a semi-state owned Sri Lankan company – JobsNet – to enter the recruitment business, as a further step to break the stranglehold on migrant workers by recruitment agencies.

Text based on:
http://www.ilo.org/actrav/about/lang--en/index.htm

Labour Recruitment Problems

A major foul play by the recruiting agencies was the sending of the recruits to places other than those promised locations. After the killing of 12 Nepalese workers in Iraq in 2004, there were several revelations by workers where they narrated gruesome experiences while they were forced to work in highly hostile terrains including active war fronts in Iraq. This is despite the fact that India and Nepal have banned its nationals to work in Iraq in the light of high security risk. It has been found by the local agencies that the workers were send to Kuwait and later send to Iraq, after creating fake documents to suggest that the workers went to Iraq by own will. Many of the workers were reported to be working in 3D situations (Dangerous, Demeaning and Dirty) without wages for proper survival and denied of basic facilities.

Conclusion

Rapid urbanization in many parts of the world has led to labour rights denials. Cheap labour and uninterrupted flow of it was one of the basic determinants of timely completion of projects and in many cases the completion was widely advertised as a national or social need. From many examples across the world, where the cities in the non-West world which are changing their character into global cities, like the urban conglomerate around Delhi or the cities of the Gulf crisis was looming over as the wage and work related factors found a decline. Violations of domestic laws on engaging labour was flagrant across the board, making it a deplorable matter where moral claim of some cultures over others in this regard remained insufficient as proof of fairness On the whole it was experience of the uninformed, migrant worker whose experience that mattered and the examples of these workers, whose life world was inextricably connected to an oppressive order of subcontracting applies to workers in the Commonwealth Games Work site in New Delhi to the hired workers in many European countries who are illegally trafficked into these countries from countries like china, India and many other Asian and East European countries. While the domestic legal systems fail to ensure the basic human rights of people, the migrant labour's experience could be linked to an absence of observing internationally accorded principles on right to life, social and physical security as well as decent wage and other benefits of the worker. Many observations in case of Gulf countries have established direct connection on the undue pace of completion due to social/national commitments and the large scale violations that occur in the process. Violations of labour rights including right to life, was the central concern in all these cases. Labour strikes in Gulf countries opened up human rights debate. Understanding the human rights possibilities in responding to this situation requires a new inventory which places the experience of labour at the centre. This is especially in the backdrop of owning the failure of supervision of rights situation by the country of origin to transit country to the recipient country. For a migrant worker referred in this study, many of the basic human rights are violated in these three counties due to the lack of accountability of states. Basic human rights are traded off for survival by the workers due to the labour arrangement processes that are controlled through non-state bodies which lack human rights approach in their practices. This lack is further added on at various levels from various stages in employment as well as state mechanisms including policy making at the highest level.

The Rights Based Approaches to Development of the United Nations suggests a no-trade off between rights and development. Development experience of manual labourers and other informal workers in the wake of rapid globalization shows a common trend of alienation across the world. Denial of living wages and other related essential rights have seen taking a beating once the project designs displaced the constitutional and social commitments in respective state, indicating to a strong role of a non-state agencies in deciding the conditions of wages, life and dignity of workers. This condition of workers also explained a situation where by the process of development usually overlooked the principal stakeholders' rights concerns due to the common mismatch between rate of growth and absence of sharing of benefits of growth to all concerned person. A classic case is the dispossession of land for development by the landowners in developing countries. While development comes through radically redefine land use, the basic rights of landowners are denied ranging from forced acquisition of land by the state to lack of providing resettlement and alternate employment. Migrants in the development age have become vulnerable to organized but invisible networks of oppressive practices. However, some initiatives have marginally successful in identifying the comprehensiveness and also in addressing the crisis with larger shared processes as we see in the case of Srilanka. Civil society pressure building as we see in Asia have also found successful in achieving policy level interventions. Worker's situation is at a cross section in the debates on rights, development, and urbanization and state policies. Starting from the right to life and livelihoods of a human person as the inalienable right of all, various stages of human rights thinking from rights based approaches of the institutional and the civil can contribute to the discussions on ensuring safe, meaningful and dignified living of workers in the Gulf. The unquantifiable pain of loss involved in the terms of engagement (i.e., forgoing better emotional and physical security as well as civil, and cultural rights at home for more income) never becomes a valid point for academic as well as official enquiries on them. Also they grapple with the classic condition of alienation of less privileged migrants, whom the agents and processes of economic and social development always looked through the lens of instrumental rationality. The initiatives in defending and promoting human rights is seen to emerge from official as well as civil locations and in many cases the processes indicate to transform, with new human rights enquiries, including the use of counter hegemonic human rights applications.

Notes

1. Immediate response to the 2004 strikes was the restrictive practices in recruitment and quota systems are introduced in different Arabian Gulf countries. This has special impact on changing the demographics patterns in migration as more workers from Srilanka and Nepal came in place of India workers. The south Asian unskilled workers influx especially after the 1991 Gulf war was looked upon as a strategy to displace politically oriented Arab workers from non-monarchic Arab countries to avoid political threat to the Arabian Gulf monarchies. The new efforts of control and putting cap on Indian labour are considered to create a new wave of labour influx from countries like Nepal and Sri Lanka where cheap labour is in abundance.Similarly, there is the issue-perhaps must be the most critical of all-seeing foreign presence as a threat to national culture and identity. The new demographic composition, which otherwise was neither so arcane nor so menacing, has got a political turn and a great deal of debate now concerns over the huge presence of Indian workers, whose population amounts to almost one million and began to upset the locals in some of the Gulf States. The demographic change was also one of the important concerns of the GCC as well recently.
2. http://news.bbc.co.uk/2/hi/middle_east/7266610.stm.
3. Testimony from Bnu Paul Migrant worker retuned to Kerala presently working as an auto rickshaw driver in Kerala who worked as labour supervisor in Bahrain in 2006-08 on the conditions of labour.
4. The following discussion is based on reference to United Nations Documents like http://untreaty.un.org/English/TreatyEvent2003/Texts/treaty2E.pdf
5. Article 6 speaks " non-discrimination based on nationality, race, religion or sex, to immigrants lawfully within its territory, treatment no less favourable than that which it applies to its own nationals in respect of the matters": relating to remuneration, including family allowances where these form part of remuneration, hours of work, overtime arrangements, holidays with pay, restrictions on home work, minimum age for employment, apprenticeship and training, women's work and the work of young persons. Article six also refers to freedom of

organization though membership of trade unions and enjoyment of the benefits of collective bargaining. It also referred to provisions for accommodation; social security according to national laws or regulations, is covered by a social security scheme to a great extent.

6. Compatibility of national regimes with standard international norms however is not a fool proof yardstick to assess human rights situation. For example, in India, despite the strong domestic regime starting from 1948 labourers, working and living conditions are highly dirty, demeaning and dangerous.
7. The present Convention is applicable, except as otherwise provided hereafter, to all migrant workers and members of their families without distinction of any kind such as sex, race, co lour, language, religion or conviction, political or other opinion, national, ethnic or social origin, nationality, age, economic position, property, marital status, birth or other status. The present Convention shall apply during the entire migration process of migrant workers and members of their families, which comprises preparation for migration, departure, transit and the entire period of stay and remunerated activity in the State of employment as well as return to the State of origin or the State of habitual residence.
8. The Forum Asia and Centre for Education and Communication Delhi (ECE) efforts in gathering public opinion and initiating a campaign for a rights based migrant policy is one of the recent actions from the civil society in India. This initiative called for a South Asian perspective in the National policy and advocated for India's ratification of various international human rights instruments having bearing on the protection promotion and dissemination of human rights of migrant workers in India. The initiative also called for the policy which is rights based as well as worker centric.
9. According to a study (Ratra Dilip and Xu 2008) worldwide flows of remittances were around US$320 billion in 2007, with remittances sent home by migrants from developing countries accounting for US$240 billion Remittances were twice as large as foreign aid and nearly two-third of foreign direct investment flows to developing countries. India is considered the biggest beneficiary of the remittance flow. With more than 10 million workers worldwide, many of them highly skilled guest workers

in the west, India's annual remittances are said to have crossed US$27 billion in 2007, followed by China (US$25.7 billion), Mexico (US$25 billion), the Philippines (US$17 billion), France (US$12.5 billion), Spain (US$8.9 billion), Belgium (US$7.2 billion), Germany (US$7 billion), UK (US$7 billion), and Romania (US$6.8 billion).

10. (Rajaram Panda 2009: 177) indicates to migrant workers contribution to Kerala economy as a back drop for advocating a more serious view of the issue of Migrant workers hailing from India. Panda cites the potential of the migrant workers as powerful economic backup for the state at the time of any economic crisis, the impact of their remittances on not just India's economy, and 'morale' of the country. Panda writes "For the longest time, the government took no note of the inflow, notwithstanding occasional stories about how the Gulf workers fuelled the boom in Kerala. It was the nuclear tests in May 1998, when New Delhi floated the Resurgent India bonds to cushion the possible impact of sanctions, which first tested the depth of the NRI commitment." RAJARAM PANDA, Migration Remittances: The Emerging Scenario, p.177 *India Quarterly 65, 2 (2009)*: 167–83.
11. Delhi Sailing in rough seas with no life saving system has led to drowning of hundreds of deaths reported, while many are unreported. The smuggling of workers happens even at the cost of being attacked by naval forces mistaking these boats as security risk. In some extreme shocking cases, refrigerated trucks were used to ferry illegal workers, where in one such incident around fifty people were found dead in France in 2008 (Interview with P Gar Craig, Professor, Social Justice at the University of Hull and Associate Director of the C. Wilbe Force Institute of Study of Slavery and Emancipation, April 12 2008).
12. A classic case is the migratory experience of workers in the Commonwealth village work sites in various places in Delhi. As per the report published by the Peoples Union of Civil Liberties (PUCL) the workers were facing extreme human rights violations including denial of right to life due to lack of safe working conditions. It was also revealed that the works were in violation of national law on minimum wages and other work related benefits and leisure, including payment of overtime allowances. Despicable conditions of living and total absence of

health care were issues highlighted. It is also interesting to see that marginal improvement in the conditions occurred after the labour unions entered into strike for few days. The urban migrant experience is also a condition where the survival and sustenance of the workers exposes an unacceptable tradeoff between human rights of the worker and the chances for the worker to continue at work.

13. The critics of the post-national citizenship thesis, Soysal (1994), have pointed out that migrants' access to rights varies across the globe and in relation to a type of migrant (Stasiulus and Bakan, 1997) and that in some cases migrants' rights have actually deteriorated as certain previously granted benefits have been withdrawn from them (Joppke, 2007).
14. In 2002, Saudi Arabia's ministry of labor and social affairs promulgated new regulations that authorized the establishment of "workers' committees" in private businesses with one hundred or more employees. International Labor Organization (ILO) director-general Juan Somavia called this development "a milestone in the labor history of Saudi Arabia," and said it was "gratifying for the ILO to be cooperating with a country which is making real efforts to promote social and labor rights." International Labor Organization, "Boost for workers' rights in Saudi Arabia," Press Release, April 18, 2002, ILO/02/17. cited in http://www.hrw.org/en/node/11999/section/9#_ftn209.
15. Ibid., Article 191 states: "Where an employee, head of an enterprise, employee or workman stops work with the object of exerting pressure on public authorities or of protesting against a decision or measure adopted by such authorities instead of having recourse to legitimate means, each such offender shall be punished with imprisonment for a terms of two to six years or a fine of 4,000 riyals to 10,000 riyals, or both." http://www.hrw.org/en/node/11999/section/9#_ftn209.
16. ('Unified Gulf plan needed to tackle labour issues' IANS, Wednesday, 10 September 2008, 12:30 hrs (inputs from comments from Mr. Mohammed Dito, of the Bahrain's labour ministry and it's Economic Development Board (EDB). He is also serving with the International Labour Organisation (ILO) Source:\latest\MIGRATION\Unified_Gulf_plan_needed_to_tackle_labour_issues-nid-46386.html).

17. On February 21, 2008, a Court in Dubai sentenced 45 Indian construction workers for six months term in Jail for their involvement in the strike it's not just in Dubai that labour unrest appears to be on the rise. In 2008 February Bahrain witnessed a week-long strike by some 1,300 workers mostly Indian workers which ended recently when they agreed to a wage rise.
18. ('Unified Gulf plan needed to tackle labour issues' IANS, Wednesday, 10 September 2008, 12:30 hrs (inputs from comments from Mr. Mohammed Dito, of the Bahrain's labour ministry and it's Economic Development Board (EDB). He is also serving with the International Labour Organisation (ILOSource:\latest\MIGRATION\Unified_Gulf_plan_needed_to _tackle_labour_issues-nid-46386.html).

References

Benhabib, S. (2007) 'Twilight of Sovereignty or the Emergence of Cosmopolitan Norms? Rethinking Citizenship in Volatile Times', Citizenship Studies 11(1): 19–36.

Bhupal Singh Structural Shifts in the Current Account of India's Balance of Payments Margin: The Journal of Applied Economic Research 2009; 3; 133.

Countries', Paper presented at United Nations Expert Group Meeting on International Migration and Development in the Arab Region, Beirut, 15-17 May, 2006.

Edward J. Malecki and Michael C. Ewers Prog Hum Geogr 2007; Labor migration to world cities: with a research agenda for the Arab Gulf 31; 467.

Habermas Jurgan.2001. "Contributions to the Discourse Theory of Law and Democracy in Steven Seidman and Jaffrey C. Alexander (eds.). The New Social Theory Reader, London: Routledge.

Habermas.1997. 'The Public Sphere' in Goodin Robert. E and Petit Philip (eds), Oxford: Blackwell.

Habermas.1999. 'Uncoupling the System and Lifeworld' in Eliot Antony (ed.) Oxford: Blackwell.

India Quarterly: A Journal of International Affairs 2009.

International Migration Report 2002, United Nations (Department of Economic and Social Affairs, Population Division).

International Organization for Migration (IOM) 2003: World migration report 2003: labour migration: trends, challenges and policy responses in countries of origin. Geneva: International Organization for Migration Press.

Jeevan Raj Sharma, Practices of Male Labor Migration from the Hills of Nepal to India in Development Discourses: Which Pathology? Gender Technology and Development 2008; 12.

Kapiszewski, Andrezej 'Arab versus Asian Migrant Workers in the GCC.

Katy Gardner and Filippo Osella An overview Migration, modernity and social transformation in South Asia: Contributions to Indian Sociology 2003; 37.

Rajaram Panda, Migration Remittances: The Emerging Scenario.

Ratha, Dilip and Zhimei Xu. 2008. Migration and Remittances Factbook. Washington, D.C.: Th e World Bank.

Sajitha Beevi Karayil Does Migration Matter in Trade? A Study of India's Exports to the GCC Countries, South Asia Economic Journal 2007; 8; 1.

Winckler, O. 2005: Arab political demography, volume 1: population growth and natalist policies. Brighton: Sussex Academic Press.

5

Water Sharing in West Asia: A Case Study of the Euphrates River System

Gazzala Sabana

Geographical Framework and Hydrological System of the Euphrates River

The Euphrates River has its springs in the highlands of Eastern Turkey, and its mouth at the Persian Gulf. It is the longest river in South-western Asia with 27,000 km, and its actual volume is 35.9 billion cubic meters. The Euphrates Rivers is formed in Turkey by two major tributaries; the Murat and Karasu. These two streams join around the city of Elazig, and the river Euphrates follows Southeastern route to enter Syria at Karakamis point. (Kolars, 1992c:107) After entering Syria, the Euphrates continues its southeastern course and is joined by two more bodies of water. These are Khabur and Balikh. Both of these tributaries have their source in Turkey. After entering Iraq, the three rivers reach the city of Hit, where it is only 53 meter above main sea level. From Hit to the delta in the Persian Gulf, for 735 km, the river loses a major portion of its waters to irrigation canals and to Lake Hammer. The remainder joins the city of Qurna, and the combined river is called the Shatt Al- Arab. (George, 1963:20-21) According to conservative estimates 88 percent of the water in the Euphrates, as it crosses the border between Syria and Iraq is derived from snow and rain that fall in Turkey, and only 12 percent from rainfall in Syria. (Shapland, 1997:103) The total length of the Euphrates in Iraq is about 1,200 km till it joins the Tigris at Qurana. Near Hit, the river enters the alluvial lowlands of Mesopotamia, it has only a little over 50 meters to fall into the Gulf in 735 km. From Nasiriya, the river divides into a number of channels some of which flow into Lake Hammar, while the remainder join the Tigris near Qurna to from the Shatt al-Arab.

Although longer of the two, the Euphrates is smaller than the Tigris in volume. (Manley, 1994, 85) The average annual natural flow of the Euphrates varies greatly. Runs of years of low flow are not uncommon: there were particularly marked periods of drought from 1958 to 1962, and from 1970 to 1975. The latter may have contributed to the tensions between Syria and Iraq which coincided with Syria's filling of Lake Assad. (Shapland, 1997:103-105) The Euphrates drains an enormous basin. Besides its two wings in Turkey, the Karasu 21,500 km and the Murat Suyu 39,700 km, whose confluence at Keban forms the Euphrates, it drains an area of 96,000 km between Keban and Jarablus, the place were it enters Syria. From Jarablus to Anah, where it enters Iraq, it drains 229,000 km, and from Anah to the point where it enters the Gulf, it drains 444,000 km. The area from which the Euphrates is fed is confined to the mountains in the north, which consist of 82,330 km only, i.e. some 20 percent of the total area of the basin. Eighty percent of the area is made up of steppe and desert. (Naff and Matson, 1984: 86) The river flows across an alluvial plain built up from eroded material upstream. The river gradient is small. In the plains region, there are wide areas of marshy lands including streams and meanders which have been abandoned. (Abbas, 1984:69) The Mountainous Mediterranean Climate zone-climate determines the flow regime of the river. Temperatures in the mountains frequently fall bellow 0^0C during the winter and the Euphrates is largely fed by precipitation falling over the uplands of Eastern Turkey, where the annual total precipitation often exceeds 1,000 mm. As most of this precipitation occurs during the winter months as snow, it tends to be locked up as snow and ice, but with rising temperatures in spring and early summer, the snow fields melt. The rainy season starts in October and ends in April. (Beaumont, 1978:35)

The semi-arid Mediterranean type zone includes those areas where there is a small winter water surplus. Such areas can be described as having a steppe type vegetation, climate and land use. Temperatures in the winter month in Urfa, Turkey, a site with a climate typical of the foothills region, range from 5^{0}C to 7^{0}C, and, in the summer, they range from 27^{0} C to 3^{0}C. The average rainfall is 300mm per annum near the Turkish-Syrian border. (Abbas, 1984:79)

Rainfall in the plain is characterized by a low average precipitation, of 150-200mm per annum which occurs mainly in the November-April winter season. The rainfall is not reliable in any part of the plains, and the records show large fluctuations from year to year. Summer in this region is intensely hot, with day shade temperatures frequently reaching a maximum of 45^{0}C in July and August and from 30^{0}C to35^{0}C in the Al-Jazira sub region. Throughout the entire basin, the winter season (December, January and February) is the most humid, with over half of the annual precipitation in the valley falling during these months, while the summer season is very dry and brings little precipitation. The average annual temperature in Turkey is 17^{0}C, in Syria 20^{0}C, and in Iraq 23^{0}C. (McLachlan, 1976:41)

The effectiveness of the winter rainfall regime is well illustrated by the Thornthwaite type of water-balance graph which potential evapotranspiration, reflecting water needs compared seasonally against precipitation. (Smith, 1970:411) The evaporation rate in the upper part of the Euphrates valley in Turkey is about 700mm per annum, and about 900 mm per annum in southern Turkey, near the border with Syria. At Deir ez zor in southern Syria the evaporation rate is 1,356mm per annum and at Haditha the evaporation rises to about 1,450 mm per annum. (Beaumont, 1978:38)

Irrigation and Development Projects

In the period between the two World Wars no conflict existed among the three countries over the use of the Euphrates water at that time. Turkey was engaged in a boundary dispute with Iraq over the Mosul province but, despite its seriousness there was no conflict of interest over the sharing of Euphrates water. (Abbas, 1984:172) Until the mid-1960s, the only country which made large-scale use of the waters of the Euphrates was Iraq. In Syria limited irrigation was practiced alongside the river, while in Turkey the waters of the Euphrates were used even less. (Beaumont, 1978:35)

An important feature of the rivers system which had a favorable effect on agriculture is that the bed of the Euphrates, from north of Falluja south wards until the two rivers meet at Qurna, is slightly higher than that of the Tigris. In modern time, as in the past, this difference of elevation has been utilized to build a network of gravity flow canals from west to east to irrigate large area of land. (Qubain, 1960: 70)

Turkey

Under the leadership of Kemal Ataturk, Turkey became the first state in West Asia to draw up a five- year development plan and, within a few years of the announcement of this initiative, Turkey embarked upon an economic experiment that was to be emulated in several countries following Second World War. (Richards and Waterbury, 1990:188) The economic development policy of Turkey has centered around state enterprise initiative and imports substitution through industrialization. Agriculture and water development, however, have received relatively little attention, with the exception of power generation projects that were needed to provide energy for new industry. This emphasis on power generation has led to the development of a number of multipurpose water projects, particularly on the Euphrates River. (Turkey 1958:5)

Throughout this period of economic development agriculture has remained the main source of employment despite the rapid growth of industry averaging 11 percent per annum. (Wilson, 1979:95) Given the current average annual population growth rate of 2.2 percent and an increase in per capital demand for food of around 1.2 percent per annum, Turkey needs to maintain an annual growth rate in food production of around 3.5 percent to meet the requirements of domestic demand. (Bilen and Uskay, 1991:4-1)

The high rate of growth in total population and the even higher rates of increase in urban population, together with changing household structures and social preferences, have led to an increased demand for water with the total water supplied for drinking and utility purposes increasing almost 2.5 times throughout Turkey .With current available water resources it would be economically feasible to irrigate an estimated 8.5 million hectares with major and minor irrigation works and a further 16.8 million hectares using advanced technology. At present both groundwater and surface flow are used to irrigate 3.2 million hectares. (Gulbahar, 1991:531) By the beginning of the 1990s, about 2.5 million hectares of irrigation infrastructure was developed in the public sector and an area of about 1.3 million hectares was provided with supplementary water by small scale, privately owned irrigation schemes, making the total area under irrigation about 3.8 million hectares or 45 percent of potential total. (Bilen and Uskay, 1991:4)

A major response to the increasing food and fiber demand in Turkey has been the expansion of irrigated agriculture sponsored largely by government agencies. In contrast to other developing countries, Turkish agriculture has undergone a complete land reform program, in which more than 80 percent of the farmers in Turkey own and work small farms of less then 10 ha. of land. (Morvaridi, 1990:304)

Because of the Mediterranean and semi-arid conditions, with a hot and dry summer, the critical growing period for most crops is during the months of June, July, and August and, during this period, most of the rivers carry base flow only. Water storage, therefore, is indispensable. At present 141 dams are in operation and 57 dams are under construction making about 70 percent of major irrigation projects fed with water from reservoirs or lakes. (Bilen and Uskay, 1991:4-2)

The Turkish government, realizing the crucial importance of a sufficient energy supply for a sustained and balanced economic development, has given priority to the energy sector in its economic policies and adjustment particularly since 1980. (Bagis, 1989:61) Turkey is steadily increasing its energy consumption, much of which must come from hydrocarbon sources beyond its border. In order to balance the regional deficiencies 220 Gwh of energy was imported in 1990 and 917 Gwh of energy was exported in the same year. In the early 1970's, the high level of dependence on imported oil was a dominant factor in the pattern of energy consumption in Turkey. (Bilen and Uskay, 1991:4-7) Nearly 39 percent of the energy consumed in the nation in 1983 was derived from imported petroleum and, when imports of coal electricity are also considered, this makes for two- fifths of the all the energy used in Turkey originating from foreign sources. Petroleum imports currently amount to some four billion dollars per year, an amount the equals approximately one third of total imports. (Kolars, 1986:53)

The share of hydro-sources has increased substantially from 30 percent at the beginning of 1970's to more than 40 percent of the total supply recently. In order to maintain this percentage, there needs to be an increase of about eight percent annum. (Kolars, 1986:53)

The country is water rich and receives about 509 billion m^3 of precipitation annually, and 38 percentage of this ends up as surface runoff, much of which into the USSR, Iraq, Syria, and the surrounding seas. Turkish estimates indicate that only a little over half of this surface runoff and a billion m^3 of groundwater can technically be used for domestic, irrigation, and industrial purposes within Turkey. The actual consumption of surface water is 25.2 billion m^3 per year indicating that only 26.5 percent of surface water development potential is consumed presently while the actual annual consumption of groundwater is 5.4 billion m^3. (Bilen and Uskay, 1991:13)

Driven by its need for new sources of energy and because only 20 percent of the hydropower potential has developed so far, Turkey has turned to the hydroelectric potential of its many river, the greatest of which is the Euphrates. With this end in mind Turkey has undertaken a gigantic development project on the river. (Kolars, 1990:59)

Syria

Syria covers an area of 185,180 km, of which about nearly half is poor steppe or semi-arid land, with 30 percent agricultural land, and only a percent of the agricultural land is irrigated. Potential irrigable land is about 1.6 million hectares with greatest potential located in the Khabur, and the Euphrates projects. (Mitchell, 1982:4) Agriculture retains its position as the mainstay of the Syrian economy despite the existence of the traditionally strong trading sector and partially successful attempts at industrialization. Irrigation is the only strategy which can make agriculture secure in dry countries such as Syria. Yields from irrigated land can be five times those on rainfed tracts, and a secure water supply enables more flexibility in cropping as well as enabling an effective high input and high output system of farming. (Allan, 1987:28)

The irrigation area was estimated at about 280,000 hectares or one eighth of the land under cultivation. Most of the water was derived from river supplies while wells and springs made only a small contribution. (United Nations, 1949:22) The 1950s and 190s saw a considerable increase in irrigated farming with the greatest change during this period occurring along the Euphrates where the use of river pumps enabled large areas of land to be brought under irrigation. (Manners and Nejad, 1985:259)

Since the mid 1980s, there has been a new expansion of irrigated land but, more than 30,000 hectares of old irrigated land were flooded in the reservoir area between 1973 and 1975, and some 4,000 hectares went out of production every year because of increasing salinity in the lower Euphrates valley. (Meyer, 1987:44)

Syria suffers from a shortage of agricultural products, which forces the authorities to increase import of food products from foreign markets. (Syria and Monde Arab, 1988, no, 408) This situation was caused by a sharp growth in population and it is predicted that the demand for food will increase by 3.1 percent annually, a figure that is higher than the annual rate of actual increase in food production which amounted in the past two decades to 2.8 percent. (Syria and monde Arabe, 1988, No. 408. 2)

Syria has the potential to feed its increasing population and even export basic food staples such as wheat the barley, but over the last thirty years, the picture in the agricultural sector, despite the bright prospects, has been one of stagnation. Some of the blame for this can be leveled at the adverse climatic conditions that have occurred from time to time, but the problem is also political. (Mitchell, 1982:22)

With population rising at a rate of well over three percent per year for several decades and with changes and improvements in domestic food consumption taking place, at the same time the need to increase food output has been inescapable. As a result policies to improve land, as well as the rural infrastructure and rural institutions associated with agricultural production, have been basic elements in national policy and planning for almost three decades. An increase in production is immediately required to meet the national demand for grain which has resulted from the rapid rise in population. (Allan, 1987a, 22)

The storage capacity of the present water projects of the Euphrates River in Syria is about 13.8 billion m^3 with the Tabqa dam having a capacity of 11.6 billion m^3 and all other dams having a total capacity of about 2.2 billion m^3. The Water Resources Ministry introduced a policy that aimed at setting up an extensive network of small to medium sized, low cost surface dams throughout the country. These dams collect rainwater during the winter, forming small lakes which water is drawn during the dry summer month. The surface dams vary in storage capacity from 700, 00 m^3 of water to more then 25 million m^3 and are mainly used to supply water for agricultural purposes, such as irrigating crops watering livestock and, to a lesser extent, as a supply of water for human use in some of the more isolated rural villages. (The Arab Economist, 1982:20)

Although, today, the Euphrates accounts for around 85 percent of the nation's surface water resources, in the 1960s probably less than one fifth of the country's irrigated area was located within its basin. Horizontal expansion is probably the one area of greatest potential for irrigation. The Euphrates and Khabur projects will carry cultivation into areas formerly too dry to be economically viable, but, combined with this; there is the effect of irrigation on vertical production expansion. Certain varieties of wheat yield twice as much under irrigation as under rainfed conditions and cotton yield on irrigated land is 4.6 times higher than on rainfed land. Horizontal expansion together with vertical expansion, as the result of not only irrigation but also a variety of other factors, holds the key to Syrian future agricultural prosperity. (Mitchell, 1982:22)

The Euphrates project has always had a high political profile for the Baathist regime. Not only is it the showcase of the Ba'ath development drive but, by having the dam-created lake named after him self, President Assad's personal prestige has been attached to it. Administratively, the project is overseen by the High committee for the Euphrates headed by the prime minister. The ministry of the Euphrates was specially created to carry out the project and was generously provided with the funds to attract the best personnel at exceptional salaries and at the expense of the traditional agricultural sector. (Hinne bush, 1989:236)

Iraq

The alluvial soils of the Mesopotamian plain in Iraq are primarily a product of man's activity during the last six thousand years. They cover more than a third of the country, and are characterized by low elevation, below 100 meters, and poor natural drainage. Large areas are subject to widespread seasonal flooding, and there are extensive marshlands, some of which dry up in the summer to become salty wastelands. Most of this plain has been covered to a depth of several feet with sediments brought in suspension by irrigation water thus the soils are not pedagogically developed in the usual sense. (Clawson, 1971:68-75)

The total area of Iraq is 43,750,000 ha, of which 11,800,000 ha., the irrigated land that is cultivated covers 1,560,000 ha., and the cultivated land in the rained area is 1,300,000 ha. (Hussain, 1990:238)

Two types of agricultural activity predominate in Iraq, one dependent upon rainfall in the north and the other dependent upon irrigation in the south. The rain zone which is watered by rain is also divided into two sub zones: the mountain area which is located along both the Iraq-Turkish and Iraqi-Iranian border, and the steppe zone. (Al-A'ni, 1977:422)

The best known agricultural product is the date, of which Iraq is one of the world's largest producers. Other crops include barley, wheat, linseed, lentils, and beans, as well as rice, sesame, maize, and millet while cotton production is hampered by soil salinity. Total agricultural production was 13.9 million tonne in 1985, compared with 13.1 million tons in 1984. (Fisher, 1989:466)

A large land area, a small rural population and a generous endowment of water resources appears to offer the possibility of rapid and rewarding expansion in agriculture.

Under proper resource management, Iraq could offer the greatest opportunities in the region for agricultural growth. (Clawson, 1971:52) The expansion of irrigation has contributed to serious drainage problems since the additional water, combined with shallow gradient of the terrain from above Baghdad to the gulf, has raised the water table and brought salts closer to the surface, affecting plant growth.

Some observers believe that as much as 65 percent of irrigated areas have had salinity problems and that 20 to 30 percent of the irrigated land has been abandoned over the years because of it. (Nyrop, 1979, 157) In fact, however despite its high agricultural potential, Iraq is not self sufficient in food production and almost 25 percent of all Iraqi imports were taken up by food in 1990. (Hussain, 1990:237)

Because of the ready availability of agricultural land, wasteful, 'extensive' farming methods which give a low yield are common; thus only one sixth of potentially cultivable territory and 3 percent of the country's total area is in use. There can be no doubt that the mounting costs of the war and the increased rural-urban migration caused by it were virtually the main reasons for the increased deterioration of the agricultural sector. (Mofid, 1990:50)

Agriculture retains its position as the mainstay of the Iraqi economy, despite the existence of a traditionally strong trading sector and partially successful attempts at industrialization. (Clawson, 1971:52)

Geopolitics of the Euphrates River Basin

A fair division of the water must be accomplished according to the need of state. Turkey and Syria are greatly in need of hydroelectric power. In Syria this situation could change because gas and oil have recently been discovered there, which would enable Syria to employ thermal energy instead. Turkey has no sources of energy apart from hydroelectric. Turkey and Syria need water for irrigation to reclaim large areas of land for their growing populations. Until recently, Iraq needed water for irrigation, but this situation could soon change because Iraq has large amounts of oil, which could be used to boost industry and so curtail agriculture.

However, in reality the three states do not cooperate, and the up-stream states make use of their advantage over the downstream state. Turkey is an upstream state in the drainage of the two rivers. Syria is a downstream state of the Euphrates relative to Turkey, and an upstream state relative to Iraq. (Saleh 1985:70-74)

A treaty of Friendship and Good Neighborliness was negotiated between Syria and Turkey in 1926 and March 1946 a similar bilateral treaty was signed between Turkey and Iraq. The latter was significant in a number of respects, Turkey, by this treaty, recognized Iraq's acquired rights, at that time some 13 bcm, to irrigate about one million hectares in the lower Euphrates. (Lupu Yonatan, Vol.14: 354-355) Iraq would have found its major water control infrastructure outside its borders, parallel to Egypt's situation if the century water scheme had been carried out in the Nile basin.

Turkey is, today, a nearly pure hegemony in the basin. With the destruction during the Gulf War of Iraq's military base, Turkey has become by far the dominant economic and military power in the basin. It can project military force throughout the basin, and more positively, can offer economic incentives to obtain acceptance of its solution. (Kolars 1991:3-9)

The World Bank has been unable to induce a solution to collective challenge in the Euphrates theater. It participated in the financing of the Karakaya dam in Turkey because this hydropower project did not appreciably affect the flow of the Euphrates, but it has refused to participate in the other dams because appreciable harm to the downstream riparian is clearly at issue.

The most recent project on the Euphrates, the Birecik dam, is to be a build–operate-and–transfer project, financed by a consortium of Turkish, Belgian, German, and French interests, with Chase Investment Bank, UK, as financial advisor. (Ali Carkoglu, 2001:61)

In the mid 1960s both Turkey and Syria began to draw up plans for exploiting their portions of the Euphrates. For bargaining purposes they put forth maximum demands: Iraq, 14 bcm; Syria, 13 bcm, and Turkey, 18bcm. These demands exceeded the annual yield of the Euphrates by 15bcm. (Waterbury 1990, 20-23) At the same time, as Turkey moved toward construction of the Keban Dam, a World Bank mission drafted a report on the water resources in the Euphrates system that became something of a baseline for all future talks. Iraq-Syrian talks in 1966 and 1967 were marked by Syria's rejection of the principle of acquired rights, although Syria accepted that Iraq was entitled to 59 percent of the Euphrates flow in normal years.

Subsequently the two countries discussed a formula that would guarantee Iraq two thirds of the flow in normal years, but invert those proportions for any excess flow in normal year. Another futile attempt was made in 1972, with Iraq invoking its cultivated surface and Syria pointing to crop water use intensities. Syria ultimately would not sign a draft agreement, and Iraq sough soviet mediation. The soviet report used the 1965 World Bank data and recommended that the Tabqa dam in Syria, which it was helping to construct, and the Keban dam in Turkey be operated in such a way as to protect Iraq's acquired rights. Syria objected to the report's findings. (Biswas, 1994:63-65)

As both the Keban and Tabqa reservoirs filled, Iraq threatened military action against Syria. The Arab league tried to mediate the dispute, but once the two reservoirs had filled. Iraq's water crisis eased. In 1980 all three riparian agreed to establish a joint technical commission for the exchange of information. It has met only sporadically since, but it represents the closest thing to a tri-partite cooperative accord in the basin. When Turkey began to fill the Ataturk dam in January 1990, leading to a month long stoppage in the flow of the Euphrates, Syria and Iraq negotiated an understanding that Syria would guarantee Iraq 290 cusecs at their border, or a 4/58 split of the 500 cusecs Syria is to receive. Turkey favors the definition of International River laid down in the Vienna conference of 1815 because it would tend to exclude from consideration tributaries to the river. Indeed, Turkey does not accept that the Euphrates is an international river, preferring the term “transboundary”. (Beschorner, 1992:56) Turkey cites the relative abundance of water in Iraq and attributes any water deficits in either Syria or Iraq to poor management and agriculture practices. (Beschorner, 1992:61)

In early 1975, Iraq complained that Syria, by filling Lake Assad, had caused it economic damage: while 15.3 bcm of Euphrates water had crossed the border from Syria in 1973 (the year in which the Tabqa Dam was completed), the flow in 1975 was reduced to 9.4 bcm. (Kienle, 1990:96-109) The dispute became a crisis. The two regimes traded accusation unrelated to the Euphrates. Syria began to give more open support to Iraqi Kurdish dissidents. Both countries sent troops to their common border in March and April 1975.

It is difficult to know whether Iraq was seriously considering attacking Syria in order to assert the rights which it claimed to the waters of the Euphrates. Given the limited nature of the military movements, it seems unlikely that either side was doing more than posturing. But such situations can develop a dynamic of their own, and deteriorate further than their creators had originally intended. Viewed from that perspective, this was certainly the nearest that the West Asia had came to armed conflict over water since Israel's attacks on the Arab project to divert the headwaters of the Jordan a decade before.

When contracts were awarded for Turkey's Ataturk dam in 1983, Syria began pressing Saudi Arabia and the Gulf States not to make financial aid available to Turkey for the project unless a water sharing agreement was reached (Naff and Matson, 1984:100). Under Syrian pressure the Arab league set up a mediation committee, which appears to have achieved nothing. In the end, Saudi mediation successfully defused the crisis by securing the release of additional water for Syria. (Kienle, 1990:97-100)

The project in southeast Anatolia will involve 22 dams, of which three have been completed and a fourth is underway, for power generation and the irrigation of some 1.6 million hectares. Two thirds of the irrigated surface will be in the Euphrates basin and the other third in the Tigris. Turkey has not obtained formal agreement from Iraq and Syria to the construction of any of these dams, and both the latter have frequently protested this fact. (Kalpakian, 2004:103) Turkey has offered a unilateral solution the "guaranteed" delivery of a flow of 500 cubic meters per second on average at its border with Syria. The guarantee applies only to the Euphrates; there is absolutely no understanding on the Tigris. The guarantees, made in 1987, were only to Syria. Iraq has been left to its own devices to assure its supply. On an annualized basis half the average annual pre- contraction discharges of the Euphrates at the border with Syria. The average annual discharge in Iraq is somewhat higher, about 33 bcm at Hit, because the Khabur and Balikh tributaries join the Euphrates in Syria. (Kolars, 1986:66-69) These also rise in Turkish territory and there is no understanding among the riparian pertaining to them.

Turkey before 1991 has large markets in Iraq, and would like to develop markets throughout the Arab world. Until 1991, Iraq could offer Turkey oil delivered through a pipeline running to a Mediterranean terminus in Turkey. Turkey closed down the pipeline during the Gulf War. The prospect of Turkey helping to develop the pipeline transport of Central Asian gas and oil to Europe may mean that this Iraqi bargaining chip has lost some value. For its part Syria partially controls Turkey's most serious internal security problem, that of the Kurdish populations of Southeast Anatolia. Syria has supported the Kurdish worker party (PKK), which has engaged in armed action against Turkish security forces and against Kurds accused of "collaboration" with the Turkish authorities. (Beschorner, 1992:38-39)

Water Crises of 1989-1990

The filling of the Ataturk reservoir began in January 1990, when Turkish engineer blocked the flow of the Euphrates through the Ataturk dam with a giant concrete plug. The filling which began on 13 January 1990 continued up to 12 February 1990. The stoppage led to strident protects Syria and Iraq who wanted to be consulted over the quantity of water to be released by Turkey. The main cause of the distress expressed in Damascus and Baghdad was probably not the economics damage done, but rather the unwillingness of Turkey to countenance any modification of plans in the face of their complaints. If Turkey would not listen on this occasion, what grounds had they to hope for better treatment in the future, when the stakes might be higher?

These fears prompted an unprecedented degree of Syria-Iraqi unity over the Euphrates. In April 1990, the two states signed an agreement that allocated the water of the Euphrates on a percentage basis: whatever the volume of water which crossed the Turkish-Syrian boundary at Jerablus, Syria would allow 58 percent of that quantity to cross its border with Iraq. At the same time, the two Arab states made a joint approach to Turkey to demand a trilateral agreement that would establish a permanent division of the waters of the river.

The agreement of April 1990 appears to remain in force: it has not been abrogated by Syria or Iraq and there have been no Iraqi complaints that Syria is not applying it. But the united front against Turkey turned out to be very short- lived: it collapsed when Syria opposed Iraq's invasion of Kuwait in August 1990. (Kolars and Mitchell 1991: 274-82)

The international isolation imposed on Iraq following that event left Syria and Turkey to continue their talks on a bilateral basis. Syria complained in March and December 1991 about temporary reductions in the flow of the Euphrates. A Joint Communiqué issued in January 1993 declared that the two countries agreed that they would sign a permanent agreement on the question before the end of the year. This goal was not achieved. Indeed, no progress to wards it had been made by February 1996, with Turkey arguing that Syria had not done enough to keep its side of the 'bargain' in terms of impeding the movement of PKK fighters across the border. In early 1995, Friction between Turkey and Syria increased when, for the first time, the PKK mounted operations in Hatay province region of Turkey claimed by Syria. (Bolukbasi, 1990:50)

In November 1995, Turkey signed a financial package that will enable it to proceed with the construction of the Birecik Dam on the Euphrates, at a location between the Ataturk Dam and the Syrian border. The project will generate power but also provide water for the irrigation of 70,000 hectares on the Gaziantep and Araban plains. Syria responded by sending diplomatic notes to Turkey, complaining of the like effect of the dam on the flow of the river, and also of the potential pollution of areas of Syria affected by return flows from irrigation in Turkey. In the background of this on going water dispute the Kurdish question once again flared up between Turkey and Syria. Both the Turkish military and the government issued statements that the country was ready to resort to military means unless Syria ends its support for Ocalan and PKK activities. But Syria's non-bellicose response throughout the crisis brought it to an end. At the same time, there were signs of a revival of the Syrian-Iraqi front on the Euphrates that had been discernible in the months before Iraq's invasion of Kuwait. Syria and Iraq called for a meeting of the Arab League to discuss Turkish actions. Iraq sent diplomatic notes to Turkey along lines similar to those sent by Syria and an Iraqi technical delegation visited Damascus to explore co-ordination between the two countries in relation to Turkey's construction of new dams on the Euphrates. (Michael Schulz, 1995: 104-120)

Conclusion

The Euphrates River has immense regional importance. As economic prosperity of Turkey Syria Iraq revolves around the Euphrates as it constitutes the principal sources of hydropower and irrigation development. The hydro politics of the

Euphrates dates back to at least the 1920's. The economic prosperity of Turkey, Syria and Iraq revolve around the two rivers as they constitute the principal sources of hydropower and agricultural development. As an upstream state Turkey has sought to exploit water in its territory, thereby causing acute concern to its downstream state. The relations between Turkey and Syria have been strained many a times mainly due to formers efforts to control the flow of the rivers. During the dry season when the Turkish and Syria dams impounded part of the Euphrates spring flood, a major crisis developed between Syria and Iraq that brought the two countries to the brink of war, Iraq and Syria traded hostile statements in which Iraq threatened to take any action necessary to regulate the Euphrates flow. In early 1980's and Syria complained against Turkey that it was holding back a part of the water from the Euphrates for its use. In 1982 joint technical committee was setup by Turkey and Iraq. Syria joined it 1983. Despite this the problem of water allocation has not been solved so far. Turkey's assertive position on the issue of Euphrates water right is uneatable both Syria and Iraq.

In the 1990's the problems of sharing Euphrates water has became more complicated as Syrian and Turkish Irrigations work are nearing completion. Growing population in also a source of concern as the demands for domestic waters use is increasing by leaps and bounds. In view of the actual or potential ethnic turmoil and separatism in the region the water issue has got inextricably woven into the politics of the region.

What kind of strategies can be developed to reduce the intensity of conflict and the danger of outright violence arising from the states that are competing for access to the Euphrates River? Confidence building measures, conflict resolution, techniques will be needed to address this urgent challenge. Preventive Diplomacy, in international relations and confidence building techniques are generally receiving greater attention in recent years. Resource management diplomacy is one form of preventive diplomacy that contains greater promise. The idea is to argue upon sustainable uses of natural resources so as reach a sensitive balance between economic development and environment protection. It is pre-condition of arriving at stable solutions that mutual interests and benefits are taken into consideration and realized.

References

Abbas, H.A.H. (1984) Managing water resources in the Tigris and Euphrates drainage basin: an inquiry into the policy process, Dissertation presented to the Graduate Council of the North Texas State university, Denton, Texas, pp. 68-79,172.

Al-A'ni, K. A.M. (1977) The Encyclopedia of modern Iraq, Vol. The Arab Encyclopedia House, Baghdad, pp. 422.

Ali Carkoglu, (2001), "Middle Eastern Studies, Vol.1, January, Published by Frank Cass, London, pp. 61.

Allan J.A. (1987) "Turkey's damming of the Euphrates could strangle Syria's agricultural Development", Mideast Mirror Extra, 20 July, pp. 28.

Allan J.A. (1987a) "Syria agricultural options", In politics and economy in Syria, (Ed. Allan J.A.), SOAS, University of London, Centre of Near and Middle Eastern Studies, pp. 21-38.

The Arab Economist (1982) "Cheap solution to water problems", The Arab Economist, Vol. 14 No. 194, February, pp. 20-21.

Bari, Z. (1977) "Syrian- Iraqi dispute over the Euphrates water", International Studies, New Delhi, Vol. 2, April-June, p. 238.

Beaumont, p. (1978) "The Euphrates River- an International problem of water resources development", Environmental Conservation, 5, pp. 35-43.

Beschorner, Natash (1992) "Water and Instability in the Middle East", Adelphi paper 273, London; International Institute for strategic studies, pp. 38-61.

Bilen, O. and Uskay, S. (1991) "Background report on comprehensive water resources management policies- and analysis of Turkish experience", The World Bank international workshop on comprehensive water resources management policies, 24-28 June; pp. 2-13.

Biswas Asit K, (1994) "International Water of the Middle East: From Euphrates-Tigries to Nile", Bombay; new: Oxford University Press, pp. 63-65.

Clawson, M., Landsberg, H.H. and Alexander, L.T. (1971) "The agricultural potential of the Middle east", American Elsevier publishing company, N.Y.; pp. 52-75.

Fisher, W.B. (1989) "Iraq: physical and social geography", The Middle East and North Africa, Thirty-fifth edition, p. 466.

Georges Roux, (1963) "The Geographical Setting Ancient, Iraq", London: Penguin publishers, pp. 20-22.

Gulbahar, N. (1991) "Supplemental irrigation in Turkey", In Supplemental irrigation in the Near East and North Africa, (Eds. Perrier, E.R. and A.B. Salkini), Kluwer Academic Publishers, Dordercht, p. 531.

Hinnabusch, R.A. (1989) Peasant and bureaucracy in Ba'thist Syria: the political economy of rural development, Westview Press, Boulder, San Francisco and London.

Hussain, H.M.(1990) "Iraq's agricultural land use program", In Agriculture in the Middle east, (Eds. Salman, A.), Paragon House, N.Y.pp. 237-238.

Lupu Tonatan (2001-2002) "International Law and the Waters of the Euphrates and Tigris", Heinonline, Vol. 14:pp. 354-355.

Kolars, J. (1986) "The Southeast Anatolia project: will it make Turkey a major food supplier to the Mildest?" Middle East Executive Reports, pp. 53-69.

Kolars, J. (1990) "The course of water in the Arab Middle East", American –Arab affairs, No. 33, summer, p. 59.

Kolars, J. (1991) "The future of the Euphrates river, Prepared for the World Bank conference, Washington, D.C, 24/26 June; pp. 3-9.

Kolars, J. (1992c), "The Challenge of Managing Mega-hydro projects: the Ataturk Dam and the Southeast Anatolia Development Project', Paper presented to the financial times conference:' world Electricity" (The Financial Time, London: 9/10 November.

Kolars, John and W.A. Mitchell, (1991), "The Euphrates River and the Southeast Anatolia Development Project (southern Illinois University Press, Carbondale; p. 317.

Manley, R.E.,(1994) "Hydrological report for environmental and ecological" study of the marshlands of Mesopotamia, p. 85.

Manner, I.R. and Sagafi- Nejad, T. (1985) "Agricultural Development in Syria", In Agricultural development in the Middle East, (Eds. Beaumont, P. and K. McLachlam.), Wiley, Chichester, p. 259.

McLachlan, K.S. (1976) "Iraq", The development agriculture of the Middle East: an overview", In Agricultural and prospects, (Eds. Burrell, R.M.S. Hoyle; K.S. and McLachlan; C. Parker.), Graham and Trotman Limited, p. 41.

Meyer, G. (1987) "Economics development in Syria since 1970", In Political and the Economy in Syria, (Ed. Alan, J.A.), SOAS, University of London, p. 44.

Mitchell, J. (1982) "Irrigation and agricultural development of the Syrian Arab Republic", University of Durham, Dissertation, pp. 4-22.

Michael Schulz.,(1995), "Turkey, Syria, Iraq: A Hydropolitical Security Complex', in leif ohlesson (eds.), Hydropolitics: Conflict over Water as a Development constraint (London: Zed Book, pp. 104-120.

Morvaridi, B.(1990) " Agrarian reform and land use policy in Turkey", Land use policy, October, p. 304.

Naff, Thomas; Matson, Ruth C. (Eds.) (1984) "Water in the Middle East: conflict or cooperation? Westview: Boulder/co; pp. 17-195.

Nyrop, R.F. (1979) Iraq: a country study, Foreign Area Studies, The American University, February, p. 157.

Qubain, F.I. (1960) The reconstruction of Iraq: 1950-1957, Atlantic Books, Stevens and Sons Limited, London; p. 70.

Richards, A. and Waterbury, J. (1990) "A political economy of the Middle East: state, class, and economic development", Westview Press, Inc., p. 206.

Saleh, W.A. (1985). "Development projects on the Euphrates," in Israel and Arab Water, A.M. Farid and H. Sirriyeh (eds.). London: The Arab Research Center, pp. 70-74.

Shapland, Greg (1997) "River of Discord: International Water Disputes in the Middle East", London: Hurst & Co, pp. 103-108.

Syrie and Monde Arabe (1988) "Syria seeks to achieve food security", Syrie and Monde Arabe, no.408, February, p. 2.

Turkey (1958) Data on Euphrates and Tigris rivers basin development plan, March, 1958, Guzal Istanbul Press, p. 5.

United Nations (1949) final report of the United Nation economic survey mission for the Middle East, part ii: the technical supplement, United Nations conciliation commission for Palestine; p. 22.

6

Aspects of Economy and Human Resource Development in Israel

Kumar Raka

Introduction

Since Independence in May 1948, Israel has fought six wars, two intifadas, a continuing terrorism threat, an economic boycott, and intermittent diplomatic isolation. In effect, most of the times in past, all of its land borders are relatively closed to trade. More generally, it is an outcast in the West Asia, deprived of any opportunity to benefit from the commerce generated by regional oil wealth but having to bear the costs of living in a neighborhood characterized by arms races and instability.

Key to Israeli socio-economic development is the human resources. The human resource development through high economic growth in Israel was mainly facilitated by the three factors: exemplary role of education, better health care services and quality of immigrants. There have been huge and massive immigration in Israel before and after establishment of the state. There is an economic cost to high levels of continuous population growth if the economy does not expand. Israel could not sustain population growth rates, retain the population and continue to attract new immigrants without extensive economic growth. Indeed, the growth of Israel's economy has widened the opportunities and generated increases in the standards of living for a growing number of people. In part, the economic changes were brought about through the increase of population by way of immigration (the human capital and resources brought by the immigrants and their contribution to production and consumption) and the increased economic investments made in Israel from outside the country. Whether demographic changes generated the economic change or vice-versa, both population size and economic production have increased considerably over time.

Human Resource Development in Israel

During the quarter century from 1950, the national product raised nine times, an average of 9 percent. (Ginor, 1986) The sharp rise reflected an increase in capital stock (11 percent per year) and the number of employed (4 percent per year); hence capital per employed increased 7 percent per year. The quality of the labour force increased dramatically after an initial decline.

Figure 6.1: GDP Growth of Israel, 1987-2006 (Annual Percentage Change)

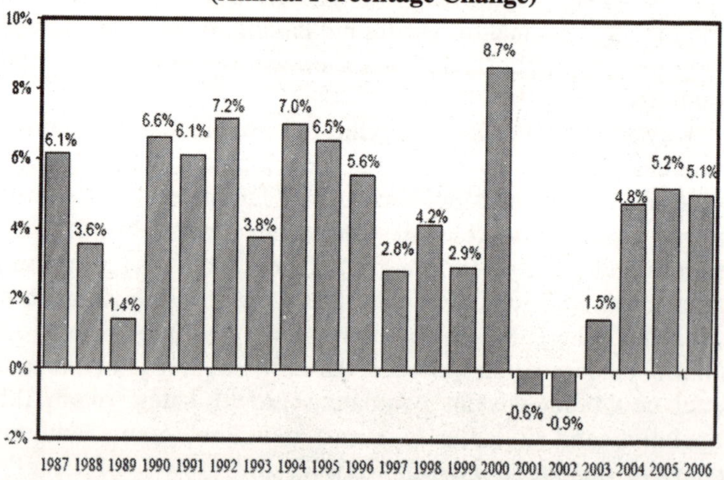

Source: Review of Economic Developments and Macro-Economic Forecasts, Economics and Research Department, Ministry of Finance, 2007.

Educational capital per employed declined by 7 percent in the first half of the 1950s, increased 22 percent in the period from 1961 to 1972 and continued to amplify in the 1970s through the 1990s (Ibid). Gross domestic product (GDP) per capita at constant prices doubled between 1950 and 1965 and doubled again between 1965 and 1990. In the half-century from the establishment of the state, the GDP increased four and a half fold. (Table 6.1)

The share of agriculture in the domestic products rose in the first years of the state, and then declined steadily with a modest rise in the share of industry. The share of trade, finance and personal services declined, and the share of public services rose, indicating the increased share in social services. The biggest rise in the capital stock occurred in the shares of public services, transport and communications indicating the expansion of the infrastructure on a modernizing basis.

Table 6.1: Selected Socio-economic Indicators in Israel, 1950-2000

Gross Domestic Product (per capita constant prices)			**Years of Schooling in percentage (Age 15 and over)**				**Food in Consumption Expenditure in percentage**
			Jews		Arabs		
Year	NIS	Index	None	13+	None	13+	
1950	2,736	100	-	-	-	-	39
1960	4,513	165	13	10	50	2	34
1970	7,474	273	9	13	36	2	31
1980	9,612	351	6	21	19	8	29
1990	11,045	404	4	29	13	9	26
2000	12,218	447	3	40	7	19	21

contd...

Source: Statistical Abstract of Israel, *various years.*

In 1950 Israel's annual growth per capita income was about one fourth the level of that of the United States and was similar to the richer Latin American countries and Italy; it was well above Japan, but only half the level of Western Europe. From 1950 to 1970, per capita income grew more than five percent annually in Israel–similar to the high rates in Europe, Taiwan and Korea–slowing considerably by 1970s. The growth after 1950 led to an increase in Israel's relative real income to over half that of the United States by 1980 and to about 75 percent of the average level in Western Europe. (Ben-Porath, 1986a)

Economic growth in Israel is directly related to changes in population. (Ben-Porath, 1986b) In the quarter-century before 1948, the Jewish population increased eight fold, with the population doubling on an average each decade. The total product of the Jewish economy in Palestine in the same period increased 25 fold, at an average annual rate of 13.7 percent; the total stock of capital increased 15 fold. Total product increased 11 fold and capital stock increased 16 fold from 1950 to 1982, with a stronger growth during the first two decades. During the pre-state and post-state periods, the correlation between the ratio of immigrants to mean Jewish population and the growth rates of gross national product (GNP) was high (0.72). A high correlation has also been documented for the relationship between immigration and the growth rate of capital stock. (Ben-Porath, 1986c)

After 1948, cycles in immigration tended to follow cycles in GNP. Immigration affected the economy by expanding the supply of labour and often the supply of capital; it generated surges in demand as well, increasing the working-age population and the labour supply. An examination of the direction of the relationship over time shows a stronger causality from immigration to economic growth in the pre-state period, and overall from 1922 to 1982. For the period 1954 onwards, immigration responded to the growth rate of per capita income and consumption. (Ben-Porath 1986c)

Table 6.2: Israel's Employed Population by Types of Occupation, 1955-2000

Year	Agr	Ind	Con	Com	Tra	Fin	Pub	Per	Total
1955	18	24	9	13	6	-	22	8	100
1960	17	25	9	12	6	-	22	8	99
1970	9	26	8	13	8	5	24	8	101
1975	6	26	8	12	7	7	27	6	99
1980	6	25	6	12	7	8	30	6	101
1985	6	24	5	13	6	10	30	7	101
1990	4	23	5	15	6	10	30	7	100
2000	2	19	6	16	6	14	31	6	100

Agr – Agriculture, forestry and fishing
Ind – Industry (mining, manufacturing, electricity and water)
Con – Construction (building and public works)
Com – Commerce, restaurants and hotels (includes banking in 1955)
Tra – Transport, storage and communication
Fin – Financing and business services
Pub – Public and community services
Per – Personal and other services
Source: Statistical Abstract of Israel, various years

Economic shifts over time can be observed in the changing structure of economic branches and in occupations. The distribution of employed people among economic branches reflects a combination of stability and change (Table 6.2). The most striking overall feature of the years between 1955 and 1990 is the relative stability of the employment distribution among various sectors. The industrial branch remained relatively steady (at about 85 percent of the employed) until 1990-2000. Commerce, transportation and personal services have also remained steady over time. The major shifts in the employment have been the decline in agriculture, from 18 percent to 2 percent, and in construction from 9 percent to 5-6 percent. At the same time, there have been increases in employment in the finance sector (doubling to 10 percent from

1970 to 1990 and increasing to 14 percent in 2000) and in public community services (from 22 percent to 31 percent).

Table 6.3: Israel's Employed Population by Profession, 1955-2000

Year	Sci	Pro	Mgr	Cle	Sal	Ser	Agr	Ski	Unsk	Total
1955	-	10	-	16	11	10	17	29	6	99
1960	-	11	-	14	9	13	17	31	5	100
1965	-	13	-	17	8	11	13	33	5	100
1970	-	16	-	17	8	12	8	32	5	98
1975	7	13	3	17	8	12	6	28	6	100
1980	8	15	4	19	8	11	6	26	4	101
1985	9	15	6	18	8	13	5	24	4	102
1990	9	17	5	17	9	13	4	24	3	101
2000	13	15	6	19	7	11	1	20	9	101

Sci – Scientific and academic workers
Pro – Professional and other technical workers
Mgr – Managers and administrators
Cle – Clerical and related workers
Sal – Sales workers
Ser – Service Workers
Agr – Agricultural workers
Ski – Skilled workers in industry and elsewhere
Unsk – Unskilled workers

Source: Statistical Abstract of Israel, various years

A complementary picture emerges from an examination of shifting occupational distribution over time in Israel (Table 6.3). There has been a clear and sharp decline in the proportion engaged in agriculture from the mid 1950s to 2000 (17 percent to one percent), modest declines in skilled labourers (from about 30 percent of the employed in 1950 through the 1970s, to about 25 percent in the 1980s and 1990s and to 20 percent in 2000). Service and sales workers have remained at about the same level over time, declining somewhat in 1990-2000. The most conspicuous overall occupation shift has been the increase in the professional, scientific and academic category (from 10 percent of the employed in 1955 to 28 percent by 2000).

Israel today ranks third in the world in the number of university graduates per capita, after the United States and the Netherlands. (Neuman, 1999) It possesses the highest per capita number of scientists in the world, with 135 for every 10,000 citizens [compared to 85 per 10,000 in the United States] (Henry and Robert Springborg, 2001), and publishes the highest number of scientific papers per capita. (Aharoni, 1991)

Economic Development: At a Glance

A range of economic indicators at the national level make it clear that Israel's economy has grown in terms of domestic production, technological developments and labour force improvements. A brief overview of Israel's economic growth over the time is indeed very interesting:

Pre-State Period: The foundations of Israel's economy date back to the pre-state Jewish settlement (*yishuv*) that began in the early 1880s. Indeed, much of the *yishuv*'s economic activity set the pattern for Israel's later development. (Elizur, 1997) With continuing immigration in the pre-state period, the *yishuv* focused its energies on building communal agricultural settlements that were meant to make the return to the land practical as well as symbolic. Numbering 12 in 1918, these collective settlements grew to 19 in 1921 and to 25 in 1925. By 1945, they reached 179. (Aharoni, 1991) The early emphasis on agriculture–in a land with a limited water supply of which two-thirds consisted of desert and barren hills (Horowitz and Lissak, 1989)–was prove lucrative in later years as Israeli agricultural productivity and innovation allowed the country to become largely self-sufficient in terms of food production, and a leading exporter of produce and agricultural technology.

Agriculture, a labour-intensive occupation, was particularly well-suited to employ the thousands of Jewish immigrants who arrived each year. From 1882 to the eve of independence, the Jewish population grew at a rate of 4.9 percent annually from immigration alone. (Neuman, 1999) Immigrant absorption, particularly the distribution of jobs, was controlled by the *yishuv* organizations and the powerful, politically active *Histadrut* trade union, which functioned not only as a labour advocate but later came to own many Israeli businesses.

In a trend that would continue well into Israel's future, the *yishuv* was financed in large part by the donations and investments of Diaspora Jews, whose money contributed to construction, manufacturing, and agricultural production, as well as public funds used to purchase land. Such ideological foreign investment was and remained vital to the *yishuv*'s, and later the state's, development given that the country attracted little foreign commercial interest until the 1990s.

The Newly Established State

Following independence, the new state's economy was structured around three basic elements: high defense costs, mass immigration absorption, and the building of new institutions such as banks, a national insurance institute, and government agencies, all of which necessitated massive infusions of public money into the economy. A formidable challenge arose with the early immigration explosion that more than doubled the Jewish population from May 1948 to 1951. Annual Jewish immigration for those years reached a rate of 22.6 percent. (Neuman, 1999) Many of the immigrants arrived from Middle Eastern and North African countries, among them a high proportion of children, and they were almost completely dependent on the state for housing, language instruction, education, job training, and employment.

The state had inherited a well-developed bureaucracy from the *yishuv* and social and economic programs of government remained on outside funding. Also lacking exploitable natural resources and offering only a small and fledgling domestic market, as well as heavy-handed government intervention, Israel attracted little foreign investment. Contributions and loans from Diaspora Jews, often in the form of low-interest Israel bonds, helped finance the state's imports of energy, raw materials, and production inputs. Far more significant was the reparations agreement that the government signed with West Germany on September 10, 1952, which provided a massive infusion of much-needed foreign currency into Israel's economy. (Aharoni, 1991) The agreement pumped about US$ 850 million directly into state coffers. German reparations helped fund continued large-scale government investment in agriculture and manufacturing through joint ventures, subsidies, loans and grants to private investors (Ibid).

Meanwhile, the Sinai campaign in which Israel joined forces with Britain and France in attacking Egypt following the nationalization and closing of the Suez Canal, led to a mini-economic boom in 1956. Unemployment declined, productivity grew (especially in agriculture and industry), and the state's balance of payments improved. (Sanbar, 1990) Similarly, the 1967 War, deliberately induced by the government, brought Israel out of the recession and following the war, unemployment was greatly reduced, productivity and private consumption began to rise, industries related to defense (from metals to computers) benefited, as did tourism, and new immigration began. Further, the domestic market expanded to include the newly occupied West Bank and Gaza Strip, which also provided a source of cheap labour (Ibid).

In sum, Israel saw tremendous economic growth in the 1950s and 1960s. Its GDP increased by an astounding 30.1 percent in 1951, and averaged a rate of 9.2 percent for the 1950-1968 period, second in the world only to Japan's 9.7 percent. (Neuman, 1999) Private consumption grew by 9 percent for the same period. (Aharoni, 1991) A World Bank mission to Israel in 1968 labeled Israel's performance an "economic miracle" given its dearth of natural resources, hostile neighbours, and large-scale immigrant absorption. The mission attributed Israel's success to two factors: human skill (a capable and determined population with a broad base of well-educated and energetic people who proved able to overcome the difficulties of economic development with great ingenuity) and foreign capital [originating chiefly from private donations of American Jews and from reparation payments by West Germany]. (Horowitz and Lissak, 1989)

Economic Ups and Downs

After the war, Israel began to produce sophisticated weapons both for its domestic market and for export. The acceleration of military production was driven by a number of factors, chiefly: necessity in light of the War of Attrition with Egypt in the late 1960s as well as continued cross-border terrorist attacks; the French arms embargo following the outbreak of 1967 hostilities, which cut off Israel's main supply of weapons; the U.S. refusal, until the 1970s, to sell Israel any major weapons' systems; and the government's desire to respond to military needs in a way that developed local industry. (Kochav, 1990) Defense spending as share of Gross National Product (GNP) doubled from 10.4 percent in 1967 to 20.2 percent in 1969 and reached 25.7 percent in 1970 (Ibid) as the government poured massive resources into research and development (R&D), boosting employment in the defense industry from 14,000 in 1966 to 34,000 in 1972 (Sadeh, 2001), and setting the industry up as a major engine of economic growth.

The 1973 War sent Israel's defense budget soaring and Israel's defense costs reached an annual average of approximately 32 percent of GNP for 1973-1976. Throughout the 1970s, Israel continued to devote about 30 percent of its national product to defense, though the numbers fell toward the end of the decade and stabilized around 20 percent throughout the 1980s. (Kochav, 1990) Despite the added jobs and export revenues generated by an invigorated defense industry, as well as a 1975 free trade agreement with the

European Community, economic growth slumped from 1973 through the 1980s. The decline was attributable to post-1973 defense demands as well as the rise in energy costs and the global recession. Israel's GDP grew a modest 2.7 percent annually from 1981-1989, with a per capita GDP rise of only 1.1 percent. (Neuman, 1999)

Inflation reached double digits by the early 1980s, as public sector employment (protected by the *Histadrut* labour union) grew to 30 percent of the labour force, forcing Israel into heavy debt to finance rising levels of private consumption in the face of stagnant output. (Aharoni, 1991) In 1985, the coalition government instituted a salutary economic program, overhauling the Israeli currency and adopting reforms designed to curb public spending. Privatization reforms paved the way for the 1990s economic boom.

Beginning of Modern Era

Since 1990, Israel experienced substantial economic growth powered by massive immigration from the former Soviet Union and evolution of a dynamic "high-tech" sector. The collapse of the Soviet Union and the ensuing political and economic turmoil drove almost 900,000 new immigrants to Israel from 1989 to 1998, augmenting Israel's population of 4.56 million people by 19.3 percent. Many of these immigrants were highly educated and assimilated fairly easily into the Israeli market. More than 55 percent had post-secondary education, and more than half held academic and managerial positions in their former countries: 15 percent were engineers and architects, 7 percent were physicians, 18 percent were technicians and other professionals, and 8 percent were managers. Their arrival contributed to annual GDP growth of 6 to 7 percent in the first half of the 1990s, one of the highest rates in the world [I993 was an exception with 3.1 growth]. (Neuman, 1999)

The unprecedented growth of the country's high tech sector achieved total annual sales of more than US$ 7 billion in 1990 and ranked among the top five world leaders in the field (Cohen, MFA website) with Tel Aviv identified as one of the 10 top high-tech centers in the world. (Ram, 2000) Indeed, as of December 2000, 9 out of every 1000 Israelis were employed in high tech research and development, almost twice the concentration of the United States and Japan. (Peled, 2001) The Middle East peace process, initiated with the Madrid Conference in 1991 and continuing through the 1993 Oslo Declaration and the 1994 peace treaty with Jordan, positioned Israel – by far the most technologically advanced country in the region–to take advantage of globalization and its corresponding international flow of capital. FDI became a novel and pronounced element of the economy totaling more than US$ 7 billion between 1993 and 1997 (Henry and Springborg, 2001), and hitting a record high in 2000 with almost US$ 5 billion. (Wasser, 2002; Shalev, 2000)

At the same time, Israel's high tech industry went global, providing the third highest number of initial purchase offerings (IPOs) on the NASDAQ in New York, after the United States and Canada, and the second highest number on London's Alternative Investment Market, behind Britain (Cohen, MFA website). Today, high tech goods and services account for one-third of Israel's exports. (Henry and Springborg, 2001)

The Middle East-North Africa (MENA) economic summits, which brought Israelis together with representatives from Arab governments and businesses throughout the decade, lent Israel a sense of legitimacy as an economic partner and helped assuage fears about Israel's precarious position in the region, both of which impacted incoming FDI flows. In addition, tourism, long a strong sector of Israel's economy, increased as a result of the peace agreements.

However, it is important to note that Israel's economy has not escaped the violence unscathed but it is hard to isolate precisely the economic impact of the terrorism. Israel's productivity started to dip in 1996, when the first wave of bombings began. But many analysts point to the Asian economic crisis of 1997-1998, followed by the bursting of the U.S. high tech bubble, as an explanation for why Israel has not yet recovered its early 1990s momentum.

Immigrant Absorption: A Key Resource to HRD

The policy of Israel has always been to encourage a high level of immigration to the country regardless of the demand for labour and the social costs of immigrant absorption. A complex system of aid which includes both direct and indirect subsidies, intensive language training, housing assistance, occupational training and income support is aimed at easing the adjustment of new immigrants.

The overwhelming magnitude of the wave of immigration which has arrived since 1990 raised problems of absorption which the country had not faced since the period of mass immigration which followed the establishment of state in the years 1948-1951. Especially in 1990, as immigration reached the level of nearly 36,000 in one month (December) it was not clear how the country would even be able to cope with the task of housing the newcomers. Solutions were found both by the state (which provided increased incentives to builders and housing renters and offered temporary solutions in caravan sites) and by the immigrants themselves, by the frequent sharing of apartments by more than one nuclear family unit. It was found that after 14 months in Israel, the immigrants from the USSR who arrived in 1990 had a housing density averaging 1.5 people per room as compared to 1.1 for the total population. In 24 percent of the households of three generations–grandparents, parents and children–were present. Nevertheless one year later 41 percent of immigrant households lived in non-institutional housing, and of them 25 percent owned the dwelling they lived in. (Ministry of Labour and Social Welfare Report, 1994)

Regarding housing, for most immigrants the "direct absorption" policy has been implemented. Rather than the government providing housing directly, immigrant households are provided with income support and rental subsidies allowing the household to make its own choices as to the nature and location of housing in response to market conditions and their own preferences. For particularly disadvantaged groups and individuals, the direct provision of housing and comprehensive services is provided in special Absorption Centers. (Ben-Moshe, 1989)

The sheer magnitude of the present immigration wave has stretched the absorptive capacity of the Israeli labour market. The immigrants entered a relatively stagnant economy, with considerable unemployment (8.9 percent) which labour force and improvement in unemployment level, which had been 32 percent for immigrants who arrived in 1990 after 14 months in the country was 19 percent one year later. By the first quarter of 1993 immigrants formed 9.5 percent of the population of labour force (age 15+), 8 percent of the employed and 19 percent of the unemployed. The economic stimulation which immigration itself provided has led, as in the past, to job expansion in the construction and service sector, where many of the jobs for the immigrants have been found. (Ministry of Labour and Social Welfare Report, 1994)

The labour force participation rate of male immigrants is similar to Israeli men and the participation rate of female immigrants is higher than that of Israeli women. A comparison of unemployment between men and women shows that the situation of female immigrants is far more worse; the unemployment level among those who were in Israel for 26 months during the first quarter of 1993 stood at 23 percent, as compared with 14 percent among male immigrants. This represents an improvement; a tear earlier the employment rate among these women had been 42 percent and among the men, 23 percent (Ibid).

So far the economy has not provided enough professional jobs appropriate to the highly skilled nature of this wave of immigration. Doctors are perhaps the most acute example of the general problem of the lack of correspondence between the immigrants' skills and the demands of the Israeli economy. The immigration of doctors in large numbers doubled the number of those already present in the country. The doctors also faced the problem of licensing and accreditation. Altogether, of those who had been scientific and academic workers in various professions in USSR, only 30 percent were employed in the same occupational category after 26 months in Israel. Problems of employment adaptation have generally been more severe for women and for older people. (Smooha, 1991)

To help overcame this disparity, many immigrants have attended occupational training and retraining courses. By the time they had been in the country for 14 months, 22 percent of immigrants aged 18-64 had attended such courses, and 16 percent had begun courses in their second year in the country. Language skills are a basic requirement for success in the labour force and these have risen over time. After 14 months of stay 47 percent of the immigrants reported that they were able to conduct a simple conversation in Hebrew freely or almost freely. After 26 months of stay 53 percent reported that they were able to write a simple letter in Hebrew freely or almost freely. Occupational training and language instructions in Israel have helped the professional immigrants to make better match between their skills and the needs of the economy of the country. (Ministry of Labour and Social Welfare, 1994)

Educational Mobility and Human Resource Development

As the state of Israel grew demographically and economically, educational levels of the population increased, networks of schools expanded, new academic institutions were established and opportunities for attending school were extended to all citizens. In fact, education has served as "an instrument of social policy" in Israel. Public elementary and high schools, collages, and universities developed to accommodate the needs of an increasing population, to educate the next generation to address the economic demands of an expanding and more diversified labour market.

The median years for schooling for the total population in 1961 was 8 years; 9 percent of the population had 13 or more years of schooling. The median increased 2.5 years by 1980, and the proportion with higher education doubled to 19 percent. Average education in Israel in the beginning of the 1990s was 12 years. By 2000, 40 percent of the Jewish population had 13 or more years of schooling. These increases are even more impressive when the educational levels of Arab Israelis are examined. Half of the Arab population age 15 and over in 1961 had no formal education, and only 1.5 percent had 13 or more years; four decades later, over 90 percent of the Arab population had more than a high school education. Among Jews, the decline at the lower level of education was from 13 percent in 1961 to 3 percent in 2000, and proportion at the higher educational level increased four during the same period. (Table 6.4)

The expansion of educational opportunities and increase in educational levels were matched by growth of the availability of jobs demanded by higher educational attainment. Job opportunities expanded and industries developed to meet the increasing number of people participating in the labour force as well as in the broader economic goals of the state. Educational and occupational opportunities developed in the new geographic areas where immigrants were living with their families. (Goldscheider, 1995)

These education shifts have transformed the employed population and their education quality (Table 6.4). In the early 1960s, 58 percent of the employed men in Israel had less than 8 years of education, and about 1 in 10 had more than a high school education. By 2000, only 1 out of 10 had less than 8 years, and 4 out of 10 had 13 or more years of education. In 2000, only 4 percent of the women employed in Israel had low levels of education, and over half had 13 or more years of education. This distribution reverses the patterns in the 1960s, when 45 percent of the employed women had less than 8 years of schooling and 15 percent has 13 years or more. (Amir,1986)

Table 6.4: Educational Level of Israel's Employed People, by Gender, 1963-2000

Years of Schooling	Percent Employed				
Men	**1963**	**1971**	**1979**	**1990**	**2000**
0 – 8	58	50	34	20	10
9 – 12	30	35	43	50	48
13+	11	15	23	30	42
Total	100	100	100	100	100
Women					
0 – 8	45	34	21	11	4
9 – 12	40	43	46	48	41
13+	15	23	34	40	54
Total	100	100	100	100	100

Source: Statistical abstract of Israel, various years

Aspects of Labour Force and Employment in Israel

The working age group (15+) increased its percentage of the population from 67.3 percent in 1984 to 70 percent in 1993. At the same time there was also an increase in the average labour force participation rate (from 50.2 percent in 1984 to 52.1 percent in 1993). As a result of these two factors the labour force grew by 33 percent from 1,400,000 in 1984 to 1,920,000 in 1993. (Ministry of Labour and Social Affairs, 1994)

The rise in the general labour force participation rate derived mainly from the significant and continuous rise in the participation rate of women. The participation rate of women rose from 36 percent in 1982 to 42.5 percent in 1992, while the participation rate of men went down during the period from 63.4 percent to 61.8 percent. The general rise in the participation rate of women derives mainly from the rise in specific participation rates of women in almost every age group and occurred both among Jewish and among Israeli Arab women. Between 1982 and 1992, labour force participation rates declined among men of all ages. The decrease was specially pronounced among men above the age of 35. Among women, rates increased for all women above the age of 25, and not noticeably for those aged 25-52 (Ibid).

Figure 6.2: Israeli Employees (in thousands), 1995-2007

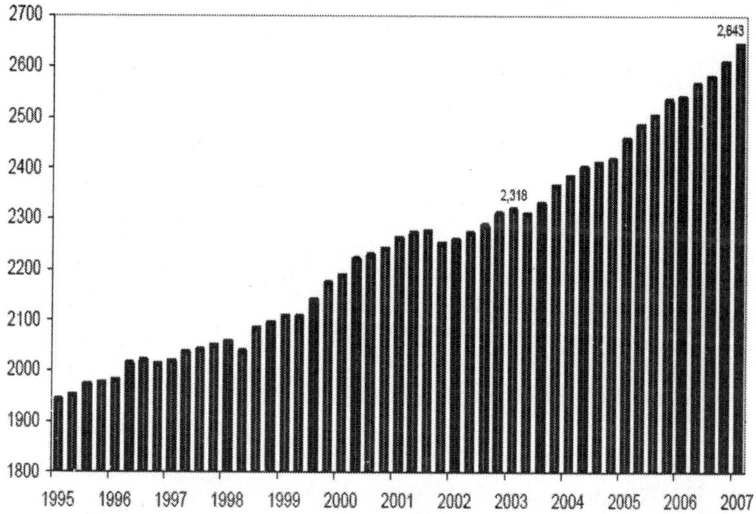

Source: Review of Economic Developments and Macro-Economic Forecasts, Economics and Research Department, Ministry of Finance, 2007.

The source of growth in the participation rate of women is partly to be found in long-term trends which originate mainly from demographic-educational changes and which are characteristic of all western countries. In addition to the long-term factors, short term-factors also strengthened the participation rates of women. Against the background of the increase of the unemployment rate during the 1990s and the loss of income, there was a trend to increase the number of earners in the household (i.e. growing participation of women in the labour force). A central factor in the increase in the participation rate of women in the next decade will be the absorption of new immigrant women into the labour force. The participation rates of these women in their countries of origin were higher than the average in Israel, and their increased entry into the labour force will contribute to a significant increase in the participation rate of women in labour force in the 1990s (Ibid).

Figure 6.3: Labour Participation Rate (age 15+), 1995-2007

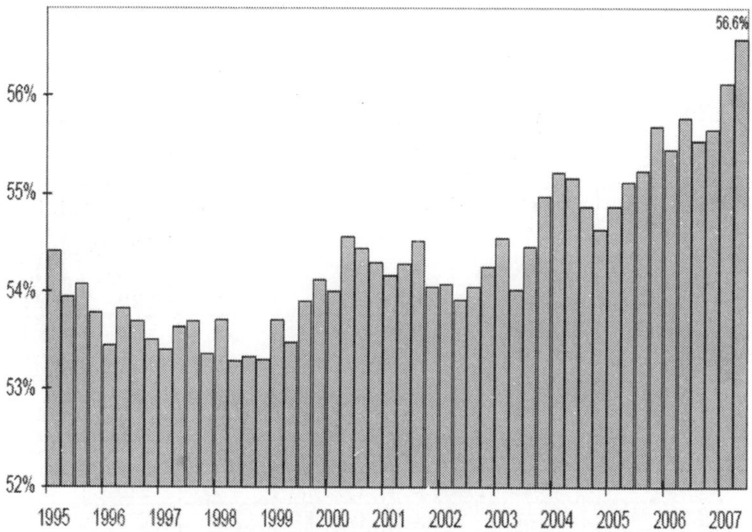

Source: Review of Economic Developments and Macro-Economic Forecasts, Economics and Research Department, Ministry of Finance, 2007.

Another important development in the Israeli labour force is the continual increase in its educational levels. The percentage of members of the labour force with 13 or more years of education rose from 28 percent in 1982 to 36 percent in 1991. (Ministry of Finance, Israel, 1998)

The rapid rise of educational levels among member's of Israel labour force is due not only to more education among the young, but also to the gradual withdrawal from economic activity of older male workers who, on average, have less schooling than their young colleagues. It is also due to the influx of women among whom the tendency to seek job rises directly with increased education. This improvement in educational levels has also affected the economies occupational structure in 1972, about 20 percent of all those employed were professional and technical workers and managers; by 1982 the proportion had reached 27 percent and by 1992 it had reached 31 percent. (Ministry of Labour and Social Affairs, 1994)

Table 6.5: Population aged 15 and over by Civilian Labour Force, 1982–1992: Characteristics and Sex

	1982	1989	1992	Average Annual Growth		
				1982–92	1982–89	1989–92
Population aged 15 and over (in thousands)	2,757.1	3,082.2	3,574.4	2.6	1.6	5.1
Civilian Labour force (in thousands)						
Total	1,366.7	1,603.3	1,857.8	3.1	2.3	5.1
Men	861.4	956.0	1,080.9	2.3	1.5	4.2
Women	504.9	647.7	776.6	4.4	3.6	6.3
Persons Employed (in thousands)						
Total	1,298.3	1,460.8	1,650.2	2.4	1.7	4.2
Business Sector	907.5	1,031.6	1,167.0	2.6	1.9	4.2
Public Sector	390.8	429.2	483.2	2.1	1.3	4.0
Percentage of Civilian Labour Force in total Population						
Total	49.6	52.0	52.0			
Men	63.4	63.0	61.8			
Women	36.1	41.3	42.5			

contd...

Percentage of unemployed Persons in the Civilian Labour Force				
Total	5.0	8.9	11.2	
Men	4.4	7.9	9.2	
Women	6.0	10.3	13.9	
Percentage of unemployed seeking employment for more than half a year	14.0	25.2	33.2	

Source: The Population of Israel, Demographic Center, Ministry of Labour and Social Affairs, 1994.

The number of employed persons increased from 1,360,000 in 1984 to 1,700,000 in 1993. The percentage of employees of total persons employed rose from 78 percent 1984 to 82 percent in 1993. At the same time the percentage employed in commerce increased from 11.7 percent in 1984 to 14.4 percent in 1993 and the percentage employed in finance increased from 8.2 percent in 1984 to 10.5 percent in 1993. The percentage of women among total employees also increased from 37.5 percent in 1984 to 44.6 percent in 1993. Average monthly wage per employees' post rose by 9.1 percent from 917 dollars in 1984 to about US$ 1,000 in 1993. (Table 6.5)

Health Care in Israel

Health care services (one of the most important factors in boosting human resource development) in Israel have been developed over the past century by voluntary health plans originally called sick funds, non-profit institutions, the government and the British Mandatory regime that existed prior to the establishment of the State of Israel in 1948. Workers' associations established the first health plan in 1911 to provide care to workers and their families and to employ immigrant doctors. This laid the basis of the health plan system, which is still a major component of the Israeli health care system. All four of Israel's health plans were formally established in the period between 1920 and the early 1940s; some of them emerged from mergers of health plans established even earlier.

The nature and the achievement of the health care system in Israel stem, to a large extent, from its foundation in organized social arrangements as well as a general consensus that society as a whole is responsible for the health of its citizens. This guiding principle has been reflected in the structure of health services in Israel, combining state activities with those of the voluntary health plans (non-profit mutual organizations).

Until the introduction of National Health Insurance (NHI) in 1995, the health plans both insured their members and provided them with most health services. By the late 1980s, approximately 95 percent of the population was insured in one of the four competing health plans, who provided their members with most curative health services either directly or by contract with other agencies. Public health and individual preventive services were provided by the government, Hadassah and some of the larger municipalities.

At present, four non-profit health plans operate in Israel: *Clalit, Maccabi, Meuhedet* and *Leumit*. Established in 1911, *Clalit* has been the dominant fund both in size and in influence, insuring more than 80 percent of the population until the beginning of the1980s. It was affiliated with the *Histadrut* (General Federation of Labour in Israel), which was established in 1920.

In general, the health of Israelis compares favorably with that of residents of other developed countries. In 1996, the average infant mortality was 6.3 for every 1,000 live births, similar to the average for countries whose per capita GNP is high. (World Bank, 1998) Life expectancy at birth is 75.5 for men–slightly higher than the average for high-income countries, and 79.5 for women-somewhat lower than the average for high-income countries (ibid). Whereas in Europe women outlive men by an average of 7 years, in Israel the difference narrows to 4 years. (ICDC, 1998) Two-thirds of all deaths in Israel are caused by heart disease, cancer, and cerebra-vascular disease–the leading causes of death in the developed world.

Israel has an extensive preventive care network of about 1,000 public Mother and Child clinics dispersed throughout the country that provide pre and post-natal care for women, well-baby care, and on-time inoculations for 91 percent of Israeli infants and children. However, some services considered primary in other developed countries-dental care, mental health services, long-term nursing care for the elderly and contraceptives for women - are not an integral part of the public health care system.

In 1995, there were 259 hospitals in Israel with 5.91 beds per 1,000 persons. The average duration of hospitalization for persons in general care has also decreased, from 7.2 days in 1976 to 4.4 in 1996. (CBS, 1997a and 1978) Annual general hospitalization days per 1,000 persons have been decreasing steadily as well: in 1996, the figure was 793 (Ibid). The average occupancy rate of hospital beds is 94 percent-indicating a high level of efficiency. (ICDC, 1997) The doctor/population ratio-461 per 100,000 persons–is among the highest in the world. Contrary to popular opinion, the latest figures indicate that Israelis do not visit the doctor more often; Israelis make an average of 6.8 visits a year. (CBS, 1997, Health Survey; Ben-Nun and Ben-Uri, 1996)

Standards of Living

Other economic indicators reveal the increased standard of living and the improved quality of life among Israelis. For example, the percentage of food consumption expenditure declined continuously from 39 percent in 1950 to 21 percent in 2000. (Table 6.1) Indicators of housing and crowding reveal the increase in the amount of household space available in 1967, 85 percent of the Jewish population lived in households in which there was more than one person in per room, compared to 58 percent in 1990; the proportion of households that had two persons or more per room declined from 31 percent to 8 percent in the same period. In 1999, only 27 percent of Jewish households had more than one person per room compared to 65 percent among the Arab population. (Goldscheider, 1995)

Increasing possession of consumer goods also indicates improvements in the standard of living and the quality of life among Israelis. In 1950, only 2 percent of the Israeli households had electric refrigerators, but one-half of the households owned it in 1960 and virtually all households by 1975. Seven percent of the households had washing machines in the mid 1950s, increasing to 43 percent in 1970 and to 80 percent in 1980. Only 4 percent of the Israeli families owned a private car in 1960, 15 percent in 1970 and 34 percent in 1980 (Ibid). According to one recent survey, almost 81 percent of Israelis own cell phones, placing it sixth in the world. Another survey found that 54 percent of Israelis own personal computers, in comparison to only 42 percent of U.S. respondents. (*Ha'aretz*, January 24, 2000) The data reveal the overall increase in the standard of living and access to modern consumption items in Israeli population.

Conclusion

Against all odds, Israel has a strong, modern, and diversified economy that in 2000 posted an annual Gross Domestic Product (GDP) of US$ 104.1 billion, 40 percent of which consisted of exports of goods and services. Growth for the Year 2000 reached six percent. (World Bank, 2002) Israel's per capita Gross National Income (GNI) for 2000, at almost US$ 17,000, placed the state ahead of Spain, Portugal, Greece, and New Zealand. (World Bank Development Indicators, 2002) No longer classified as a "developing country" by the World Bank, 54-year-old Israel now ranks as a high-income economy and was identified as one of the most global emerging markets by Foreign Policy magazine's Globalization Index. Over the past decade, Israel's high-technology industry, second only to California's Silicon Valley in concentration of firms, powered economic growth and attracted massive Foreign Direct Investment (FDI) to the country, a figure that reached US$ 4.4 billion in 2000. (Wasser, 2002)

Apart from growing economy, the present status of education in Israel is also excellent. Health services in the country are equal to any other developed country. And immigration in Israel was not merely the source of population growth which was needed for the survival of the Jewish state, but it was also an instrument of human capital accumulation. Israel received a highly educated and trained manpower, particularly in the form of European-American immigrants. Other categories of immigrants were brought within the ambit of education, training and planned development by a large network of vocational and technical schools. Health care facilities have further provided a boost to the planned development of the country.

References

Aharoni, Yair (1991), *The Israeli Economy: Dreams and Realities*, London: Routledge, p. 3.

Amir, S. (1986), "Educational Structure and Wage Differentials in the Labor Force in the 1970's", in Yoram Ben-Porath (ed.), *The Israeli Economy*, Cambridge: Harvard University Press.

Ben-Moshe, E. (1989), "Marriage Squeeze and Marriage Patterns in Israel", in Uziel O. Schmelz and Sergio Dellapergola (eds.), *Papers in Jewish Demography 1985*, Jerusalem: The Hebrew University, pp. 87-95.

Ben-Porath, Yoram (1986a), "Diversity in Population and in the Labour Force", in Yoram Ben-Porath, (ed.), *The Economy of Israel: Maturing through Crises*, Cambridge, Mass.: Harvard University Press.

Ben-Porath, Yoram (1986b), "The Entwined Growth of Population and Product, 1922-1982", in Yoram Ben-Porath, (ed.), *The Economy of Israel: Maturing through Crises*, Cambridge, Mass.: Harvard University Press, pp. 27-41.

Central Bureau of Statistics (1981), Government of Israel, *Projection of Population and Households in Israel up to 2000*, Jerusalem.

——(1983), Government of Israel, *Census of Population and Housing: 1983*, Jerusalem.

——(1994), Government of Israel, *Use of Health Services Survey*, Publication No. 970, Jerusalem, January-March 1993.

——(1994a), Government of Israel, "Households of Immigrants from U.S.S.R. who arrived in Israel in October-December 1990: A Follow-Up Survey, Two Years after Immigration", *Supplement to the Monthly Bulletin of Statistics*, 45 (10): 59--108, Jerusalem.

——(1994b), Government of Israel, "Employment of Immigrants from U.S.S.R. who arrived in Israel in October-December 1990: A Follow-up Survey, Two Years after Immigration", *Supplement to the Monthly Bulletin of Statistics*, 45 (4): 157-204, Jerusalem.

——(1995a), Government of Israel, "Households of Immigrants from U.S.S.R. who arrived in Israel in October-December 1990: A Follow-up Survey, Three Years after Immigration", *Supplement to the Monthly Bulletin of Statistics*, 46 (12): 131-190, Jerusalem.

——(1995b), Government of Israel, "Employment of Immigrants from U.S.S.R. who arrived in Israel in October-December 1990: A Follow-up Survey, Three Years after Immigration", *Supplement to the Monthly Bulletin of Statistics*, 46 (6): 71-128, Jerusalem.

——(1995c), Government of Israel, *Family Expenditure Survey 1992/93, Part D: Immigrants' Households*, Publication No. 1002, Jerusalem.

——(1996), Government of Israel, "Employment of Immigrants who arrived from the Former U.S.S.R. in October-December 1993", *Current Briefings in Statistics, Findings from Recent Surveys*, No. 24, Jerusalem.

——(1997a), Government of Israel, *Income Survey: 1996*, Jerusalem.

——(1997b), Government of Israel, *Socio-Demographic Characteristics of Infant Mortality, Based on Data for 1990-1993*, Jerusalem.

——(1997c), Government of Israel, *Health and Demographic Profile of the Settlements in Israel: 1990-1994*, Jerusalem.

——(1997d), Government of Israel, *Health Survey: 1996/97, Advance Data for the Period April-September 1996*, Jerusalem.

——(2002), Government of Israel, *Israel 2001 – Social Report*, Publication No. 5, Jerusalem.

——(2003), Government of Israel, *Jews and others, by origin, continent of birth and period of immigration*, Accessed on 04 April 2006, URL: http://www1.cbs.gov.il.

——(2004), Government of Israel, *Pupils in Grade XII, Matriculation Examinees and Entitled to a Certificate*, Accessed on 14 November 2006, URL: http://www1.cbs.gov.il/shnaton56

——-(Various Years), Government of Israel, *Immigration to Israel: Various Issues*, Jerusalem.

——(Various Years), Government of Israel, *Statistical Abstract of Israel: Various Issues*, Jerusalem.

Ben-Porath, Yoram (1986c), (ed.), *The Economy of Israel: Maturing through Crises*, Cambridge, Mass.: Harvard University Press.

Elizur, Yuval (1997), *Economic Warfare: The One Hundred Year Economic Confrontation between Jews and Arabs*, Israel: Kineret, (Hebrew).

Ginor, Fanny (1986), *Socio-Economic Disparities in Israel*, Tel Aviv: Transaction Books.

Goldscheider, Calvin (ed.) (1995), *Population, Nation-Building, and Ethnicity*, Boulder: Westview Press.

Henry, Clement M. and Robert Springborg (2001), *Globalization and the Politics of Development in the Middle East*, Cambridge: Cambridge University Press, p. 202.

Horowitz, Dan and Moshe Lissak (1989), "The State of Israel at Forty", in Peter Medding (ed.) *Israel: State and Society, 1948-1988*, Jerusalem: Studies in Contemporary Jewry, Institute of Contemporary Jewry.

Israel Center for Disease Control, (1997, 1998), *The Condition of Health in Israel*, Tel Hashomer (Hebrew).

Kochav, David (1990), "The Influence of Defense Expenditure on the Israel Economy", in Moshe Sanbar ed. *Economic and Social Policy in Israel*, Lanham: University Press of America, p. 41.

Ministry of Finance of Israel (1998), *The Israeli Economy Achievements and Potential: Tel Aviv Hailed as One of the World's Top Hi-tech Centers*, November, 1998, URL: www.jewishagency.org/

Ministry of Labour and Social Welfare Reports, Government of Israel, Accessed on 21 March, 2002, URL: http://www.tamas.gov.il/NR/exeres/9034396F-AC64-4C44-9466-25104B45FBB1.htm.

Neuman (1999), "Aliyah to Israel: Immigration under Conditions of Adversity", Bonn: Institute for the Study of Labor (IZA), Discussion Paper No. 89, p. 22.

Neuman, Shoshana (1999), "Aliyah to Israel: Immigration Under Conditions of Adversity", Bonn: Institute for the Study of Labor (IZA), Discussion Paper No. 89, p. 22.

Peled, Dan (2001), "Defense R&D and Economic Growth in Israel: A Research Agenda", paper prepared for Samuel Neaman Institute for Advanced Studies in Science and Technology, Technion-Israel Institute of Technology, p.18.

Sadeh, Sharon (2001), "Israel's Beleaguered Defense Industry", *Middle East Review of Foreign Affairs, (MERIA) Journal*, 5(1): 1.

Shalev, Michael (2000), "Liberalization and the Transformation of the Political Economy", in Gershon Shafir and Yoav Peled (eds.) *The New Israel: Peacemaking and Liberalization*, Boulder: Westview Press, pp. 139-140.

Smooha, Sammy (1991), *Arabs and Jews in Israel*, Vol. 2, Boulder: Westview Press.

Wasser, Dani (2002), "The Effects of Current Events on the Israeli Economy and Investments", Power Point Presentation on April 4, 2002, Investment Promotion Center, Ministry of Industry and Trade.

World Bank (Various Years), *World Development Indicators: Various Issues*, Washington, D.C.

World Bank (Various Years), *World Development Report: Various Issues*, Oxford University Press, New York.

7

Situating the Hobbesian State of Iraq in Contemporary International Relations

Arshi Khan

An underlying fact about the emergence of the modern state system is that it must follow certain important principles of legitimate governance and uphold the sovereign status of the state. As a result, the state system, both in terms of being a Nation-State and a Federal-Nation, elected or monarchical, was held responsible for upholding human security and the right to participate in the public life of the country. In other words, the state system was conceived as the main regulator of 'justice' to its citizens. Similarly its behavioural pattern recognized by the United Nations and other regional security arrangements of post-World War II era, affirms the legitimate right of an independent country to maintain its internal supremacy. This kind of status granted to the state was meant for protecting and promoting the rights and interests of its own citizens. Thus we find that the purpose of an independent and sovereign state is to justify its policies, programmes and actions for the legitimate purpose of democratic demands of the people and to set its corresponding goals in international relations.

Preservation of sovereign states emerged as one of the major principles of maintaining security, peace and order in different regions. They also became the constitutive units of balancing relations in international politics. At the same time they were presupposed to follow the code of conduct for not usurping the rights of any other states. In contrast to Thomas Hobbes, Bodinian sovereignty is of course in favour of absolute and perpetual power of the Republic but forbade it to become irresponsible. Later John Austin, conforming to the Hobbesian state, called international law as 'positive international morality'. French thinker, Jean Bodin (1530-1596), seemed to be better than 'liberal intitutionalists' as his system of fundamental law included (a) natural law; (b) the *leges imperii*, or constitutional law defining the royal office; and (c) certain laws considered fundamental to the structure of a particular society, which to Bodin meant the sanctity of private property and of the family. [1]

For this purpose, sovereign states created several regional and international organizations to set their pattern of acceptable behaviour, policies and actions in international politics. As a result, the position of 'sovereign states' was supposed to remain intact despite the legitimate claims of the individuals and international organizations. It is, therefore, important to mention that security in the region or in any part of the world depends mainly upon the role of the constituents of International Relations. On the other hand, sovereign states were supposed to maintain 'self-restraint' in terms of their actions affecting the interests of others. The United Nations was developed as a corporate entity, as the hallmark of liberal internationalism, to perform a set of functions which are of value to the whole group. It has no independent means of action. Its policy decisions are simply the decisions reached in common by the representatives of its member states. It is a kind of organized diplomatic round-table for all its members to act in ccllective interests.

On the contrary, Hobbesian-Austinian concept of state seems to endorse the Realists approach to international politics to provide space to the mighty states to pursue mainly their interests and not law or international morality. What is disturbing to note is that the Hobbesian view dominated international politics during the Cold War era and more aggressively after fall of the Berlin Wall in 1989. The tacit endorsement of the Hobbesian and Machiavelli's views seem to provide a rationalization of imperialism and aggression in terms of national mission. This was also echoed in the celebration of the march of "Idea"/ "Reason" in teleological process. Self-proclaimed moral values of a mighty state gets prioritized vis-à-vis international laws. This happened in the Fascist Italy and Nazi Germany before 1939. Those who opposed the aggressive and expansionist impulse of the European Nation-State, became the founding fathers and mothers of the Cold War era in which power-politics characterised international relations.

The so-called liberators of Europe from dictatorial regimes caused irreparable damages to humanity in Korea, Vietnam, Congo, Angola, Latin America and in many other places. It is also important to recall here that the same forces were instrumental in the unlawful take-over of the Palestinian territories through various means which caused massive humanitarian crises in the Mediterranean. Now it is resurfacing its dragon teeth in the midst of international politics since the First Gulf War. Juridically, liberal democracies accept that states are equal, coordinate entities in a society of states but they differentiate between 'equal before law' and 'equally entitled to the protection of international law'. [2] The moral value of Manifest Destiny and international enforcement of Western civilization, in different forms, have become more dangerous in the existing Unipolar world in which unilateralism is bound to belittle the United Nations and regional organizations of non-western basic units.

Wailing Iraq

This paper is mainly intended to analyze the contemporary trends of unilateralism to understand the extent of threats directed at the Asian security. More than one-forth of the population of the country is directly affected by the policies and actions of the invaders and occupiers. The Associated Press have recently estimated 4335 deaths of the US soldiers. The case of Iraq is the most important example as well as an academic reference for many of us who wish to rethink over the legitimacy of the liberal paradigm of resetting Iraq on the pretext of democracy. Oldest democracies like the UK and the US have proved to be more disastrous and monstrous than the attack of Chengiz Khan earlier. The present predicament of the Iraqi people also show that the real cause of bombing and occupying Iraq was not to unseat its President Saddam Hussein but to regain control over Iraq for geo-strategic and geo-economics purposes. Since March 2003, Iraq has been loosing its vitality for emerging as a viable stable united sovereign state. It is a country where the foreign nationals are more safe than the native people. It is a land where psychological operations and massive media campaigns are in full swing to divide Iraqis by all means. Not a single day is left without the painful news of Iraqi bloodshed. Security and development have become only paper-works. Right to life, other civic rights and the right to seek justice have no meaning in today's Iraq. The barbarians are responsible for the inhuman situation in this land of civilizations.

The ongoing destructions and military occupation of Iraq with massive human rights violations are most dangerous signals of turbulence, instability, insecurity and divisive threats for Asia. The case of Iraq is extremely important for two very important reasons. First, the brutal destruction of Iraq through illegal invasion and continuing murderous role of the 'Coalition of the Willing' led by the United States in Iraq can be attributed to the behaviour and policies of the invading entities. So the first factor is the unlawful and anti-human policies, plans and actions of non-Iraqi states against Iraq for which Iraqi ruler cannot be held responsible which resulted in the uncontrolled chaos, human insecurity, massive destructions of human life, properties and irreparable damages manifesting beyond Hobbesian state of nature. As a result, these illegal actions of the coalition of invaders have created global security concerns dangerous to the region in particular and to the whole world, in general. Dangerous security situations created by the invasion, occupation, continuous bombings and military operations in Iraq are worse than any kinds of threats so far posed by non-state terrorist actions. This can be understood apparently as the violent face of naked unilateralism propagated as peace/liberation operations on the pretexts of peace, freedom, democracy and human rights.

The other is the legitimacy and the role of the new state and government created by the occupying forces. Destruction of Iraq can be partially compared with the situation of collapsed Germany soon after 1945. However, unlike Iraq, Germans had not been deprived of basic rights caused by any genocidal economic sanctions and indiscriminate killings, kidnappings, displacement, tortures, detentions, civil wars and other crimes as Iraqis suffered. Soon after the collapse of Germany, real economic recovery of Germans started which soon brought positive results of reconstructions. On the contrary, the occupying power politicized the term 'reconstruction' to have claims over the Iraqi oil and natural resources. Therefore, the agenda of the occupying forces is to decapitate Iraqis not only in terms of security and defense but also in terms of managing economy and polity on their own. As a result, the occupying forces have been destroying all the supportive infrastructures required for capacity building of the Iraqis to manage their affairs including the required social harmony to build a political union or a commonwealth.

This systematic destruction of the Iraqi State and the Society can be looked into three phases. The first phase is the phase of genocidal sanctions of over 12 years which crippled Iraq. Simultaneously, the US-UK coalitions' military actions gradually demolished conventional defense capacity of Iraq. Eric Hoskins, a Canadian doctor who was also the coordinator of the Harvard team on Iraq, reported that the bombardment of 1991 had "effectively terminated everything vital to the human survival in Iraq—electricity, water, sewage systems, agriculture, industry and health care." [3] Before the full invasion of Iraq in 2003, round-the-clock bombing began for four days December 16-19, 1998 which was called Operation

Desert Fox. Peacetime bombing of Iraq (1991-February 2003) had lasted longer than the US invasion of Vietnam or the war in Laos. [4] The second phase occurred at the time of brutal invasion of Iraq in March 2003 with the use of all the weapons of mass destruction in major cities with massive media operations resulting in the collapse of the Iraqi State. The third phase of destruction is now going on to germinate all sources of difficulties, despair and damages which could never build a united, lawful, progressive, democratic, manageable and viable state of Iraq.

It is in this context it would be important to recall the warnings of the famous Roman philosopher Marcus T. Cicero against the present-day-Iraq-like State. In his opinion, when there is no justice, there is no law and thus no state. To him simply the existence of government and the rules/laws is not the qualifying criteria for being a state. It is the just law and the legitimate government which makes the state. In the case of Iraq, we find government, laws and the constitution but serious questions can be raised over their legitimacy. Do they exist in the interest of the people in general? Have they been dictated by the occupying forces? Who engineered the elections? How the elections were held? Who managed and monitored the elections? What is the condition of justice in Iraq? What about the life and security of a common Iraqi? Is any one safe even in the hospital, university or in private dwellings? Hair-splitting of such questions can raise many valid points of objections and disappointments over the future prospect of Iraq.

Situation in Iraq needs to be a serious concern for India which is one of the most potential countries of the Asian continent. Owing to its historical ties and quite friendly relations with Iraq's pre-occupation legitimate governments, India can define its constructive role in the larger interests of Asian security. Pre-March 2003 Iraq was neither a terrorist state nor possessor of the weapons of mass destruction. However, the continuing aggression on different provinces of

Iraq has uprooted over 25 percent of its population with the acute shortage of basic necessities, stability, national security, freedom of speech, movement and freedom of privacy. About two million Iraqis were killed so far. Practicing trifurcation of Iraq, control over its oil-wells and building of over a dozen military bases inside Iraq have also significant message for India which has sensitive regions, national minorities, and ethnic violence.

Similarly we can find Western involvement in Shii-Sunni violence in Iraq, *de-facto* partition of Iraq into three pieces (earlier promoted through safe-haven and no-fly-zone methods (during 1991-2003) which warn some important lessons to India. The armed forces of the North Atlantic Treaty Organisation is next to our borders, Afghanistan. Most friendly Iraq is fully occupied. India's good-old neighbours in Central Asia are deeply penetrated by the foreign military bases. India is also under external pressures to support pro-Western forces against the Myanmar's regime. Its close-door neighbour, Pakistan is the strategic ally of the US and we are also constrained to minimize terms with Iran. The National Security Strategy (NSS) of September 17, 2002, along with the *Quadrennial Defense Review* Report give a pretty clear picture of U.S. policy in the Middle East-which is essentially to control the natural resources and the shipping lanes. Some of the Iraqi cities were declared "free fire zone," meaning they gave soldiers license to shoot anything they wanted. The NSS declared its preparedness to intervene unilaterally, if needed, on behalf of democratic values, human rights, and its own security anywhere in the world. It decided not to hesitate to act alone if required. It reaffirmed what the American President George Bush had told the Congress that the advance of human freedom depended on the US. In the State of the Union Address on January 28, 2008, declared to support freedom in countries from Cuba and Zimbabwe to Belarus and Burma. So the US is not ready to accept the world as it is today. It is also important to mention that democracy and human rights are now the parts of the US foreign policy. This type of priority of the US is bound to affect the Asian security in the time to come.

It would not be irrational to state that India's security is also the constituent of Asian security as the Iraqi security was for West Asia. There are lessons for many of us how the occupying power has been trying to impose its choice and will over each and every provision of the sponsored Iraqi constitution ranging from citizenship to the control over oil. It was the genocidal policy of the economic sanctions which disabled the middle class of Iraq. Later aggressions and continuing military operations (on the pretext of the Baath party followers, the Al-Zarqawi and Al-Qaeda) against the Iraqi people have created chaos. At present, future of Iraq is to eliminate all resisting forces and to sponsor like-minded administrators with controlled elections and embedded journalism. It is in this context, Asian security can be discussed in the larger interests of India and the region. India has a lot to contribute to Iraq provided such intentions are accepted by the occupying powers.

It is also important to recall here that the genocidal killings in Iraq should not be termed as war or humanitarian intervention or war on terror. It is basically none of them. It is the case of a naked aggression on Iraq without any provocation to the aggressor. The aggression had neither the mandate of the United Nations nor any worsening humanitarian crises except those of the genocidal effects of the UN Sanctions against which the Saddam government was trying hard to overcome. Iraqi government was doing its best to cooperate with the politically motivated team of UN weapon inspectors. Iraq was open to all international agencies to verify the possession of the weapons of mass destruction whereas another country in the same region was free from all such pressures of inspections and WMD despite possessing over 200 thermonuclear weapons and occupying sovereign territories of neighbouring states.

Thus Iraq is the case of multiple war-crimes caused by aggression, style of governmental engineering, psychological operations, engineering of civil wars and explosions in religious and civilian areas and total disablement of Iraq. Aggression on Iraq and the policies of the occupying forces have serious implications within and outside Iraq in the areas of national security, national sovereignty and independent economic policies. The major goal of the occupying forces in Iraq is neither the establishment of democratic governance, nor the protection of human rights nor political stability but to enable the United States and its closest ally in the region to set the rules of the game of hegemony and control over the oil wells and unexplored oil fields. The immediate goal is three: to secure green-zones, to fuel civil war and to perish Iraqi resistance forces. The intermediate goal is to sponsor government of its choice for creating conformist political actors, institutions, and procedures. The ultimate end is to gain control over its vast natural resources and to secure strong military bases within Iraq to patrol all over West Asia. In such a situation, the aggressor and the planners would have material future of Sophists and Benthamites while the rest in this region would have the status of Anglo-Saxon slaves.

Such unlawful actions ever experienced in human history would have security implications for Asia. Most of the Asian countries had to pay a heavy price due to colonial misrule for a long time. After their independence, they were encircled by the rival nuclear camps of the Cold War era. Their Non-Aligned movement was also seriously affected by higher conspiracies. When they were about to breathe fresh air of freedom after the end of the Cold War, they got alarmed by the interventions of the European defense arrangements known as NATO in the case of Yugoslavia. This socialist country was dismembered on the pretext of democracy, human rights and ethnic nationalism. Similarly, Iraq was attacked on the pretext of preventing threats from the WMD. Later, the excuse was shifted to bring democracy and freedom in Iraq. Then the occupation forces switched over to fighting Baathist forces. Then they claimed fighting against Zarqawi and Al-Qaeda. Now they don't repent at all over what they did in Iraq. It is the saddest moment in the history of the 21st century in which the main victims are Political Protestants beginning with Iraq. Soon it became apparent that this invasion had domino effects on the whole region having serious implications for the contiguous neighbouring countries.

Looking into the Questions

It is imperative to investigate into the question of Iraq with the following questions. How to situate Iraq? What to situate in the context of Iraq? In what way the study on Iraq is relevant to analyze its implications for India? What is the political, cultural and social identity of Iraq and India among their respective territories, region and the world? What was the role of the United Nations and the US? How should we address the Iraqi question in the context of international politics? Should we trust the US and legitimize its war crimes for the democratization of Iraq? Or should we take it as the politics of 'American internationalism' to control and guide the Arab world in its domestic affairs? What should we select or reject in our day-to-day discussions on Iraq? Should we hold the Iraqi Government headed by President Saddam Hussein or the American interventionism responsible for looking into the genesis of the Iraqi tragedy since 1991 and March 2003? Should we take Iraq as the major victim of the New World Order (Willing Coalition led by the US) and the "Third Millennium" (Project of New American Century) in which the Western Europe is both a competitor and collaborator of the US in Iraq?

Situating Iraq in international politics is both a difficult and an easy subject for many of us. Those who adhere to the Americanism are supportive of what the US has done in the name of democracy, human rights, peace and freedom. But there are a large number of people who believe in the institutional dynamics and reality of international law and its agencies, and reject the use of war machines and all the acts of criminality against the sovereign Iraqi State and people. This paper is an attempt to discuss the subject of Iraq within the principled boundaries of international law in which the external imposition in any kind is prohibited and considered an international taboo in the internal affairs of the State unless and until it becomes murderous calling humanitarian intervention mentioned under the exceptional provision of the UN Charter. There is also an attempt to deny any legitimacy to those emerging theorist and policy makers who are devising several holes to puncture the ball set by the UN Charter in 1945. They are calling for the triumph of Liberal World Order, Liberal Millenarianism, [5] and democratic entitlement [6] theory vis-à-vis international law. In other words, there are many attempts to turn down the customary international law or use it on selective basis or to manipulate it for vested interests. As a result, the ground reality in the context of Iraq is that either international law failed to address the Iraqi question before and after March 2003 or it was forced to be a party in the dispute.

Politics of Benign Neglect

Since long particularly after early 1991, the West pursued the policy of benign neglect vis-à-vis Iraq. It is still in vogue. On the pretext of liberating Kuwait from the Iraqi occupation of only seven months, the US pursued three kinds of engagement. It damaged Iraqi defense capacity and civilian infrastructures beyond expectation in 1991 bombings. It expanded its military base and increased its number in the Gulf region including water-ways. It started the politics of dividing Iraq and to dismantle the Iraqi society. These were achieved by imposing illegal 'no-fly-zones' in north and south and 'safe-haven' for the Kurds. The US funded and facilitated anti-Iraqi elements within and outside Iraq to sabotage the Iraqi Government. As a result, northern Iraq became a major point of anti-Iraqi activities and many US sponsored Iraqis were later offered high positions in the US-sponsored government in occupied Iraq.

On many occasions, the Western liberal democracies ignored the Iraqi claims of eliminating all weapons of mass destruction. But the Western world believed the US statements and the media which unfortunately played a partisan role against Iraq. Even on the issue of the war on terrorism since 9/11, the West largely believed in the US version linking everything with Al Qaeda. As a result, we find West's military engagement in Afghanistan and non-military engagements in Iraq at many levels. Therefore, the Western Europe which differs with the US on Iraqi occupation remained largely engaged in all the efforts of the US, such as organizing donor conference, preparation for the constitution and elections in Iraq and providing all necessary supports to the US. This can be further witnessed in their behaviour and policies in European forums and in other regional and international agencies which speak of the threat of terrorism rather than the threats created by the occupation of Iraq.

Despite many cases [7] of violation of human rights, rights of prisoners, civilians, women, children and freedom of press which were committed beyond all limits of precedents in Iraq, the North American and West European leadership in raising human rights issues largely ignored or failed to highlight the issues as they have been doing in different places. As a result, human right champions and humanitarian activists stand suspect today in Iraq for their deliberate silence. It is also sad to note that the most badly affected agencies are media and information sectors which are denied access even to release minimum basic information. Media giants owned by the Western tycoons have completely controlled almost all information related to different news and views in Iraq. In other words, even the Western countries which have not participated in military invasion of Iraq, have also either failed or ignored the need to contain psychological war carried out by the media agencies. It becomes very clear from a common set of statement by the European leaders, opposed to the war that invasion is wrong but Saddam had to go. He was a butcher. This is a 'disclaimer'. Now the NATO has almost agreed to join the US politics of reconstruction.

Americanization of the UN

In the case of Iraq, the US has taken the services of the UN and its agencies as a client. [8] There is not a single evidence in the last 15 years of the UN activism in Iraq (since 1991) that shows judicious decision of the UN. There are many areas such as drafting resolutions, manipulation of votes in the Security Council, involvement of UN agencies, reports of the inspectors and US assessment of the Iraqi compliance of the UN resolutions, etc in which the UN acted more as a 'client' of the US than like an embodiment of international law. Before the occupation, the UNSC passed over 62 resolutions against Iraq, mostly drafted and decided by the US. After the illegal attack on Iraq since March 19, 2003, the UN Security Council passed more than 5 resolutions, most of them legitimizing the belligerents directly or indirectly. Not a single member of the UNSC could veto any resolution against Iraq whereas the US used veto over 32 times in the UNSC in favour of Israel. The UN Secretary General's involvement in the Madrid Donor Conference and UN engagement in aiding the US in forcing elections on Iraq, where election would only strengthen aggressors, clearly show Council's conformity with the US. Let us briefly look at the role of the UN.

What is more painful today is the role of the United Nations Security Council vis-à-vis Iraq [9] which in many aspects are questionable and against the very essence of the UN Charter. Two questions can be raised here. Has its role been objectively pursued? Or is it also engaged in strategies to somehow achieve the US agenda? There can be many examples to substantiate one's doubt about the UN's rationality towards against Iraq. How did the UN respond to the US attack campaign and the working of the United Nations Monitoring, Verification and Inspection Commission in the matters of Iraq? Most of the US anti-Iraq campaigns were launched from the UN platform which provided legitimacy to propaganda. It was the statement of US Secretary of State, Colin Powell with LCD presentation in the Security Council on February 5, 2003, which showed the Iraqi truck carrying the WMD. It later appeared completely false, which finally opened doors for the US to attack Iraq. He showed pictures, phone intercepts and al Qaeda linkages which were denied by Iraq. Powell made a case of war against Iraq merely on the basis of its intelligence reports. One can be sure that US intelligence vis-à-vis Iraq was certainly unfair as the former was hostile to Iraq since 1980s. Intelligence reports could not have been made the criteria of launching attack on Iraq. Such a case was engineered by the US against Nicaragua which has three million populations.

If we go little back to the history of the role of the Security Council in the case of Iraq, we can find many issues such as the continuation of the economic embargo, weapon inspectors and other non-UN methods which have neither been rejected nor reviewed in the premise of international legality. There are also examples of direct indulgence of the CIA in UNSCOM [10] and tremendous US pressure on the International Atomic Energy Agency findings related to Iraq. *The Washington Post* reported in December 1998 how the US officials played 'a direct role in shaping Butler's text (UNSCOM chief who presented it next day at the Security Council) during multiple conversations with him at secure facilities at the US mission to the UN.' It has been quite common for chief inspectors to spend long hours with the officials of US and UK before and after their visits to Iraq.

However, the end-result of the Security Council which forced Iraq to comply with several avoidable resolutions, has been its failure in the following areas: lifting economic embargo and protecting Iraq from US-UK bombings in no-fly-zones before March 2003, preventing US invasion of Iraq, failing to declare unlawful presence of the US and its allies and illegality of post-March rulers of Iraq and finally to do the needful for mobilizing rehabilitation and relief works for Iraqi people. In return to its adherence to UN resolutions Iraq has been punished with sanctions, militarization of the Middle East region and military colonization of Iraq.

Similarly the US threat of Iraq invasion forced the UNSC to pass resolution 1441 which is quite distinct in the UN history. It put the entire onus on Iraq as it was done soon after the 1991 Gulf War. First of all the passage of this resolution weakened Iraq further by vesting all powers of 'certification' of WMD in the hands of the UNMOVIC whose credibility is quite questionable. Role of Inspectors and their reports on January 27 and February 14, 2003 became instrumental in complicating the issue of disarmament in Iraq. [11] But it certainly provided more space to the two groups for further manipulations. Warmongers took Hans Blix's reports as a failed attempt at the disarmament of Iraq. The other came with the plan of increasing periodicity and strength of the inspectors. It has also proposed for UN armed personnel to back the inspectors.

In order to avoid attack Iraq fully cooperated with the UN and submitted all documents, offered all sites, accepted inspectors' demand of flying U-2 and other planes for surveillance and encouraging its scientists for appearing in interviews. Before invasion, about six kinds of planes and helicopters are engaged in surveillance. UNMOVIC raised the issue of some questions on the suspicion of some chemical and biological materials whose documentary proofs do not exist. UNMOVIC raised the issue of *al-Samoud* II missiles which had no guidance system. It also raised the issue of some reconstructed casting chambers and aluminum tubes within Iraq. Even if they existed in Iraq, they were technically incapable of making Iraq a WMD threat.

Iraq consistently maintained about its effective implementation of UNSC Resolutions particularly 687 and 1441 under which Iraq accepted the UN demand of the elimination of WMD on unconditional basis. Accordingly it opened all doors and premises which were called by the inspectors. As of February 4, 2003, they made 575 inspections on 371 sites since November 2002. Since February 6, 2003, Iraqi scientists, who were not prepared to give interview in private due to the factors of self-respect and manipulations by the UNMOVIC, started appearing for private interviews. Iraq also allowed U-2 to fly over Iraq. In fact about 700 'no-notice inspections' were made at all the places which were supposed to be based on US intelligence sources. Previously 3845 UN inspectors consisting of 276 teams of inspectors were engaged in Iraq for eight years under Resolution 687 who inspected thousands of sites. They also held hundreds of interviews with scientists, students, and others. 665 sites were identified for monitoring with sensors and cameras which were destroyed by heavy bombings over Iraq on December 16-20, 1998.

Therefore, some questions can be raised over unidimensionality of the operational aspect of the UN Security Council which has regularly compromised over the acts and policies of the violations of the sovereign rights of Iraq on the one hand and exposing itself as not only ineffective but also "collaborative" to the anti-Iraqi fronts, on the other. In the case of Iraq, weapons inspectors were made crucial actors in the "theatre show of WMD" whose clearance certificate was made mandatory for the lifting of the UN Sanctions against Iraq. Before September 11, US-UK alliance was maintaining "status-quo" policy against Iraq by somehow continuing with Sanctions against which Iraq had protested time and again to the UN.

After 9/11, there occurred a shift towards controlling the State and Society in Iraq. Thus the issue was not the elimination of WMD but the "regime change", 'on come what may criteria' in Iraq. This was really a serious matter for the larger world where the "US choice" can be imposed without any respect for the institutions and procedural aspects of the concerned country. In case of Iraq, the alliance acted either on its own or through the UN. In latter's case, the alliance was active on all fronts to pressurize and influence inspectors to produce results in congruence with the objectives of the alliance. As result, most of the sites which were inspected in Iraq by UNMOVIC had been identified earlier and informed by the alliance intelligence networks. Therefore the main question today is to how to assess the UN jurisdiction over international law in case of Iraq or in other similar cases? Why did the UN fail to take up the Iraqi issue in its own jurisdiction? In what way US succeeded to hatch the Iraqi issue as an agenda of the Bush-Blair alliance which prevailed over a decade? What would be the end-result of the kind of policy of the "alliance" against the larger world which has so far been timid and tolerant to "intolerant alliance"?

American Super-positivism

Benign neglect on the part of the Western world certainly provided a historic opportunity to the United States 'to do whatever it wants' against Iraq on varying pretexts such freedom of Kuwait, freedom of the Kurds, freedom of the US and the free world, humanitarian factors, human rights, democratic entitlement and freedom of Iraqi people and free society in Iraq. In fact Iraq became an acid test for the international law and human rights organizations for their political and moral commitment to the basic fundamental rights of a sovereign state and people since 1991. The results so far are so demonstrative of the fact that the 'liberal fraternity' ultimately failed to be responsive to the Iraqi question. Massive violation of human rights and war crimes almost on daily basis in Iraq is a painful reality, which has not been addressed at all by international law.

At the public opinion level, the West established its role in influencing media to the extent of becoming an Americanprotégé. It highlighted the negative image of the non-conformist Iraq with play card of being a rogue state, evil state, and Saddam Hussein as the most dangerous man of the world. The Iraqi State was projected as the store-house of the WMD. Saddam Hussein's WMD or the links between the Iraqi regime and al-Qaeda was invented as a scare to go alongside the notion of an 'evil' regime whose arsenal must evoke deep fear. [12]

The US has been using all means-- form diplomacy, massive embedded journalism to war-machines through all channels—its weapons, the UN, Europe, Iraqi agents and other agents, since 1991, to impose a new set of rule of polity, economy, justice, culture and foreign policy. The US misused international law and violated the UN Charter. Misuse of international law by all means was basically an exercise to create "disablement" of Iraqi State and Society". There are a number of instances since 1991 when the US abused its powers and misused the UN as well as the regional Middle East politics to bring back Iraq to pre-industrial age. Who should be held responsible for bringing total anarchy in Iraq with various symbolic acts of humiliations and disregards to Iraqi culture, religion, family values and individual rights?

Till March 2003, both State and society was targeted and later the larger society has been facing the American crimes since mid April 2003. The US adopted the strategy of "systematic failure" of Iraqi State and society and then finally "bulldozing" the remaining edifice of the State in March 2003 invasion. This was done in the following "scrapping" style. Massive bombings of the civilian infrastructures (90 percent of the US targets) in early 1991 were supplemented by the tough economic sanctions which continued till the existence of the lawful Iraqi State. The US drew no-fly-zones in 1991 and 1992 in north and south with 'safe-haven' for the Iraqi Kurds. This was the creation of secessionism in Iraq. Since 1991, the US continued with periodic bombings on Iraqi defense installations (unlawful), demonization campaign against the

Iraqi leader President Saddam Hussein and manipulation of the UN in Iraq. The US seized 90 percent of Iraqi sovereign space and over 40 percent of the Iraqi sovereign territory with several satellites monitoring over Iraq. It restricted the movement of Iraqi people with the exception of the Kurds. This resulted in the decline of the capacity building of the Iraqi society. All these constituted 'dual criminality' against the Iraqi people and the State.

Since Iraq was capable to revive after the lifting of the sanctions due to its over 3 million human resources and rich natural resources, its main regulator—the State, was dismantled in the first phase of the invasion. [13] Later the US targeted those sections and sectors of society, which could have resisted the occupation forces. Breakdown of Iraqi State is not only dangerous for seizing the rights of legitimate Iraqi government in international agencies but also catastrophic in terms of its supervision, welfare activities and control vis-à-vis the Iraqi people. The US invasion and brutal use of force against the Iraqis brought about 'total collapse' of the State thus affecting the large number of Iraqis badly. The whole purpose of the State is to serve the people. International law is basically meant to protect a sovereign State to exercise its powers to maintain rule of law, law and order and security of the State.

The Election Fiasco amidst Insecurity and Bombings

In the last four tragic years of crimes by the occupation forces, Iraqis have faced several challenges ranging from the daily killings, bombing of civilian settlements, illegal detention and Abu Ghraib tortures, humiliations caused by enchaining the Iraqi President, suicide bombings, murders and hostage killings. Over 250 university teachers, 110 journalists, mostly Iraqi nationals, and over 300 scientists have been murdered since occupation. However, this is not the latest estimates. Like the earlier strategy, there are again conspiracies to divide Iraqis along the sectarian lines. Clerics have accused the US for the killings and all the devastations they are facing every day. Since occupation, hundreds of Shii notables and Sunni clerics belonging to the Association of Muslim Scholars have been killed. Hundreds of them are under detention excluding the detention of 70,000 Iraqi civilians and several scientists. On the other hand there are also attempts to terrorize general Iraqis. Explosions are engineered at many religious sites and public places over several times. External forces are working out shii-Sunni cleavages inn addition to the problems of medicine, food, lootings, insecurity and lawlessness.

It is not only Falluja and Ramadi but most parts of Iraq are engulfed into the crisis of governability and instability. It is also tragic to note that several major Iraqi cities and towns have been converted into fierce battlefields and bombing zones where international law and the so-called international community have remained silent and inactive. Areas of resistance are immediately converted into graveyards. Pretexts for military operations have been Baathists, Sunni insurgents and Al-Qaeda but civilians have always suffered. For example, The US made bombardment on the Arab Jubour district in Diyala province just 15 kilometres south-east of Baghdad on January 10, 2008. In the space of 10 minutes, B-1 Stealth bombers and F-16 fighter-bombers pounded 47 targets with 47,500 pounds of high explosive bombs. The attack on Arab Jubour is part of a broader offensive in the first weeks of 2008 called Phantom Phoenix. The US commander in Iraq, General David Petraeus, has ordered increasing use of air strikes in order to meet the Bush administration's desperate demands for reduced US casualties and the suppression of the ongoing insurgency. In 2007, there were at least 1,119 air strikes, according to the US Air Force, compared with 229 the previous year. The US military did not state how many casualties resulted from this bombardment. [14] The towns, villages and hamlets of Arab Jubour have been a major battleground between the US occupation and insurgents, and in the civil war between rival Sunni factions. The area, which had a pre-war population of more than 100,000, is now a wasteland of bombed-out buildings, dried-up channels and abandoned fields. It was once renowned for its intricate and centuries-old irrigation systems which fed off the Tigris River and supplied productive date and fruit orchards. Its beauty, rural charm and proximity to Baghdad made it a desirable location for the homes of better-off Iraqis, including officials of the Baathist government and military officers. [15]

It was only after passing over four resolutions, the UN Secretary General called Iraq war illegal. Now it looks that the US target was not really the unseating of the Iraqi leader but the use of force against those Iraqis who resisted American agenda of 'control' on the pretext of democracy and freedom. The US later included the name of Abu Musaab al-Zarqawi and Muqtada Al-Sadr after demonizing Saddam Hussein. Similarly it is now alleging Al-Qaeda and foreign terrorists after blacklisting the Baath party of Iraq. The US President George Bush, his envoy Paul Bremer, his other representatives like Zalmay Khalilzad, Negroponte and Iraqis head of the sponsored government from Iyad Allawi to Maliki have termed the problem of Iraq as terrorism and civil war. Both John Kerry of the Democrats and the Iraqi religious and intellectual persons refused to accept this claim as legitimate. Kerry had already called this invasion as the result of the incompetency of the federal executive.

It seems that deceptions have prevailed all over Iraq. Soon after occupation, serious call and appeal of Baqar al-Hakeem, Ali Sistani and many others for holding free and fair elections were simply ignored and a combination of military rule-CPA was imposed on Iraqis. More than 15 political parties were opposed to this election. But the Iraqi people's rights were determined by the US and its agents in Iraq. The occupying power also imposed a handy but quite dangerous interim constitution to justify further manipulations in future. The stage-managed transfer of powers from the CPA to the Iraqis was now fully exposed to the extent of being a calculated hoax. The way Iraqi premier and president and ministers were installed prove that people loyal to Pentagon and State Department, and not to the Iraqi people were rewarded to rule over Iraq. Their participation in governance has not minimized Iraqi sufferings and losses. Similarly the members of the council were selected amidst rockets and bombs raining in Baghdad several weeks ago.

Today Iraqis look completely bewildered than ever before. There are following serious reasons for this. At the international level, so-called major democracies like UK, Italy and Australia have not withdrawn their forces despite knowing the fact that Iraq had neither WMD nor violated the resolution 1441. France and Germany have been cooperating with the US along with indirect involvement of the NATO. Iraqi neighbours are already tamed and threatened to be either quiet or to side with the US. In particular, Kuwait further earned Iraqi anger no matter what government comes to power in future. Moreover, the US had invaded Iraq for replacing WMD with D (democracy) which is exposed false on both fronts. There were no reasons for invading Iraq, say many investigations. What may be shocking to the Iraqis and others is the Bush response to a question to Kerry—what would he have done 18 months ago had been president? Bush replied: "Knowing what I know today, I would have made the same decision." [16]

At the home, Iraqis are bewildered and vulnerable due to the timing, method and policies related to elections for National Assembly in Iraq to elect 275 members. It is known to many that fair and free elections in Iraq, for which the Western civilization is known, would reject most of the ministers and so-called representatives. Certain restrictions mentioned under Articles 30-31 of the Interim Constitution disqualified many significant Iraqis to contest in January 2005 elections. The occupying forces managed the elections at over 4000 polling sites which were self explanatory vis-à-vis fairness. So who were the election monitors? Who listened to the grievances related to poll riggings?

Disturbing Implications

In the midst of such disturbing moments, India seems to face complex situations created by those realists who are determined to define the premise of international and regional politics both in the present and future by themselves. The very first sentences of the State of the Union Address on January 28, 2008 mention: "Seven years have passed since I first stood before you at this rostrum. In that time, our country has been tested in ways none of us could have imagined. We faced hard decisions about peace and war, rising competition in the world economy, and the health and welfare of our citizens. These issues call for vigorous debate, and I think it's fair to say we've answered the call. Yet history will record that amid our differences, we acted with purpose. And together, we showed the world the power and resilience of American self-government." [17]

On the other hand, they claim to represent the interests of the whole world community while in reality it is only a talk than intent. 21st Century has begun with major national destructions, war against occupied nationalities, politically motivated car bombings, insecurity, invasions, massive media manipulations and threats to the notion of state sovereignty. However, reality is presented otherwise. It was said in the State of the Union Address: "In the last seven years, we have witnessed stirring moments in the history of liberty. We've seen citizens in Georgia and Ukraine stand up for their right to free and fair elections. We've seen people in Lebanon take to the streets to demand their independence...In Iraq, the terrorists and extremists are fighting to deny a proud people their liberty, and fighting to establish safe havens for attacks across the world". [18] At this juncture, democratic polities are under risks while preferred monarchies and conformists have been upheld. Examples exist on our border where the military regime was embraces with progressive pursuits. Elected government in Iran is referred as 'extremists', 'evil', 'terrorists' and 'failed state' while the most-abused elections in the occupied Iraq and hand-picked individuals were called democratic. This is the tragedy of this century. Recently the US President said: "We've seen jubilant Iraqis holding up ink-stained fingers and celebrating their freedom. These images of liberty have inspired us." [19]

Therefore, it is important to understand that the 21st Century's international politics has finally shifted focus from Europe to the 'developing polities'. It is neither the manifestation of the clash of civilization nor any alternative super-power. Today is not the question of the West versus Muslims only. "America opposes genocide in Sudan. We support freedom in countries from Cuba and Zimbabwe to Belarus and Burma." [20] Elements hostile to peace, harmony and good neighbourly relationship have their own agenda of 'controlling vital resources and social dynamics' by using the trump card of war on terrorism. His speech clearly says: "We are engaged in the defining ideological struggle of the 21st century. The terrorists oppose every principle of humanity and decency that we hold dear. Yet in this war on terror, there is one thing we and our enemies agree on: In the long run, men and women who are free to determine their own destinies will reject terror and refuse to live in tyranny. And that is why the terrorists are fighting to deny this choice to the people in Lebanon, Iraq, Afghanistan, Pakistan, and the Palestinian Territories." [21]

Recently an expert analysis by outstanding US medical epidemiologists Professor Burnham (Johns Hopkins University) and Professor Roberts (Columbia University) in which they commented trenchantly on the latest UK-based Opinion Research Business survey, indicating over 1 million violent post-invasion Iraqi deaths. The following analysis reveals that the total violent and non-violent post-invasion Iraqi excess deaths now total 1.5-2.0 million and that the total excess deaths in the Bush I and Bush II Asian Wars now total 8 million. [22] Following responses to ORB's earlier work, which was based on survey work undertaken in primarily urban locations, it conducted almost 600 additional interviews in rural communities. By and large the results are in line with the 'urban results' and it now estimates that the death toll between March 2003 and August 2007 is likely to have been of the order of 1,033,000. If one takes into account the margin of error associated with survey data of this nature then the estimated range is between 946,000 and 1,120,000. [23]

At present, the US invasion has produced over 4.5 million orphaned Iraqi children. It is the report of the Iraqi Ministry of Labour and Social Affairs. The ministry also announced in January 2008 that there are an estimated 500,000 orphans now living in Iraq's streets without accommodation or an appropriate care provider, as the Iraqi news agency Voices of Iraq reported, that there are only around 459 orphans who are currently residing in Iraqi government funded orphanages. There is uncertainty as to how many children are actually being held in "detention" inside of prisons in Iraq, or even information relating to the welfare of children who are now resident in refugee camps as a result of the crisis. There also exists no record of those children who have been kidnapped by criminal gangs and whose lives are being held hostage for use in the now booming sex trade. [24]

The Iraq Solidarity Campaign does hold the regime of the ruling Labour Party fully responsible for these abuses and we would urge that people in Great Britain, see the elections on May 1st as being an opportunity to demonstrate your solidarity with the children of Iraq and use the power of your ballot to remove those responsible for these crimes. Over 513 Iraqi children have been imprisoned by the Americans in Iraqi jails. A December 2007 UNICEF report stated that 2.2 million Iraqi children lack adequate nutrition and an estimated 75,000 children are living in tents because of displacement caused by the war. The UN has also reported that 80 percent of Iraqi families can't separate sewage water from water used for other household needs and that 70 percent lack access to potable water but as Britain combats terrorism, the campaign of fear is used solely to distract attention away from the 400,000 Iraqi children who are suffering from "wasting", which is characterized by chronic diarrhoea and high deficiencies of protein. [25]

It is in this context, difficulties can be understood between the two set of principles, one carried out by those who are creating humanitarian catastrophe and the other who regards international politics as a common field for all sovereign states. India has a strong heritage of anti-colonial movements. India neither approved World War II nor did it value polarization of world politics during the Cold War era. India has historically been concerned with the legitimacy of the United Nations and International Law which are now threats of the few. On the other hand, India has also been criticized by the few over the question of Jammu and Kashmir. Foreign financers helped militancy in Punjab. India's neighbourhood and region around it are on the verge of instability. The occupation of Iraq and emerging threats to Iran are bound to affect us in several ways. Thus there is a need to estimate what the world lost in Iraq.

What do we mean by the destruction of the State in Iraq? It has a long list. Only one of the factor would be reasonable to explain the tragedy of State destruction. This is the State function of the 'rule of law', 'law and order' and security in the country. Rule of Law becomes a historic joke and an illusion in a situation where the judiciary and enforcement agencies and their roles of a country is being defined by an occupying power that too with the interests of some people on subjective and selective basis. Independence of judiciary is indispensable for the survival/operation of the rule of law. Another aspect is the respect for the rule of law is also linked with the kind of authority and the sources of its legitimacy.

In the context of the occupation of Iraq, one can raise certain questions particularly related to the subject of rule of law [26], state making and constitution making [27] to achieve democracy. What is the law in Iraq? Where is the rule of law, and law and order in the country? Who are exercising the powers of the State in Iraq? Why the so-called Iraqi premier thanks the US for liberating Iraq? Why do his people selected by the US call the resistance force as terrorists? Who are terrorists in Iraq? What are the investigation agencies involved into various explosions in the country particularly in the religious places? What is the legitimacy of the set-up imposed after military invasion of Iraq? What is the source of legitimacy of the Transitional Administrative Law of Iraq of 8 March 2004? What are the provisions for citizenship, participation in elections and. election procedures? How the permanent constitution of Iraq will be made? Who will make it? Who is recognizing illegitimate institutions and structures made after March 2003?

The main question is—What about the rights of the people of Iraq for determining the policies of the country, which were already decided by the interim constitution of Iraq? How the legitimate ruling institutions and persons of Iraq are being treated by the invading agencies? What do we mean by handcuffing the Iraqi President, or showing the AbuGharib humiliation or annihilating the beautiful town of Falluja? Look at how the Iraqi State is being built? What is the nation building process? What is constitution making? What do they mean to occupiers? Answer to these questions is required to situate Iraq in international politics. What matters here in today's discussion are the State making, constitution making and nation making exercise in Iraq and the sources of legitimacy. Is colonization guiding democratization process in the country? Who is accountable for this? Whither State sovereignty, rights of the people for self determination guaranteed in the UN Charter? Is not the case of the suppression, elimination and political exclusion of the people in nation making? Who has legitimized the illegitimate institutions and elements in Iraq after March 2003? Have we ever counted upon the cost of recognizing these unlawful sources of legitimacy?

Readings on the Iraqi interim constitution would be sufficient to understand the implications of the new set up to the Iraqis, region and other countries. Pre-March 2003 Iraq is accused of internal mismanagement leading to the violations of human rights. Do other countries not have the issues internal mismanagement? Iraq is accused of WMD. Is it not true that India is also under continuous pressure for signing the NPT? Iraq is accused of suppressing the Kurds? Have we not been accused by the West of the violation of human rights, ethnic problems and conflicts in Jammu and Kashmir and North-East? Iraq is accused of invading Kuwait. Do we not have some weaknesses in the affairs of Sri Lanka and the creation of Bangladesh? Who instigated our neighbour for border crossing and Kargil engineering? Which forces nurtured and funded the extremists in Afghanistan and Pakistan for defeating Russians and to de-stabilize some other countries. Which country supported the Sikh terrorists during the Khalistan movement? Who is helping the Christian terrorists in the North-East against India's sovereignty? Who helped military take over and military rule in neighbouring Pakistan? There are many factors that put India in a vulnerable position. India is now witnessing extremely new trend within its territory. After moving towards some sort of normalcy in Jammu and Kashmir and peace talks over the North-East, enemies have been engineering bomb explosions within temples and mosques. It is certainly of the foreign origin. The EU Commission has already shown its deep interests in the Gujarat riots of 2002 which is clearly interference in the internal affairs of India.

Whatever is happening in Iraq is a great lesson for many of us. A gas cylinder under Saddam cost 1,500 Dinars (US$1.20) whereas now it has become 16,000 Dinars. Oil during this heavy winter - has reached 20,000 Dinars. One liter of gasoline, for example, equals US$1, whereas under Saddam it used to be 3 cents per liter. [28] Increase in salary has no positive results due to extremely high inflations. Iraqis are deprived of basic necessities. The government of Iraqi Kurdistan started signing independent oil extraction contacts with foreign companies, in total disregard of the Baghdad government. To date, more than 20 contacts have been authorized, prompting Oil Minister Hussein al-Shahristani to call these contracts "illegal". [29]

Former US president Jimmy Carter -a stern critic of the Bush Administration - was prescient when he declared on February 3, 2006: "There are people in Washington ... who never intend to withdraw military forces from Iraq and they're looking for ten, 20, 50 years into the future ... the reason that we went into Iraq was to establish a permanent military base in the Gulf region, and I have never heard any of our leaders say that they would commit themselves to the Iraqi people that ten years from now there will be no military bases of the United States in Iraq." [30]

The US is spending over a billion dollar per annum to build military base military in Iraq In the years since the invasion, there have been numerous journalistic accounts of the mammoth bases the US has built, and continues to expand. There is the giant Al Balad base covering 16 square miles, some 40 miles north of Baghdad, formerly the Iraqi Air Force Academy. It houses 40,000 US troops, contractors, special operation types, and Defense Department employees. As the *Washington Post's* Tom Ricks, who visited Balad *back in 2006*, pointed out -- in a rare piece on one of our mega-bases -- it's essentially "a small American town smack in the middle of the most hostile part of Iraq." [31]

The ongoing flightline projects at Balad AB consist of concrete pad extensions that will provide occupation surfaces for multiple aircraft of various types. Here's just a taste of what's been going on recently at Balad, one of the largest bases on foreign soil on the planet, and but one of perhaps five mega-bases in that country When asked back in the fall of 2003, only months after Baghdad fell to U.S. troops, Lt. Col. David Holt, the Army engineer then "tasked with facilities development" in Iraq, proudly indicated that "several billion dollars" had *already* been invested in those fast-rising bases. Even then, he was suitably amazed, commenting that "the numbers are staggering." Imagine what he might have said, barely two and a half years later, when the U.S. reportedly had *106 bases*, mega to micro, all across the country. [32] There is the even bigger Al Assad base covering 19 square miles; the Al Tallil base; the Al Sarq base; the Al Qayyarah base in the north and many others. Shortly after its invasion, the US established 110 bases in Iraq. The present plan seems to be to consolidate these into 14 "enduring bases" in Iraqi Kurdistan, at Baghdad airport, in Anbar province and in the southern approaches to Baghdad. [33] Besides, the presence of over 140,000, there are 180,000 contractors. [34]

It is also important to know that majority of Iraqis have no access to food. Iraq's food rations system was introduced by the Saddam Hussein government in 1991 in response to the UN economic sanctions. Families were allotted basic foodstuffs monthly because the Iraqi Dinar and the economy collapsed. The sanctions, imposed after Saddam Hussein ordered the invasion of Kuwait, were described as "genocidal" by Denis Halliday, then UN Humanitarian Coordinator in Iraq. Halliday quit his post in protest against the U.S.-backed sanctions. The imminent move will affect nearly 10 million people who depend on the rationing system. "The monthly food ration was the only help from the government," local grocer Ibrahim al-Ageely told IPS. "It was of great benefit for the families. The food ration consisted of two kilos of rice, sugar, soap, tea, detergent, wheat flour, lentils, chick-peas, and other items for every individual." According to an Oxfam International report released in July this year, "60 percent (of Iraqis) currently have access to rations through the government-run Public Distribution System (PDS), down from

96 percent in 2004." The report said that "43 percent of Iraqis suffer from absolute poverty," and that according to some estimates over half the population are now without work. "Children are hit the hardest by the decline in living standards. Child malnutrition rates have risen from 19 percent before the U.S.-led invasion in 2003 to 28 percent now." [35] Whereas the sanctions regime demonstrated the success with which the US turned the UN into a multilateral proxy. [36]

In April 2007, *Aljazeera* published an interview with the former leader of the Iraqi Republican Guard, Saif al-Deen al-Rawi, who was charged with organizing the defenses of the capital during the 2003 invasion. Al-Rawi claimed that US forces used neutron nuclear bombs against the Iraqi Army during the battle for Baghdad's airport. Al-Rawi said that his units were decimated by neutron bombs which, he added, neutralize soldiers without damaging buildings and equipment. Al-Rawi also claimed that large 9-ton bombs and phosphoric weapons that can cover large areas were used during the battle. The battle for Baghdad's airport was the turning point of the war, and the quick defeat of the elite forces that defended the area opened the way for the general collapse of the Iraqi Army and the subsequent fall of Baghdad. The former commander affirmed that the elite units that were engaged in the battle "fought till death" and that there were no survivors among them. Al-Rawi is still on the list of major Ba'thists wanted by the US army, and ranks as number 14 on the list. [37]

At present India is more vulnerable than ever in its history. Middle East is full of US military bases. Iraq is occupied. Syria is silenced. Iran is under tremendous pressure to be in US conformity. Central Asia is again under the American military presence. Afghanistan is already occupied by the US. Pakistan is already most special non-NATO friend of the US and instable country on India's border. Ethnic conflicts in Srilanka and political disorder in Nepal are already disturbing trends on borders. In this situation India must abstain from engaging itself in strengthening illegitimate institutions and

US sponsored elections. For that India needs to have a fresh look at the viable foreign policy with vigilant diplomacy and military preparedness to build its destiny in the environment of desirable peace and order. As Iraq was important to the stability of the region of West Asia, India is the pivot of Asia as it had been rightly mentioned by the First Prime Minister of India Pandit Jawaharlal Nehru and Sri Aurobindo earlier.

Owing to its good image in Iraq, India can play a vital role in Iraq as there is no mediating space left due to the policies of the occupying forces. Participation of India and the United nations can give some hopes to Iraqis who have been left unattended in Iraq. When a truck bomb tore through U.N. headquarters four months into the occupation, killing special envoy Sergio Vieira de Mello and 19 others, pro-consul Bremer suggested two possible culprits: "Saddam loyalists or foreign insurgents". The interim government's Ahmed Chalabi, however, had received prior notice of the attack the week before. Chalabi had been warned that a "soft target" was to be attacked, although it would be "neither the Coalition Authority nor coalition troops". But the UN, whose security had been withdrawn that day, was never warned. [38]

India needs to be careful about the sinister plan in West Asia. In June 2003, the US Defense Department's journal, the Executive Intelligent Research Project, republished well-known American historian Bernard Lewis's thesis on partitioning the Middle East into more than 30 ethnic and sectarian states. Another dangerous strategic study was conducted by Oudid Yinon. This was presented to the Israeli foreign and defense ministries, and was published in February 1982. Its danger lies in Yinon's view of the Camp David accord with Egypt as "a sin committed by Israel". He says that redressing it "would require a consistent effort towards dividing Egypt into four mini-states: a Coptic mini-state in the north, a Nubian mini-state in the south; a Muslim mini-state with Cairo as its capital and a fourth mini-state under Israel's dominance. Yinon also spoke about partitioning Lebanon into seven cantons, Sudan into three and Syria into four, and called for "the disintegration of Iraq because its strength constitutes. This plan also includes the fragmentation of Iraq into three mini-states. In 1985, the Israeli army published a book that included Yinon's study, and touched upon "Israel's efforts to deal a blow and divide Iraq". It further detailed Israel's plans "to disrupt Syria, Lebanon, Algeria, Sudan and the Gulf". And in this context, reference can be made to a seminar held at the Dayan Centre for Middle East and Africa Studies in Tel Aviv University in 1990, under the title The Disintegration of the Arab World, and to a symposium at the Bar Ilan University in 1992, which recommended an intensification of efforts for the fragmentation of Arab states. [39]

Problems range from food security to water, electricity, medicine, sanitation, education, training, internal displacement of Iraqis and rebuilding of Iraqi polity and elections. According to the United Nations Children's Agency (UNICEF), 2007, about one in 10 children, under five, in Iraq are underweight and one in five are short for their age. Poverty and insecurity are said to be the main causes of the children's deteriorating diets. This means that some 4.5 million children in the country are under-nourished. In some these areas, India can do a lot for Iraqis provided occupying forces want it to do so in the larger interests of humanity. India's strength is its democratizing polity, rising economy, composite culture and federal political set up in the country.

Notes

1. Lennox A. Mills and Charles H. McLaughlin, *World Politics in Transition* (New York: Henry Holt and Company, 1956), p. 28.
2. Ibid., p. 32.
3. Mahmood Mamdani, *Good Muslim Bad Muslim: Islam, the USA, and the Global War against Terror* (Delhi: Permanent Black, 2005, p. 184.
4. Ibid., p.185.
5. Susan Marks, "International Law, democracy, and the end of history", in Gregory H. Fox and Brad R. Roth, eds., *Democratic*

Government and International Law (Cambridge: Cambridge University Press, 2000), pp. 532-566.
6. Thomas M. Franck, "the emerging Right to Democratic Governance", *American Journal of International Law*, 86 (1992), p.46; Anthony D'Amato, "The Invasion of Panama was a Lawful Response to Tyranny", American Journal of International Law, 84 (1990), p. 516.
7. Arshi Khan, "US Policy bitten by the Iraqi bug", *The Pioneer*, August 24, 2000, Foreign Page; " A sanctioned killing", *The Telegraph*, June 12, 2003, p.9; "They'll Stay back", *The Telegraph*, 13 April 2004, Edit Page; "Issue of Iraq in International Politics", *Mainstream*, 33 (2002), pp. 15-18.
8. Arshi Khan, "Politics of UN coup against Iraq", *The Pioneer*, 22 February 2003, Op-ed page; "UN dogged by P5's parochial interest", *The Pioneer*, 21 Sept.2000, p. 11; "Iraq Done In With Sanctions", *The Telegraph* (Fifth column), February 16, 2000, p. 10; "Iraq ki Tabaahi mein Eqwam Mtahada ka Kirdar", *Rashtriya Sahara*, August 17, 2003, p. 4.
9. Aftab K. Pasha, *Iraq: Sanctions and Wars* (New Delhi: Sterling Publishers Pvt. Ltd., 2003, p. 82-113.
10. Amin Saikal, " Iraq, UNSCOM and the US: A UN Debacle", Australian Journal of International Affairs, 3 (1999), pp. 286-293.
11. Arshi Khan, "Politics of Making a Case for attack on Iraq", *Mainstream*, 10 (2003), pp. 4-5, 35; "Question of who Blix first", *The Pioneer*, February 4, 2003, Op-ed page.
12. Mahmood Mamdani, Good Muslim Bad Muslim, p. 199.
13. Arshi Khan, "Continuing Agony of Iraq", *The Observer* (ed. page), February 5, 2000, p.6; "How a Society Being Annihilated", *The Observer*, August 10, 2000, p.9; "Iraq Done In With Sanctions", *The Telegraph* (Fifth column), February 16, 2000, p.10."Bombing Baghdad", *The Pioneer*, February 21, 2001, Op-ed page.
14. James Cogan, "US carries out massive bombing on outskirts of Baghdad", dated January 12, 2008, www.wsws.org/articles/2008/jan2008/bomb-j12.shtml.
15. Ibid.
16. Coverage made by the CNN during the Presidential Debates in October 2004.

17. The US President George Bush's State of the Union Address to the Chamber of the US House of Representatives on January 28, 2008, released by THE WHITE HOUSE, Office of the Press Secretary and circulated by the US Embassy at New Delhi on January 30, 2008.
18. Ibid.
19. Ibid.
20. Ibid.
21. Ibid.
http://www.countercurrents.org/burnham230907.htm.
http://globalavoidablemortality.blogspot.com.
http://globalbodycount.blogspot.com.
http://mwcnews.net/content/view/1375/247.
http://mwcnews.net/content/view/17066/42.
22. www.opinion.co.uk.
23. Available on the web page of Iraqi Solidarity Campaign.
24. Hussein Al-alak, the Iraq Solidarity Campaign, "Remember! Remember!", June 12, 2008, iraqsolidaritycampaign.blogspot.com/2008/06/remember-remember.html.
25. Lidija R. Basta Fleiner, et al., eds., Rule of Law and Organisation of the State in Asia: The Multicultural Challenge (Bale, Geneva, Munich: Helbing and Lichtenhahn, 2000).
26. Nicholas R. L. Haysom, Constitution and Nation Building", in Raoul Blindenbacher and Arnold Koller, eds., Federalism in a Changing World: Learning from Each Other (Montreal, London: McGill-Queen's University Press, 2003), pp. 216-239.
27. Sami Moubayed, "The clock ticks for Iraq's time bomb", *Asia Times*, January 3, 2008, available at http://www.uruknet.de/?p=m39781&hd=&size=1&l=e.
28. Ibid.
29. Patrick Seale, "US is building bases in Iraq", Special to the *Gulf News*, June 4, 2007.
30. Tom Engelhardt, Finally, the U.S. Mega-Bases in Iraq Make the News, June 15, 2008, http://www.uruknet.de/?p=m44914&s1=h1.
31. Ibid.
32. Patrick Seale, "US is building bases in Iraq", Special to the *Gulf News*, June 4, 2007.
33. http://www.uruknet.de/?p=m37377&hd=&size=1&l=e.

34. Ahmed Ali and Dahr Jamail, “Saddam Provided More Food Than the U.S.”, dated December 27, 2007, available at www.uruknet.info?p=39578,ipsnews.net/news.asp?idnews=40613.
35. Mahmood Mamdani, *Good Muslim, Bad Muslim*, p. 180.
36. Amer Mohsen Iraq Papers Mon: "US Army Used Neutron Bombs" *Former General Speaks, Recounts the Battle for Baghdad* Iraqslogger, 8 April 2007.
37. *Asia Times*, August 20, 2003.
38. As'ad Abdul Rahman, “A sinister plan for the region”, Special to *Gulf News*, November 30, 2007. Professor As'ad Abdul Rahman is the Chairman of the Palestinian Encyclopedia.

8

Oil, Democracy and Terrorism: An Inevitable Nexus in the Gulf

Vrushal Ghoble

Albert Einstein once said, "I know not with what weapons World War III will be fought, but World War IV will be fought with sticks and stones". [1] This is the predicament, the rate at which the energy resources are being exhausted. Without oil, the Second World War could never have been won. The oil once processed was used to run transportation and not to mention guns and machinery. There is a strong belief that the next World War is going to be for resources, i.e. Water, but there is another strong contender, that's called Oil. Infact, the cold energy war has already begun with the external stakeholders striving for energy supplies. In addition to the West, countries of rising Asia like India and China have joined the scramble for these resources, undoubtedly in the Gulf. Oil has played a very significant role since the Second World War. Oil is a strategic asset and as demand exceeds supply, making it a scarce commodity. In that sense, having a strategic petroleum reserve (SPR) will not suffice to the growing demand. Hence, as the global consumption specifically the US, Europe and Asian countries like India and China is growing rapidly, there will be a greater competition for these resources. A country having SPR might be a good political option, but is bad economics because without a threat pulling out huge petroleum stock will create artificial scarcity in the market, hiking prices. For e.g., in past disruptions, note that shortages of only 5 percent in supply caused 400 percent increases in its price. [2] Democracy promotion has been on the top of the US foreign policy, however externally forced democracy has not shown positive signs in the Gulf. Understanding the present situation of democracy and terrorism in the region, the question of a link between oil and these factors has become more timely relevant than ever.

Significance of the Gulf Oil

Oil is worlds' most valuable and finite energy resource. In the future, much more environment friendly fuel could be used to fuel our vehicles, but as of now, the world needs oil. Today, oil has become a global commodity, without which no industrialized economy can survive. Hence, its secure supply must be guaranteed and if need be a strict military force could be used. Oil played a significant part in both World Wars – indeed, Iraq is an artificial state created by a young Winston Churchill in the aftermath of World War I exactly because of the growing importance of oil to the ebbing British Empire. [3] The Gulf dominates world energy exports today and will do so for years to come. The recent war on Iraq did create a sense of insecurity, but had little impact on the energy supplies, except for a short-term cut in the Iraqi production.

According to British Petroleum, Iraq & Kuwait together have more than 100 years of Reserves to Production (R / P) ratio. The largest reserves are held by Saudi Arabia, Iran, Iraq, Kuwait, UAE and Qatar, followed by Oman, Yemen and Syria. With respect to Natural Gas, its Qatar, Iran, Iraq and Kuwait that have gas resources. Apart from these states, UAE and Yemen also have gas reserves that account for more than 100 years. This can be understood in detail in Table 8.1.

The Gulf dominates the world energy market today. The significance of the Gulf is steadily attempting to increase its profit margins by producing and exporting refined oil products than selling crude. The Gulf resources are the cheapest to produce in the world. The percentage of this oil that flows from the Gulf to the US is in much less volume, but, the region provides more than a quarter of the world's oil, mostly to Europe and Asia. "... the U.S. Department of Energy (DOE) estimates that the Gulf averaged 15.4 MMBD worth of exports in 1995, which equaled 41 percent of all world exports versus 47 percent for the entire Middle East.

Table 8.1: Middle East Energy Reserves & R/P Ratio [4]
(Oil - '000 Million Barrels / Natural Gas – Trillion Cubic Feet)

	Oil		Natural Gas	
Country	**Reserves**	**R/P Ratio**	**Reserves**	**R/P Ratio**
Bahrain	-	-	3.00	7.4
Iran	138.4	86.2	981.75	*
Iraq	115.0	*	111.95	*
Kuwait	101.5	*	63.00	*
Oman	5.6	21.3	24.37	28.6
Qatar	27.4	62.8	904.06	*
Saudi Arabia	264.2	6905	253.03	94.4
Syria	2.5	17.4	10.17	54.7
UAE	97.8	91.9	215.07	*
Yemen	2.8	22.7	17.23	*
Other Middle East	0.1	10.9	1.73	18.5
Total Middle East	755.3	-	2585.35	-

* More than 100 years.
Source: British Petroleum (BP) (June 2008), *BP Statistical Review of World Energy*, p. 6.

DOE estimates that the Gulf will average 37.2 MMBD in exports by 2020, which will equal 56 percent of all world exports compared to 60 percent for the entire Middle East". [5] The total Gulf exports to the industrialized nations will fall further. According to EIA, the share will fall from 57 percent in 2001 to 45 percent in 2025. [6] This shift will occur primarily due to the rise of modern industrialized economies in Asia. China alone, is likely to import about 5.9 million barrels per day from OPEC by 2025, virtually all of which is expected to come from Gulf producers. [7]

Saudi Arabia is one of the largest and most important exporters in the Gulf. It has produced more than 8 million barrels per day since 1991 – roughly 30 percent of total OPEC crude production. [8] Saudi surplus production capacity has made it a swing producer that can increase its exports to maintain stable supplies in the market. Iraqi proven oil reserves are the third largest in the world. Since the fall of Saddam Hussein, various other sources have talked about a much more rapid expansion to levels of 6 MMBD, 9 MMBD, and even 12 MMBD. [9] "...problems at Iraqi oil fields include: years of poor oil reservoir management; corrosion problems at various oil facilities; deterioration of water injection facilities; lack of spare parts, materials, equipment, etc.; damage to oil storage and pumping facilities; and more". [10] There are some critical problems with Iraq namely, population explosion, unemployment, law and order, oil income and foreign investment. US sanctions have limited the growth and development of the Iranian energy sector. Iran has potential to increase its energy production capacity. Iran produced 6 million bbl/d in 1974, but has not surpassed 3.8 million bbl/d on an annual basis since the 1978 / 79 Iranian revolution. [11] However, inspite sanctions, "...Iran has ambitious plans to double national oil production -- to more than 7 million bbl/d by 2015 or so. The country is counting on foreign investment to accomplish this, possibly as high as US$ 5 billion per year".

The Greater Burgan area of Kuwait is widely considered the world's second largest oil field, surpassed only by Saudi Arabia's Ghawar field. The U.S. Department of Energy estimates that Kuwait will expand its production from 1.7 million barrels per day in 1990, and 2.4 million barrels per day in 2001, to 2.8 million barrels per day in 2005, 3.3 million barrels per day in 2010, 3.9 million barrels per day in 2015, 4.5 million barrels per day in 2020, and 5.1 million barrels per day in 2025. [12] Kuwait is one of the two major oil exporting powers that can rapidly increase production in an emergency, and its role as a swing producer may increase over time. The UAE is one of the world's largest oil producers. Abu Dhabi holds 94 percent of this amount or about 92.2 billion barrels, and Dubai contains another 4.0 billion barrels. [13] The U.S. Department of Energy estimates that the UAE will increase its production capacity from 2.5 million barrels per day in 2000, to 3.0 (2.6 - 3.2) million barrels per day in 2005, 3.7 (2.8 - 4.0) million barrels per day in 2010, 4.4 (3.1 - 4.8) million barrels per day in 2015, and 5.1 (3.5 - 5.6) million barrels per day in 2020. [14] Bahrain has proven oil reserves of 125 million barrels. Oman and Bahrain's reserves are very small. Bahrain has only one field, Awali, producing this output and its reserves are declining. "The Bahrain Petroleum Company has announced a US$ 900 million modernization program that will allow Sitra (Bahrain's only oil refinery) to produce a wider range of petroleum products. Because Bahrain consumes as much as is produced, Qatar and Bahrain signed a Memorandum of Agreement in 2002 indicating Bahrain's intentions to purchase natural gas from Qatar". [15] Qatar has their largest natural gas reserves in the world after Russia and Iran. Most of Qatar's gas is located in its North Field, which contains 380 Tcf of in - place and 239 Tcf of recoverable reserves, making it the largest known non - associated gas field in the world. [16]

Table (8.2) represents Gulf's oil trade with the world. The table clearly shows, Gulf's rising exports to Asia and Pacific than to other regions.

The Gulf region has been and will continue to play a critical role in meeting the global demand. It is also an important source for simple and straightforward reasons, i.e., it has the largest reserves of oil and gas and is cheaper to produce in large amounts. "...the Persian Gulf share of worldwide petroleum exports is projected to increase gradually to 66 percent by 2025. In the low oil price case, the Persian

Gulf share of total exports is projected to reach 76 percent by 2025". [17] The pattern of US imports from the Gulf states is different from the Asian imports that have advantage of the lower shipping costs from the region, while US seeks oil with lesser transportation costs from Africa and Latin America. The Gulf is also a significant gas exporter. Gulf gas exports are also in the form of liquid natural gas (LNG). Hence, the global economy will grow far more dependent on the Gulf energy in the future.

Table 8.2: Direction of Oil Exports (2007) (000' b/d) [18]

From	From				
	US	Western Europe	Africa	Asia & Pacific	Total
Iran	-	847.4	148.1	1469.1	2464.6
Iraq	593.4	326.3	-	605.3	1525
Kuwait	111.9	109.0	43.7	1347.4	1612
Qatar	-	-	-	615.1	615.1
Saudi Arabia	1528.5	838.5	196.6	3989.5	6553.1
UAE	4.2	20.3	33.2	2276.9	2334.6

Source: *OPEC Annual Statistical Bulletin 2007,* pp. 83-86.

Oil Companies, Concessions and the Rentier States

By the twentieth century, oil had become world's dominant interest in the Gulf. The first half of the twentieth century was dominated by few American and British oil companies. The combination of factors–foreign (western) oil companies in the region and the significance of the Gulf as a leading source for world's oil, increased Gulf's significance. It was the discovery of oil in Bahrain in 1931 that caught attention and interests of the oil firms (British) in exploring the oil resources in the Gulf. The discovery of huge oil reserves in the Gulf countries (Iran, Iraq and Saudi Arabia) prompted the oil firms to obtain concessions in the Gulf and gradually transformed themselves into giant oil multinationals. Whoever, got hold of these reserves was bound to become rich. It was Rockefeller in the 70s and then the Seven Sisters, the great oil majors ruled the oil market from the 1920s to 60s. The Gulf states were either under direct colonial rule or semi - colonial control, for e.g., Iraq, Bahrain and Kuwait were under the British. Iran was divided into spheres of British and Russia. Saudi Arabia was also under a form of semi - colonial rule of the US. The oil concessions covered vast areas and were granted for the long-term. The royalty payments to the host governments (four gold shillings per ton – originally about one eighth of the per barrel price) were fixed by contract and for the duration of the concession. [19] In the Gulf, "the companies could easily hand over to their rulers as much as 90 percent of the net profit and still enjoy a return on capital of over 40 percent". [20] Between 1950 and 1960, imported oil supplies sourced from American and British oil companies in Kuwait, Saudi Arabia, Qatar and Iran rose from 114,000 barrels per day to 310,000 b/d. [21] "By 1960, five of the seven giant multinational oil corporations which dominated the Gulf were US companies – Exxon, Chevron, Mobil, Gulf and Texaco. Between them, these companies controlled 60 percent of the 164 billion barrels of proven Middle East oil reserves, with shares ranging from 23.75 percent in Iraq and Qatar, to 100 percent in Saudi Arabia". [22]

Each oil concession's agreement of the Gulf States was signed under the protection of the British. Britain used its political clout to win large concessions. Britain also insisted that the rulers of these countries grant exploration concessions only to companies under British control - until U.S. pressure caused it to withdraw the "nationality clause" in 1930. [23] "The first document to be signed was usually, though not necessarily, a commercial agreement between the company and the Ruler. A second stage usually saw a political agreement between the British Government and the oil company. This stage would ideally be endorsed by the Ruler through an exchange of letters with the appropriate British authorities in the Gulf". [24] The oil concessions brought the Gulf rulers into limelight and showered great significance upon them. Unaware of their bargaining power, the rulers did not ask for huge bonuses or fees, but most of the time asked for protection. For e.g., the ruler of Qatar, secured a formal guarantee of protection from Britain against attack by an external power before signing the May 1935 commercial agreement. [25] This can also be seen as, with the capturing of most of the Arabian Peninsula, Ibn Saud established the kingdom of Saudi Arabia in 1932. In order to maintain peace and govern his newly formed kingdom, he needed financial guarantee. Hence, "....in 1933, he signed a concession agreement with Chevron which, in return for exploration rights to 360,000 square miles of territory with a duration of sixty years, provided the King with a loan of £ 155,000 in gold to be paid in installments and repaid out of the royalties which the King would receive once production of oil had commenced". [26] However, the western (US) governments tried to expand their assets in the Gulf. Yet the US oil companies had limited access. Soon, the US government realized that something else was required to cement the rulers' confidence in the oil companies. And, "in February 1945, shortly after the Yalta Conference, President Roosevelt met with King Abdal - Aziz Ibn Saud on a US warship in the Suez Canal...it is generally believed that Roosevelt offered Ibn Saud military support to put down any external attack or internal challenge to his rule in return for privileged access to the Kingdom's vast oil resources – in other words American, not British or French oil companies would get the oil. To further cement the alliance between the USA and the House of Saud, in 1946 a US$ 10 million loan to the Kingdom was arranged". [27] Gradually, the National Oil Companies (NOCs) came into being, which took over the operations from the private companies. For e.g., "The Saudi government gradually bought up the Arabian - American Oil Company (Aramco). It acquired a 100 percent participation interest by 1980; and in 1988, it established the wholly state-owned Saudi Arabian Oil Company (Saudi Aramco), thereby taking over Aramco's activities". [28]

The rentier Gulf states were absolute welfare states which provided free health care, subsidized commodities and free education. The rentier nature of these states have brought them enormous wealth but also made them lethargic and low performers. The states are run by autocratic rulers that have very little opposition. With the discovery of oil, the Gulf states could not diversify any other sector apart from oil. The Gulf states having bountiful of energy resources could not manage their oil revenues and diversify their economies. The oil revenues or rent that the ruling class seeked from the oil companies made them corrupt and big spenders without thinking of the state and people. The revenues also made the government officials and elites to maintain the highest position in the state to further enjoy the benefits of their natural resource. This corruption and non-transparency in the deals made between the ruling families and the oil companies have undermined the democratization process in the region. The oil wealth in the Gulf states have encouraged the factor of 'free money' among the people, giving them an easy access to quick money. As more oil was discovered, the Gulf states became more revenue hungry and involved itself into lavish lifestyle and increasing its military might to strengthen its position in the region as well as against any uprising within the state. The rulers became extreme autocratic and suppressed any democratic movement of the people. Hence, rent from external sources made them less accountable towards the people and instead of gaining legitimacy from the people through taxation, the rulers became autocratic and sought legitimacy from oil rents. Saudi Arabia is a classic example, as it derives nearly all of its income from oil exports and does not tax its people, as oil rents tend to displace other sources of revenue. The oil rent or revenue was also used to suppress any protests by the people by pleasing them with money. Massive amounts of oil revenues were accredited by the foreign oil companies turned the Gulf oil producing states into a rentier economy.

US Intervention and the Democratization Process

Lack of reforms in the Gulf countries has hampered the process of democratization. It is believed by the policymakers that democracy is absent in the countries where energy resources are in abundance. Rulers in these countries have been successful in consolidating an authoritarian rule. However, in other countries, the unequal distribution of oil wealth have caused bloody uprising causing political instability and civil war. Hence, it can be rightly said that the, "The price of oil and the pace of freedom always move in opposite directions in oil-rich petrolist states". [29] An authoritarian state will respond to the people's mobilization against the state, thereby threatening their power. Thus, conflict over the current and future distribution of rents can increase the incentives of elites to stage coups or block democratization. [30] However, there have been sparks of democratization in the Gulf countries. For e.g., the first steps of people's participation occurred in Bahrain, before it became a monarchy in 2002. "In 2001, close to 300 political prisoners were freed before a referendum was held. A parliament was elected in due course, with Islamist groups dominating it… five women, a Christian and a Jew (were appointed) to the Shura Council to complete the process". [31] While, in other countries the democratization efforts were not much successful. For e.g., "prominent Saudi reformers led by Abdullah al - Hamed , along with Matruk al - Faleh and Ali al - Diminni and thirteen other activists, was arrested in March 2004, … Remarkably, the tone of Saudi reformists was non-confrontational, even respectful towards the Al Saud. In December 2003, in June 2004 and again in September 2004, several rounds of National Dialogue were held to discuss, at times with unabashed frankness, sensitive questions. Saudis from all walks of life debated their religious differences, educational concerns, some of the causes leading to extremism, gender matters and municipal elections". [32]

Today, the west (US) has been trying hard to establish democracy through military intervention. One study of regime change in the 20th century found that only 4 of the 16 operations in which the United States was involved in effecting a change in government resulted in the establishment of democracy. [33] However, no democracy can be enforced, it is a process. The US efforts to spread democracy in the region have not been successful. Moreover, the policies of external players in the Gulf should not be democracy per se, but rather to build a more tolerant, peaceful and liberal society. The US invasion of Iraq in 2003, has led more casualties than to have democracy. "...James Akins, the former US ambassador to Saudi Arabia, likewise commented in early 2003 that 'what they [the Bush administration] have in mind is denationalization, and then parceling Iraqi oil out to American oil companies. The American oil companies are going to be the main beneficiaries of this war". [34] Although, Iraqi oil revenues could be used for its reconstruction, but it could also lead to conflicts if there was unequal distribution of oil revenues causing civil war delaying democracy. Talking about war on Iraq, "Dr. Edward Luttwak, the internationally renowned author, lecturer, historian, military strategist and Pentagon consultant said,

Saddam is not like the Saudi Princes who spend the bulk of their lives outside of their country, and who fritter away the Kingdom's oil profits on prostitutes and bottles of champagne in Paris. No, Saddam is building railways! Creating electrical networks! Highways and other important elements of a serious State infrastructure! After eight years of war against the Iranian regime of Khomeini, he desperately needs to demobilize his Republican Guard, which incorporates so many of his technical elite, in order to rebuild the war-devastated country. These people are his technicians, his engineers. If they are put to work in the way Saddam wishes, they will rapidly make Iraq the most advanced power in the region, and we cannot allow this to happen". [35]

US intervention has not led a genuine democracy in the region but, it has further increased chaos. In Iran, Mohmmad Mossadegh nationalized the country's oil sector and reacted against the Western imperialism and exploitation. His nationalization policy greatly undermined the US and British oil interests in the region and Iran in particular. Thus, Mossadegh and his government were deposed by the west and the ousted monarchy of Shah of Iran was reinstalled. Thus, the western interest in promoting democracy in the region is pretentious and rises out of its need for oil.

The obvious reason for such policies of external players is huge oil and gas resources in the region. For e.g., "Iraq's oil is the world's cheapest to produce, at a cost of only about US$ 1 per barrel. The gigantic 'rent' on Iraq's oil, during decades of production, could yield company profits in the range of US$ 4 -5 trillion...Assuming fifty years of production and 40 percent royalties, Iraq could yield annual profits of US$ 80-90 billion per year, more than the total annual profits of the top five companies, …". [36] The oil companies feel convenient and prefer to deal with the clergy and corrupt officials who don't know the significance of oil and have no vision and plan to revolutionize their societies and liberalize them. Hence, the oil corporations benefitted and profited from the deals. Oil has been a critical factor in the US intervention in the Gulf. Dollar's significance as the global transaction currency was also related to the Gulf oil, democracy promotion and war on terrorism. Oil is not just the most important commodity, but is also a lifeline of the west and the developing countries. Oil is traded in dollars globally. Countries have to change their currencies to dollars, before buying oil. This virtually meant that the US controlled the international oil market. OPEC's shift from dollars to euro would result in downfall of US dominance. In 2000, 'Saddam Hussein has caused international turmoil by demanding payment for its oil in euros rather than dollars, the industry's accepted form of payment'. [37] The war on Iraq was not about WMDs or a war against a tyrant. It was about a threat that other regional powers would follow Iraq and shift from 'dollar' to 'euro', resulting into the fall of the US as an economic power. Another OPEC member Iran, is also considering the option. "...the Central Bank of Iran is looking into a switch away from dollar payments–with the euro a favoured alternative" said an Iranian oil industry source. [38] Since then, it has been included into the list of countries fostering terrorism.

US have been a dominant power in the Gulf. US policies and its interventions in the region had one main aim, i.e. to secure cheap and plentiful energy supplies. Despite the fact that, new oil discoveries have been made in other parts of the world in Caspian region and Africa, the Gulf remains the hub of energy resources to the world as its oil is cheap to pump and produce. The US has also been dependent on the regional powers like its ally in the Middle East, Saudi Arabia and Israel to maintain its military presence in the region. For e.g., "...as the threat of Arab nationalism rose after Mossadeq's and Nasser's rise to power in the early 1950s, U.S. aid to Israel began to increase. Whereas in 1951 the U.S. gave Israel only US$ 100,000 in grants, the coup in Egypt the following year prompted the U.S. to give Israel US$ 86.4 million". [39] Also, US gave billions of dollars to Saudi Arabia, not just to prevent entry of other players for Saudi 'oil', but also to resist domestic unrest. The US will to spread democracy in the region has not worked its magic. Saudi Arabia is one of the most authoritarian societies in the world. "Amnesty International, Middle East Watch, the Minnesota International Lawyers Association and other human rights organizations have documented endless cases of imprisonment, torture and elimination within the kingdom. Solitary confinement for years on end is a regular happening, kidnappings and disappearances are common, political executions without proper trial are frequent...and even women are not spared torture and humiliation. In February 1996 a ten- year old child was left in the sun tied to a rope in front of a police station. In six hours he was dead, the victim of the merciless desert sun. The boy had criticized the House of Saud". [40]

The human rights abuses have long been off the records and with the US intervention the suppressive monarchies in the region have sustained to be in power. US has been promoting dictatorial regimes in the region. It has been very easy for US to deal and manipulate with the monarchies, having no idea of the value of their resources and in turn receiving huge orders of military equipment. US virtually own the Gulf oil through its agenda of democracy. Hence, the US promotion of democracy in the Gulf pose new risks for the region.

Oil, Islam and Terrorism

The most significant development in the Gulf has been the growth of Wahhabism, the strictest form of Islam. "The name Wahhabi (was) derived from Muhammad ibn Abd al Wahhab, he studied Hanbali law, usually considered the strictest of Islamic legal schools, and continued his studies in Medina and then in Iraq and Iran". [41] Later on, after having captured most of the Arabian peninsula, Ibn Saud established the kingdom of Saudi Arabia (possessing largest oil reserves in the world). This further intensified the Wahhabi fanaticism and provoked the Arab states to unify. The Wahhabi's wanted to go back to the pure form of Islam. They were fiercely anti-western and did not like the increasing foreign presence in the region and Saudi Arabia in specific. The strict conservatives have been anti-west that threatened their pure form of Islam. However, despite criticism of foreign presence in the Gulf (Saudi Arabia) region, the Gulf countries allowed commercial oil production. Hence, the Gulf became home for the western oil firms. Also, "the existing owners – Chevron and Texaco – lacked sufficient refining capacity in the USA to process the future oil production from the Saudi fields. On the other hand, Exxon and Mobil had the US refining capacity but insufficient reserves of crude". [42] This saw the first union between Saudi Arabia and US forming Arabian - American Oil Company (ARAMCO) in 1947, based in Saudi Arabia, owned by the US. To accompany the workforce, the western housing compounds were created. The strict Islamic laws enforced outside the compounds did not apply inside and the compounds were given western look and freedom. In addition to Ibn Saud and other local sheiks sustaining themselves from royalties given by the oil companies, US proposed Marshall Plan for Saudi Arabia, to support the weak state.

"By 1960, five of the seven giant multinational oil corporations which dominated the Gulf were US companies – Exxon, Chevron, Mobil, Gulf and Texaco. Between them, these companies controlled 60 percent of the 164 billion barrels of proven Middle East oil reserves..." [43] Still, there was a stiff competition for the US oil companies by other players in the region and Saudi Arabia in particular. Hence, to consolidate the US influence on the energy resources, President Roosevelt offered huge loan and military assistance to King Ibn Saud. The agreement between the Gulf rulers and the oil companies further denied openness in the region. While, the oil companies continued to give huge loans and fees for the oil concessions, the US claimed that the Gulf states, primarily Saudi Arabia wants them on its land for their security. Thus, US practiced the idea of 'oil for protection' for the Gulf states. This made the Gulf economies dependent on the oil revenues. The Gulf rulers and elites became notorious big spenders and lost credibility amongst the religious conservatives. "To give some sense of how this tremendous oil wealth was spent, Ibn Saud spent US$ 2 million in 1946 to maintain his garages, Saudi spending on education in the same year amounted to US$ 150,000. Today, the ruling Saud family, for whom Saudi Arabia is a piece of family real estate, consists of several thousand members. Of them, more than 50 are billionaires. The king's palace alone is estimated to be worth US$ 17 billion, and the royal family's budget is US$ 6 to US$

7 billion". [44] The religious fanatics held the western oil firms responsible for misleading their rulers. This became a prime bone of contention between the west and the religious fundamentalists within the region.

While, the US support of Israel in the Arab-Israeli war, forced Saudi monarchy to stop pumping oil, leading to the oil embargo in 1973 which quadrupled the oil prices. "The Iranian Revolution of 1978 reduced the flow of Middle Eastern oil by around 3.5 million b/d for six months, and was followed by a second world oil price surge". [45] This further emphasized the overreliance of US dependence on the Gulf oil and took the western world hostage. This acted as a fuel against the western imperialism. Oil was the national security priority for the US as the industrial nations were dependent on the Gulf oil. The oil embargo redefined the balance of power between the oil producing states and the consumer nations. Adding to the catastrophe, Kuwait asked for the repayment of its war – time loans to Iraq after the Iran-Iraq war. "In a further intensification of the crisis, Saddam Hussein dusted off old territorial claims against Kuwait and charged it with 'stealing' oil from a major Iraqi field lying on the Iraq-Kuwait border. Then, on 2 August 1990, after Kuwait had rejected all Saddam Hussein's demands, 100,000 Iraqi troops poured over the border". [46] To this, Osama bin Laden (a Saudi national) offered to bring its forces from Afghanistan to fight the Iraqi's. However, the Saudi monarchy used the US troops and Iraq was driven out of Kuwait, with the help of US. While withdrawing, Iraq burned Kuwait's oil fields. Offer rejected, acted as a spark between the Osama bin Laden, the monarchy and the west (US). This dependency of the Gulf and especially Saudi monarchy on the west (US) was denounced by the jihadi terrorist organizations, not to mention Osama bin Laden. Since then, terrorism has been a major concern in the Gulf states as terrorists have lashed out against the Gulf monarchies, the west and their alliance.

Oil is a valuable resource and energy infrastructure is a natural hostage in a strategic confrontation and involves far less provocation than civilian attacks. An effective destruction of a key energy facility could also produce a serious mid to long- term blow to the global energy supplies. There have been terrorist attacks in Riyadh (Saudi Arabia), Nairobi (Kenya), Dar es Salaam (Tanzania) and USS Cole (Yemen) which have caused fears of global terrorism. "The November 13, 1995 truck bombing of the National Guard Headquarters in Riyadh killed five U.S. service men and two Iranians. The June 25, 1996 bombing of the Khobar Towers killed 19 U.S. servicemen, and it involved a massive device. The attacks on the U.S. Embassies in Kenya and Tanzania involved massive numbers of innocent casualties – 247 dead and over 5,000 wounded in the case of Kenya, and 10 dead and more than 75 wounded in the case of Tanzania. These attacks involved truck bombs with 600 - 800 pounds of explosive". [47] Terrorism is not the only factor that has reduced the production and exporting capacity of these countries, but war and conflicts in the region has also disrupted the global oil supplies, for e.g., during Iran – Iraq war 3 months (3.3 mmbd) and Iraqi invasion of Kuwait 3 months (4.6 mmbd) oil supplies were disrupted. When it came to light that 15 out of the 19 hijackers were Saudi's in the 9/11 attacks, that caused a rift and suspicion between the two powers (Saudi Arabia and US). These attacks showcased the great division between the pro-west Gulf and the Islamic extremists in the region.

The Gulf energy exporters and consumers need a smooth flow of energy that must be delivered reliably on a day-to- day basis and needs to be expanded over a period of time to meet the global demand. However, till now the terrorist organizations have rarely made direct attacks on energy facilities. This might be because most of the fundamentalist groups see energy export earnings as serving national needs and not just the western interests. There have been attacks on the foreign oil company's residential compounds in Saudi

Arabia in ways that could have a future impact on the foreign expertise that Saudi Arabia needs for some aspects of its oil and gas production. However, even an unsuccessful attack can push up the oil prices. For e.g., "even though unsuccessful in causing disruption, the attempt by al – Qaeda to attack the Abiqaiq oil complex in Saudi Arabia immediately resulted in a US$ 2 rise of oil price". [48] Energy infrastructure like pipelines was sabotaged during the Iran - Iraq war. In 2007, total world oil production amounted to approximately 85 million barrels per day (bbl / d), and around one - half, or over 43 million bbl/d of oil was moved by tankers on fixed maritime routes. [49] The global market is dependent upon reliable transport of energy. Any disruption in these supplies can cost in billions. Hence, maritime security has become an important issue as these straits are easy targets. The Gulf though rich in energy has been prone to risks emanating from within the region and external intervention. There are other set of issues that portrays risks in the Gulf oil. For e.g., "Over reliance on production from a small number of large but ageing oilfields…Rate of depletion (e.g., all five major oil producing Saudi fields use water drive to create high levels of oil flow and avoid the normal rate of depletion. The last major commercial success occurred in 1989. It was Hawrah field in central Arabia, which produced 200,000 b / d. It has problems with corrosive aquifer water and bacteria contamination). The future leadership should be capable and experienced (e.g., Sultan Qaboos of Oman is childless...Therefore, under these circumstances it is far from clear who will succeed him and what his competence and experience would be). Prolonged U.S. economic sanctions will affect energy investment in key exporting states (e.g., ILSA in 1995)". [50] The high prioritization and securitization of the Gulf, predominantly by the west has led to flow of arms in the region, thereby promoting terrorism. The recent terrorist activities in the region have made it far from clear for the global community to help resolve the Gulf's regional issues.

The Gulf oil will remain central to the global energy security. While, the rising instability and external intervention in the region will have tremendous impact on oil prices, the Gulf states also suffer from acts of terrorism at varying degrees, also added by religious and sectarian conflicts. The impact of terrorism on tourism, financial institutions, democracy and most importantly energy has received a considerable attention after 9/11. [51] All of these issues make energy security centric to every country's development. Many of the people in the Gulf countries follow a narrow and rejectionist approach, unfortunately towards accepting democracy. The liberal groups in the region can show the extremists, how democracy can be fruitful, thereby changing the mindset of groups who are less inclined to support democracy. If really, the west wants to promote democracy in the region, it should talk of equality, good governance, human development and freedom. The US's Greater Middle East Initiative is one such initiative focusing on the bi-lateral FTAs and development of democracy in the region. The initiative focuses on economy, education, politics and women. "Informal parts of the Initiative include substantially increased funding for the Middle East through such organizations as the National Endowment for Democracy. The National Endowment for Democracy, for example, received an additional $ US 40 million in 2004 targeted for the Middle East. The Administration has committed more than US$ 290 million to the MEPI". [52] Although, the US intentions to establish democracy in the region are moral, it cannot be ruled out that its oil that lead these interests. Its initiative to transform monarchy into democracy will take some more time.

Notes

1. Steinberg, John (6th July 2005), "WORLD WAR III - The next war has already started", Accessed 26th May 2009. See, http://peakoil.blogspot.com/2005/07/world-war-iii-next-war-has-already.html.
2. Ibid.

3. Ibid.
4. British Petroleum (BP) (June 2008), *BP Statistical Review of World Energy,* [Online: Web] Accessed 27th May 2009, URL: http://www.bp.com/liveassets/bp_internet/globalbp/globalbp_uk_english/reports_and_publications/statistical_energy_review_2008/STAGING/local_assets/downloads/pdf/statistical_review_of_world_energy_full_review_2008.pdf.
5. Cordesman, Anthony H. (15th September 1999), "Geopolitics and Energy in the Middle East", *Centre for Strategic and International Studies,* Washington, p. 26, Accessed 25th May 2009, See, http://www.csis.org/media/csis/pubs/meenergy[1].pdf
6. Cordesman, Anthony H. (March 15, 2004), "Energy Developments in the Middle East", Draft for comment and Review, *Centre for Strategic and International Studies,* Washington, p. 174, Accessed 28th May 2009, See, http://www.csis.org/media/csis/pubs/meep_fullreport.pdf.
7. Ibid.
8. Ibid, p. 180.
9. Ibid, p. 199.
10. Ibid, p. 200.
11. Ibid, p. 208-09.
12. Ibid, p. 219.
13. Ibid, p. 225.
14. Ibid, p. 225-26.
15. Ibid, p. 230.
16. Ibid, p. 238.
17. Cordesman, Anthony H. (March 15, 2004), "The Growing Importance of Middle Eastern Energy, Draft for comment and Review, *Centre for Strategic and International Studies,* Washington, p. 34, Accessed 28th May 2009, See, http://www.csis.org/media/csis/pubs/growing_importance.pdf
18. *OPEC Annual Statistical Bulletin 2007,* p. 83, 84, 85 & 86, Accessed 29th May 2009, See, http://www.opec.org/library/Annual percent20 Statistical percent 20Bulletin/ pdf/ASB2007.pdf.
19. Ibid, p. 28.
20. Rutledge, Ian (2005), "Addicted to Oil: America's Relentless Drive for Energy Security", I. B. Tauris: London, p. 6.
21. Ibid, p. 20.
22. Ibid, p. 34.

23. Marcel, Valerie (2006), "Oil Titans: National Oil Companies in the Middle East", Royal Institute of International Affairs: London, p. 18.
24. "Near & Middle East Titles: Oil Concessions In Five Arab States 1911–1953: Kuwait, Bahrain, Qatar, Trucial States And Oman", Cambridge Archive Editions, Accessed 30th May 2009, See, http://www.archiveeditions.co.uk/titledetails.asp?tid=71.
25. Ibid.
26. Rutledge, Ian (2005), "Addicted to Oil: America's Relentless Drive for Energy Security", I. B. Tauris: London, p. 29.
27. Ibid, p. 30-31.
28. Marcel, Valerie (2006), "Oil Titans: National Oil Companies in the Middle East", Royal Institute of International Affairs: London, p. 29.
29. Dunning, Thad (2008), "Crude Democracy: Natural Resource Wealth and Political Regimes", Cambridge University Press: UK, p. 1.
30. Ibid, p. 100.
31. Kéchichian, Joseph A. (Winter 2004), 'Democratization in Gulf Monarchies: A New Challenge to the GCC", *Middle East Policy Council Journal*, XI (4), p. 40, Accessed 4th June 2009, See, http://www.mepc.org/journal_vol11/kechichian.pdf.
32. Ibid, p. 42-43.
33. Preble, Christopher (2004), "Exiting Iraq: Why the US mush end the Military Occupation and renew the war against Al Qaeda", *Report of a Special Task Force on Exiting Iraq*, CATO Institute, Washington D.C., p. 46.
34. Philips, Kevin (2006), "American Theocracy: The Peril and Politics of Radical Religion, Oil, and Borrowed Money in the 21st Century", Penguin Group: USA, p. 92.
35. O'Huallachain, D. L. & J. Forrest Sharpe (eds.) (2007), "Neo-conned! again: hypocrisy, lawlessness, and the rape of Iraq : the illegality and the injustice of the Second Gulf War", IHS Press: US, p. 29-30.
36. Philips, Kevin (2006), "American Theocracy: The Peril and Politics of Radical Religion, Oil, and Borrowed Money in the 21st Century", Penguin Group: USA, p. 91.
37. "A Look At The World's Economy: Iraq Could Become The Spoiler" (22nd December 2000), *CBS News*, Accessed 6th June 2009, See,

http://www.cbsnews.com/stories/2000/12/22/2000/main259203.shtml.

38. "Iran may switch to euro for crude sale payments" (5th September 2002), "Alexander's Gas and Oil Connections", 7 (17), Accessed 6th June 2009, See, http://www.gasandoil.com/goc/news/ntm23638.htm.
39. D'Amato, Paul (December 2000 - January 2001), "U.S. Intervention in the Middle East: Blood for Oil", *International Socialist Review,* Accessed 10th June 2009, See, http://www.isreview.org/issues/15/blood_for_oil.shtml.
40. Ibid.
41. "Kuwait: Wahhabi Islam in the Gulf", Accessed 11th June 2009, See, http://atheism.about.com/library/FAQs/islam/countries/bl_KuwaitIslamWahhabi.htm.
42. Rutledge, Ian (2005), "Addicted to Oil: America's Relentless Drive for Energy Security", I. B. Tauris: London, p. 31.
43. Ibid, p. 34.
44. D'Amato, Paul (December 2000 - January 2001), "U.S. Intervention in the Middle East: Blood for Oil", *International Socialist Review,* Accessed 10th June 2009, See, http://www.isreview.org/issues/15/blood_for_oil.shtml.
45. Rutledge, Ian (2005), "Addicted to Oil: America's Relentless Drive for Energy Security", I. B. Tauris: London, p. 48.
46. Ibid, p. 50.
47. Cordesman, Anthony H. (September 15, 1999), "Geopolitics and Energy in the Middle East", *Centre for Strategic and International Studies,* Washington, p. 94-95, Accessed 12th June 2009, See, http://www.csis.org/media/csis/pubs/meenergy[1].pdf.
48. Ghoble, Vrushal (2009), "European Union and India: Contesting for Gulf Energy", Regal Publications, New Delhi, p. 18.
49. Energy Information Administration (EIA) (January 2008), "World Oil Transit Chokepoints", *Country Analysis Briefs,* Accessed 12th June 2009, See, http://www.eia.doe.gov/cabs/World_Oil_Transit_Chokepoints/Background.html.
50. Ghoble, Vrushal (2009), "European Union and India: Contesting for Gulf Energy", Regal Publications, New Delhi, p. 13-14.
51. Ibid, p. 17.

52. Candland, Christopher, "The U.S. Greater Middle East Initiative: Implications for Persian Gulf Economies and Polities (1)", p. 1-2, Accessed 12th June 2009, See, http://www.wellesley.edu/Polisci/Candland/USGMEI.pdf.

9

Islamic Responses to the Western Modernity Project: Within and Beyond

Kundan Kumar

Modernity is a situation of unending transit in which the uncertainty of what it means to be modern is never eliminated. To radicalize the project of modernity is to sharpen and renew this uncertainty, to create new possibilities for modernity always to be able to be something different and something more. [1]

Modernity, being distinctively a Western project [2] due to its European roots [3] and close association with Euro-American power and imperial expansion overseas [4], is neither an exclusively Western nor an exclusively Eastern phenomenon as its histories and experiences goes beyond the confines geography, ethnicity, class, nationality, religion and ideology.' [5] But the events of the 20th century like the First World War, the rise of Fascism, the Second World War, the Cold War, the fear of nuclear destruction of life from the planet, and then the collapse of the Communist utopia in 1989 paved a way for the intellectual reconstruction of the concept of modernity, as the historians of modernity have been trying to do by placing it between social, cultural, and political renewal expressed theologically, traditionally, and dynastically; and the far-reaching action and reform justified in secular, non-theological, and non-customary ideological terms. [6] The domination of the world's political, economic and cultural life by the 'West' rests at least partly on the discursive construction of a worldview that sees such domination as natural, inevitable and appropriate. [7] This history of 'modernity' continues to have direct institutional legacies for the Arab Islamic world as well as for Arab perceptions of 'modernity'.

The distinction between Islam and modernity has to be located in the ongoing debate between modernity and tradition in the Islamic societies of the new globalized world. [8] The Enlightenment modernity, imposed as the sole model of modernity at the cost of local values and beliefs, has alienated the Islamic landscape. Islam's compatibility with modernity cannot be ascertained due to the lack of consensus among historians and Islamicists about the nature of the Islamic belief system and the experience of historical Islam. [9] "Generations of Muslims themselves have felt that the ambiguities of lived experience are illumined by the articulation of a conflict, however evaluated, between Western modernity and Islam." [10] The literature on multiple modernities [11] shows that the contemporary use of the terms 'Islam' and 'modernity' negates the validity of the concepts like 'multiple Islams' and 'multiple modernities.' There are several unequal and sometimes contradictory forms of modernity [12] as it is in the process of being rejected, supported and negotiated. [13]

Islam, unlike Christianity, is considered by Western scholars as an obstacle to development [14] without taking into account the important differences between the origin and foundation of two cultural worlds: the rise of Christianity within the Roman Empire and the rise of Muhammad in a context where he had to construct a political, economic and social order. [15] In this way, Huntington's 'clash of civilizations' thesis, according to which conflicts and threats to world peace and security in the 21st century will be carried out along civilizational fault lines [16], has been denied by scholars such as John Esposito who argues that such visions of the future rest generally on an exaggerated and distorted understanding of Islam and a misunderstanding of the nature of diversity and the complexity of social change. [17]

Islamic political thought, a part of a larger intellectual response to 'general societal decay and the oppression by

Western powers', [18] took multiple forms, ranging from the wholesale acceptance to the total rejection of modernity and the West, which feeds the distinction made by many Western social scientists between rational, modern, Western thought and irrational, tradition-bound, Islamist ideology. [19] Islamic thinkers has been branded as reactionary ideologues who, in the words of Bernard Lewis, attribute all evil to the abandonment of the divine heritage of Islam by advocating a return to a real or imagined past. [20] Many scholars, however, also disagree with Lewis' view. [21] Denying to analyze the theoretical merits of conceptual categories such as 'tradition' and 'modernity' at face value or as "rigid and mutually exclusive categories of thought," [22] the vast majority of nineteenth and twentieth centuries' Islamic thinkers perceived the West, and its novel form of social organization, as a "political, religious, and intellectual problematic and threat." [23]

Western literature and scholars operate on assumption that Muslims, having one creed and thereby one culture, collectively share a disdain for modernity and reject democracy as a formula of governance. Huntington argues that Islam is not hospitable to democracy [24]; Pipes claims that "[N]early all Muslim subjects kept away from politics and became actively engaged only when they had a chance to apply the law or battle non-Muslims" [25]; Lewis declares that Muslims' "dominant political tradition has long been that of command and obedience, and far from weakening it, modern times have actually witnessed its intensification" [26]; Fukuyama argues that 'there does seem to be something about Islam, or at least the fundamentalist versions of Islam that have been dominant in recent years, that makes Muslim societies particularly resistant to modernity.' [27] Such representatives of the 'New Orientalism' reflect the conventional wisdom of both the social sciences and policy-makers in the West [28] based on the assumption that Muslims share the 'same values legitimating social practices' that are inherently un-democratic. [29]

Islamic Responses

Practicing itself in different ways within a vast array of cultures [30], Islam, right from the 19th century, has shown certain threads of its accommodation to change as well as its reactions and responses to the Western ideas, institutions, and values in its relationship with the new demands of the modern world on religious, political, economic, and social levels. [31] Responding to the question of Western modernity, Muslim intellectuals and religious scholars such as Sayyid Jamal al-Din 'al-Afghani [32] of Iran and Muhammad Abduh [33] of Egypt concluded that a reformation and a new interpretation of Islam were needed in Muslim societies. 'Abduh, inspired by Comtean positivism, [34] questioned "whether someone who lived in the modern world could still be a devout Muslim" [35], and argued that 'man has unlimited capacities, unlimited desires, unlimited knowledge and unlimited action, which are required to be used to demonstrate that Islam is fully compatible with the demands of modernity.' [36] The re-envisioning of community and identity that took place in the Middle East in the last two hundred years comprises a complex and multifaceted phenomenon. [37] The first serious and comprehensive response to European conceptions of nationalism from an Islamic perspective was propounded by Jamal al-Din al-Afghani in whose view, "...norm of human action is no longer the service of God; it is the creation of a human civilization flourishing in all its parts." [38] Muhammad Abduh followed his "Islamic reformism." [39] Earlier even Muhammad Ali articulated modern Europe as "a dynamic society rationally exploiting its resources and administering its affairs with national strength as the criterion of law and policy." [40] The reforms that these Islamic thinkers advocated were aimed at reconciling Islam and modernity and to promote individual freedom, social justice, and political liberalism.

The Islamic thinkers and intellectuals sought to avail their societies the fruits of modernity while fortifying their own traditions, so as to ensure their independence from the West [41], and in this process they, rather than staging an attack on modernity, sought to oppose its oppressive and exploitative version promulgated by European colonial regimes. They tried to cultivate a movement that could transform Muslim society by reframing traditional Islamic categories into a modern sociological existence by their writings and speeches during late 19th and early 20th century and inspired the development of an entire lexicon of Islamic idioms to meet the challenges of economic, political, and social subordination by the West. 'Islam became a channel through which persons who had failed to become integrated into the secular system were engaged in their own project of boundary expansion, and search for freedom' [42] and in this process, Muslim intellectuals claimed religious/moral authority in the name of Islamic Law (Sharia). [43]

Islamic challenge to modernity "requires a serious exploration into the genealogy of the Western narratives of modernity and its dichotomizing representation of non-Western cultures and societies" [44] without negating the reconciliation of "the tension between modernity's promise of openness and inclusive qualities and the blatant Eurocentric narrative of modernization that forecloses the possibility of real "local" experiences and of their contribution in the realization of modernity." [45] "Religious intellectuals are the architects of a critical theoretical framework for understanding the dialectic of tradition and modernity. The focus of this critical perspective is the tension between modernity and religion." [46] The confrontation between tradition and modernity is easier in Islam than in Christianity, where "tradition" is tied up with the idea of the church as the vehicle of sacred history. [47] Islam is faced with the problem of 'defence or innovation' regarding western modernity. [48] Muslim intellectuals and *ulama*, engaged in protracted and highly contentious disputes on how to respond to the challenge of Western modernity and democracy, fall into three categories: traditionalists, modernists and secularists [49]: one thread believes that the religion of Islam is incompatible with modern thinking and scientific rationality, the second supports the opposite view, and the third view is that there are some elements that can be incorporated, adapted, and adopted by the Islamic world simultaneously rejecting other elements of modernity.

Islamic Reformism/ Islamic Modernism/ Salafism

Emerged in the late 19th century due to attempts at modernisation and reform from above both in the Ottoman and Persian Empires to catch up with Europe, and direct confrontation and connection with the powerful European forces, this political ideological movement was a response to the direct confrontation with the European expansion from the mid-19th to the early 20th centuries embodied in Great Britain, into the Islamic lands [50], and its main ideologues were Seyyed Jamal al-Din Afghani [51], Mohammad Abduh [52], and Ayatollah Muhammad Hussein Na'ini. [53] The Muslim thinkers criticised the rulers as despots and ulama as fanatics and opposed the Western materialism and secular culture, believing that only by imitating and naturalising both Western technique and thought could strong independent politics and society in the Islamic world be achieved. They reinterpreted early Islamic injunctions to make them compatible with Western liberalism on matters such as the parliamentary system based on a constitution. [54] While some of them advocated *Westernization* and secularization as the surest way to compete with Europe, others advocated an *Islamic Modernism*, arguing that Western methods and key institutions, legislatures, bureaucracies and banks could be revised along the lines of Islamic law. [55] In their view, if Muslims refute Darwinism, Marxism or the contributions of Freud and Kant; this is not because everything they said was wrong, as some of what they said may be useful and thus deserve to be studied. [56]

The modernists, including al-Afghani and Abduh, [57] tried to interpret the Islamic texts in terms of Western science, rationality, and modernity. Al-Ghazali praised the 1923 Egyptian constitution that mainly was imported from the West as practically more Islamic than most of the so-called Islamic constitutions. [58] In modernists' view, a mature Muslim can read un-Islamic and non-Islamic philosophies and pick and choose what is compatible with his/her ethics and creed [59] and thus should not refute the wisdom contained in the books of the "people of falsehood." [60] While some modernists maintain that most of what Muslims learn from others mainly is what others previously had learned from Muslims [61], others even give the right of *ijtihad* to all Muslims, who have the right to choose among the differing *ijtihad*s of *ulama*. [62] Thus modernists aim at advocating "modernization without encouraging servility to the West and discouraging confidence in one's own cultural resources." [63] By emphasizing the possibility of attaining the truth through the use of human reason as well as the need for liberty in the interpretation of the *shari'a,* a number of thinkers and philosophers of Islam have undoubtedly stridden along toward a kind of European Enlightenment. [64] However, the momentum which they initiated was not strong enough to alter in a durable manner the traditionalist perceptions about the role of religion in social and political life, such as expressed by Hanbal and Al-Ghazali. [65]

Islamic Revivalism/ Islamism/ Radical Islam/ Islamic Fundamentalism/ Wahabism/ Traditionalism

Developed and continued until its structural crisis in the late 1980s and 1990s, [66] the main ideological representatives of Islamic traditionalism were Hasan al- Banna [67], Rashid Rida, Seyyed Abdullah al-Mawdudi, Seyyed Qutb [68], Ali Shari'ati [69], Mohammad Baqir Sadr and Ayatollah Ruhollah

Khomeini. [70] It was a radical reaction to the intensification and expansion of the Western capitalism mainly after World War II and its socio-economic, political, and more importantly, cultural consequences in the Islamic world. Due to colonial reasons [71] and due to the failure or suppression of Westernizing strategies in Islamic states, conservative religious responses grew more pronounced generating various Islamic fundamentalist movements in the 20th century which constituted a response to Westernised and modernised authoritarian regimes and their socio-economic and cultural modernisation programmes in the Islamic world, and also to the rapid social changes, stresses and strains of the secular culture of modernity which, devoid of a religious base, can be seen as existing without transcendental meaning. [72] It translated Islamic tradition and symbols into a popular language to secure the support of the wide urban-based social classes and groups.

In addition to al-Wahhab, there were many other articulate fundamentalist authors of the 20th century, whose works have served as the ideological pillar for the radical movements. Al-Banna believed in achieving modernity by linking economic reform with spiritual one, and advocated reforms based on Islamic culture. [73] Mawdudi supported reforms to meet the challenges of modernity, propounding that Islam was self-sufficient and could modernize without foreign interference. [74] Advocating a Pan-Islamic nationalism for the entire Muslim world [75] and arguing that 'Islam cannot be rightly practiced in isolation from society and its people cannot be Muslims if they do not put it into effect in their social, legal and economic system' [76], Qutb was inspirational to Muslims disillusioned by European colonialism. [77] So the language and symbols of returning Islam to its triumphant were also used for escaping foreign domination. [78] Without taking into account the different academic propositions on the issue of Islamic modernity as, for example, given by Gran [79] and Schulze, [80] it can be seen that Islamist movements have mobilized mass support by constructing and transmitting an understanding of Islam as the answer to modernity. [81]

Despite their critique of modernity, fundamentalist groups are thoroughly modern in that the concerns of their leaders are shaped and formed in reaction to the modern situation. They are directly opposed to cultural modernity and its democratic heritage, the political culture of pluralism, human rights and liberal tolerance, yet they selectively use the resources of modernity to promote their particular concept of political order. [82] Therefore while Christian fundamentalism is the product of a reaction, in the face of the forces of modernity and secularism, to a loss of Christian autonomy and social, cultural and political hegemony, the phenomenon of Islamic fundamentalism, especially in its more violent expressions, is an appeal by non-Western Islamic societies for recognition of their sovereignty and social realities. [83]

Islamic Secularism

Emerging from the late 1980s, its main intellectual representatives are Mohammad Iqbal [84], Mehdi Bazargan, Abdolkarim Soroush [85], Fazlur Rahman, S.M. Zafar, Rachid Ghannouchi, Muhammad Shahrour, Chandra Muzaffar, Mohamed Talbi, Yusuf Qaradawi, Mohamed Arkoun, Abdullahi Ahmed An-Na'im, and Nurcholish Madjid. Its criticism of Islamism and Islamic radicalism, and more importantly its criticism of Islam as political ideology show its tendency towards democracy, by means of defending civil society in general and human rights in particular and more importantly its support for secularism. [86] Rahman argues that the *Ulama* did not share with the modernists the idea of the comprehensive nature of Islam and its compatibility with modernity when he says "it is the belief of the *Ulama* that the medievally formulated traditional beliefs can be kept intact and immune from modern influences, which is directly responsible for secularism in the Muslim world." [87] Political interpretations of a comprehensive Islam necessitated the rejection of the West and separation of politics from religion which, however, pushed political Islam [88] to a gradual theologization of political concepts.

According to Abduh, while Islamic texts mandated specific rules regarding the worship of Allah, they included only broad principles on how humans should relate to each other, thus leaving it up to humans to apply these in specific circumstances and this not only allowed but also required the application of *ijtihad* (independent reasoning) in the development of legal codes [89] as happening in Turkey. [90] This new agenda, one that is still self-acclaimed as Islamist and not secularist albeit departing from the old Islamist strategies, [91] is an attempt to turn the underlying principles of Islamism on its head by emphasizing rights instead of duties, plurality in place of a single authoritative voice, historicity rather than fixed scriptures, and the future instead of the past. It wants to marry Islam with individual choice and freedom, with democracy and modernity, to achieve what some have termed "an alternative modernity." [92]

Turkey depicts an example which not only exhibits the tensions that exist between the religious and the secular, tradition and modernity, but also the possibility of cohabitation, change, and compromise, which helps discern the conditions under which Islamic political and social movements may achieve compatibility with liberal democratic norms and modernity. [93] As contemporary Wahabi scholars not only reject the notion of cultural exchange with non-Muslims but even refuse to "interpret the divine law from a historical, contextual perspective and treat the vast majority of Islamic history as a corruption of the true and authentic Islam," [94] secularists reject this traditionalism by arguing that Muslims need to follow the paths of the most successful to outdo them, exactly as the West did by learning from ancient Muslims and others. Taking into account the growing gap between Muslims' power and the flourishing Western democracies, [95] some secularists blame the failure of attempts to catch up with the West in part on the absence of a worldview that respects other civilizations and learns from them. [96] In their view it is not possible to import Western materialist products and outcomes without understanding and adopting the system of beliefs and ideologies behind them. They put before modernists the question as how it is possible to "import from the West what is compatible with our values and leave the rest. [97] In fact, they contend that interaction and learning from other civilizations cannot succeed without emancipation from the power of the "holy" interpretations and traditions that come as a package with the sacred texts. [98] Thus secularists consider the adoption of ideas and institutions from other civilizations to be a very important sign of the perseverance of Muslims and their capacity to make up for what they missed.

Islamic Response to the Question of 'Democracy'

Democracy in terms of popular sovereignty never became a social-political practice in Islamic societies despite traditions of social justice and tolerance because "the European Renaissance, Reformation and Enlightenment were relatively unknown and European innovations in technology, philosophy and commerce had little impact on early modern Islamic societies." [99] Without going into the debates of whether any conflict may come about as a result of the absence of democracy in a given society but not of cultural differences [100]; whether high religiosity is more likely to be found in less developed societies, while more aesthetic values are more likely to be found in rich and developed societies [101]; whether Islamic liberalism in political culture would not be authoritarian or conservative, as in the case of Christian Democratic parties in the European experience [102]; I wish to point out that the lack of democracy in the Middle East is seen as a natural concomitant of the failure to embrace modernity. In the years following the end of the Cold War, a certain triumphalism emerged concerning democratic politics, what Francis Fukuyama so precipitously called 'the end point of mankind's ideological evolution'. [103] The Western efforts to suppress Islamic traditions of openness to change, tolerance, democracy and equality [104] introduced a troubling new solidarism into the discourse: if there is only one end point of human political evolution – capitalist liberal democracy – then any different vision becomes an illogical, unacceptable other. Democracy in the post-Cold War world became the hallmark of legitimate government and a part of a new 'standard of civilization.' [105]

The equation of political pluralism with a democratic government has been a persistent subject in the writings of secular intellectuals – both liberal and autocrat – in the Middle East for about 100 years. [106] Liberal secularists are close to the Western concept of liberal democracy while autocrats are associated with most intellectuals who earn their living through glorifying and defending rulers in Muslim countries. [107] According to autocratic secularists, illiteracy, tribalism, apathy, emotionalism, and nostalgia are not conducive preconditions for democracy, [108] which can be seen in the case of Lebanese democratic experience which ended up in a severe civil war; [109] in the democratic political opening in Egypt in the 1980s which led to massive violent fundamentalism [110]; in the rebellion against Siyad Berri in Somalia which ended up with chaotic state breakdown [111]; and in free elections in Algeria which led the country into civil war with tens of thousands of deaths and causalities. [112] Hafez al-Assad's autocratic policies managed to break the vicious cycle of coup d'etats by systematic removal of his opponents for "the interest of Syrians and all the Arab umma." [113] Liberal secularists argue that limits on the right of participation are disallowed, which is why their main target of criticism is not Islamists in opposition but the autocratic rulers, whether Islamists or secularists.

Liberal secularists have the weakest voice in the Muslim world [114] as they cannot offer the baksheesh that autocratic rulers can. [115] Modernists accept new ideas, mechanisms and values as far as they do not contradict authentic and well-established *sharia*. As in modernists' view most aspects of democracy are compatible with Islam, they challenge doctrines which stipulate that Islam and democracy are incompatible (but remain with the dilemma of how to reconcile Islam with modernity). [116] Thus Lewis's argument that "Islam is incompatible with liberal democracy" [117] has no firm basis. Secularists find in the holy texts little of relevance with respect to how to run modern societies and argue that all texts and issues are subject to human scrutiny with no immune zones.

Following modernists from the 18th and 19th centuries, such as Rifaah Rafi al- Tahtawi of Egypt, Khayr al-Din Tunisi of Tunisia, Abdul Rahman al-Kawakebi of Syria, Jamal al-Din al-Afghani of Iran, and Mohamed Abduh of Egypt, who called upon Muslims to learn non-Islamic discoveries and inventions from Europe, [118] modernists today argue that if there is anything not Islamic by origin but necessary to establish Islamic goals such as justice, it can be imported and Islamized. Modernists, in contrast, are more open to competitive elections [119] as political parties are expected to be loyal to the regime and respect the autocratic authority either through joining a coalition with the ruling party or by posing no threat to the dominance of the autocrat. [120]

Conclusion

Muslims have a plurality of readings and interpretations of Islam. While traditionalists and modernists share similar assumptions and doctrines regarding the role of Islam in politics arguing, "Islam cannot but be political," [121] secularists, acting as intellectual competitors to monopolized learning and intellectual activity [122] of *ulama* perceive Islam as a relationship between God and the believer, not between God and the government, causing disagreement. [123] While traditionalists reject anything beyond Islamic teachings, modernists think that most aspects of democracy are compatible with Islam. Secularists do not consider much of value in the holy texts regarding how Muslims should govern modern societies. 'Contemporary Muslim thinkers continue this line of analysis, leading to the conclusion that "Islamic doctrine, as embedded in the text and traditions, is conducive to democratic thought in many compelling ways," and the "greatest periods of Islamic rule have been precisely those in which Islam's structural and intellectual developments were the most democratic."' [124]

Finally, one can say that in the process of creating an alternate Islamic modernity by way of adapting, re-appropriating, negotiating, contradicting, and defying the Western modernity, Islam has, in consonance with all other faiths and religions, been in the constant struggle to reshape the concept of modernity which is already in crisis today.

Notes

1. Néstor García-Canclini, *Hybrid Cultures: Strategies for Entering and Leaving Modernity,* Minneapolis: University of Minnesota Press, 1994, p. 268. For more views on modernity and its problematic connotations see, Marshall Berman, *All That Is Solid Melts Into Air: The Experience of Modernity*, New York: Penguin Books, 1988; H. Lefebvre, *Introduction to Modernity*, London: Verso, 1995; H. Foster, (ed.) *Postmodern Culture,* London: Pluto Press, 1985; Jurgen Habermas, 'Modernity: An Incomplete Project,' in Hal Foster (ed.), *The Anti-Aesthetic: Essays on Postmodern Culture*, Seattle: Bay Press, 1983, pp. 3-16; and Z. Bouman, *Modernity and Ambivalence*, Cambridge: Polity Press, 1991.
2. See A. Giddens, *The Consequences of Modernity*, Cambridge: Polity Press, 1991.
3. Lauren Langman & Douglas Morris, "Islamic Modernity: Barriers and Possibilities", *Logos*, Vol. 1, No. 2, 2002, pp. 61-62. See J. Habermas, *The Philosophical Discourse of Modernity*, Cambridge: Polity Press, 1987.
4. See, Lewis Hanke, Aristotle *and the American Indians: A Study in Race Prejudice in the Modern World*, London: Hollis and Carter, 1959; Julia Kristeva, *Strangers to Ourselves*, New York: Columbia University Press, 1991; Tzvetan Todorov, *The Conquest of America*, New York: Harper & Row, 1984; Max

Horkheimer and Theodor W. Adorno, *Dialectic of the Englightenment*, Amsterdam: Amsterdam University Press, 1997; Ali Mirsepassi, *Intellectual Discourse and the Politics of Modernisation: Negotiating Modernity in Iran*, Cambridge: Cambridge University Press, 2000; Ashis Nandy, *The Intimate Enemy – Loss and Recovery of Self Under Colonialism*, Oxford: Oxford University Press, 1984; D. Lyon, *Postmodernity*, Buckingham: Open University Press, 2nd ed., 1999; M. Foucault, "What is Enlightenment" in M. Drolet (ed.), *The Postmodernism Reader: Foundational Texts,* London: Routledge, 2004.

5. See Marshall Berman, op. cit.
6. See Jonathan I. Israel, *Enlightenment Contested: Philosophy, Modernity, and the Emancipation of Man 1670–1752*, New York: Oxford University Press, 2006. See also, David Harvey, *The Condition of Postmodernity*, Cambridge, MA: Blackwell, 1990. For more anti-Western articulations of modernity, see, Stephen N. Hay, *Asian Ideas of East and West: Tagore and his Critics in Japan, China, and India,* Cambridge: Harvard University Press, 1970; Ali Rahnema, *An Islamic Utopian: A Political Biography of Ali Shari'ati,* New York: I.B.Tauris Publishers, 2000; and Marc Gallicchio, *The African American Encounter with Japan & China: Black Internationalism in Asia, 1895–1945,* Chapel Hill: University of North Carolina Press, 2000; Cemil Aydin, "The Politics of Conceptualizing Islam and the West", *Ethics & International Affairs*, Vol. 18, No. 3, 2004; Prasenjit Duara, "The Discourse of Civilization and Pan-Asianism," *Journal of World History,* Vol. 12, No. 1, 2001, pp. 99–130; Michael Adas, "Contested Hegemony: The Great War and the Afro-Asian Assault on the Civilizing Mission Ideology," in Prasenjit Duara, (ed.), *Decolonization,* New York: Routledge, 2004, pp. 78–100; Mark Bradley, *Imagining Vietnam and America: The Making of Postcolonial Vietnam, 1919–1950,* Chapel Hill: University of North Carolina Press, 2000; and Erez Manela, "The Wilsonian Moment and the Rise of Anticolonial Nationalism: The Case of Egypt," *Diplomacy & Statecraft,* Vol. 12, No. 4, 2000, pp. 99-122.
7. Sophie Bessis, *Western Supremacy: The Triumph of an Idea*, translated by Patrick Camiller, London: Zed Books, 2003.
8. For broader debates of religion and modernity, see, Ian Richard Netton, *Islam, Christianity and Tradition: A Comparative*

Exploration, Edinburgh: Edinburgh University Press, 2006; Linda Woodhead and Paul Heelas (eds), *Religion in Modern Times: An Anthology*, Religion and Modernity Series, Oxford: Blackwell, 2000; Paul Heelas (ed.), *Religion, Modernity and Postmodernity*, Religion and Modernity Series, Oxford: Blackwell, 1998; David Smith, *Hinduism and Modernity*, Religion and Modernity Series, Oxford: Blackwell, 2002; A.H. Ziadi, "Muslim Reconstructions of Knowledge and the Re-enactment of Modernity", *Theory, Culture and Society*, Vol. 23, No. 5, pp. 69-91; and James Beckford, "Religion, Modernity and Post-Modernity", in Bryan Wilson, ed., *Religion: Contemporary Issues*, London: Bellew Publishing, 1992, pp. 11-23.

9. Mansoor Moaddel, "The Future of Islam after 9/11", *Futures*, Vol. 36, 2004, p. 961.
10. Chistopher Houston, "ISLAMISM, CASTORIADIS AND AUTONOMY", *Thesis Eleven*, Number 76, 2004, p. 50.
11. See Dilip Parameshwar Gaonkar, "On Alternative Modernities", *Public Culture,* Vol. 11, No. 1, 1999, pp. 1 – 18; Ibrahim Kaya, "Modernity, Openness, Interpretation: A Perspective on Multiple Modernities", *Social Science Information,* Vol. 43, No. 1, 2004, pp. 35- 47; Timothy Mitchell, *Questions of Modernity,* Minneapolis : University of Minnesota Press, 2004; and Charles Taylor, "Two Theories of Modernity", *Public Culture,* Vol. 11, No. 9, 1999, pp. 153 – 174; Bjorn Wittrock, "Modernity: One, None, Many? European Origins and Modernity as a Global Condition, *Daedalus*, Vol. 129, No. 1, pp. 31-59; Peter J. Taylor, *Modernities: A Geohistorical Interpretation*, Cambridge: Polity Press, 1999; Charles Taylor and Benjamin Lee, *Multiple Modernities Project: Modernity and Difference*, Chicago: Centre for Transcultural Studies, 1998; Robert W. Hefner, 'Multiple Modernities: Christianity, Islam, and Hinduism in a Globalizing Age' *Annual Review of Anthropology*, 27, 1998; Shmuel N. Eisenstadt (ed.), *Multiple Modernities*, New Brunswick and London: Transaction Publishers, 2005.
12. Néstor García-Canclini, op. cit. p. 182. See also, Marwan M. Kraidy, *Hybridity, or the Cultural Logic of Globalization,* Philadelphia, PA: Temple University Press, 2005.
13. See Leszek Kolakowski, *Modernity on Endless Trial,* Translated by Stefan Czerniawski, Wolfgang Freis and Agnieszka Kolakowska, Chicago: University of Chicago Press, 1997.

14. See Bernard Lewis, (ed.), *The World of Islam: Faith, People, Culture,* New York: Thames and Hudson, 1992.
15. A. Greif, *Institutions and the Path to Modern Economy –Lessons from Medieval Trade,* Cambridge: Cambridge University Press, 2006, p. 206.
16. Mehdi Parvizi Amineh, 'Globalization and Political Islam: The Challenges of Modernity', in F. W. Russell (ed.), *Dialogue among Civilisations*, United Nations Educational, Scientific and Cultural Organization: Paris, 2006, p. 114.
17. Trish Madigan Op, "The Threat of Fundamentalism? Some Christian and Muslim Perspectives", *Compass Review of Topical Theology*, Volume 38, No 2, 2004, p. 14. See also, J. Esposito, *The Islamic Threat, Myth or Reality?* New York & Oxford: Oxford University Press, 1992, pp. 4-5.
18. Yvonne Yazbeck Haddad and John Esposito, *The Contemporary Islamic Revival: A Critical Survey and Bibliography,* New York: Greenwood Press, 1991, pp. 3-4.
19. Roxanne L. Euben, *Enemy in the Mirror: Islamic Fundamentalism and the Limits of Modern Rationalism: A Work of Comparative Political Theory,* Princeton: Princeton University Press, 2002, p. 154. See also, Robert Wuthnow, "Understanding Religion and Politics," *Daedalus,* Vol. 120, No. 3, 1991, pp. 1-18.
20. Bernard Lewis, *What Went Wrong? The Clash Between Islam and Modernity in the Middle East,* New York: Oxford University Press, 2001, p. 159.
21. John Esposito, *Islam and Politics,* Syracuse: Syracuse University Press, 1998, p. 54. See also, R.A. Euben, *Enemy in the Mirror: Islamic Fundamentalism and the Limits of Modern Rationalism*, Princeton: Princeton University Press, 1999, p. 155.
22. Ibrahim M. Abu-Rabi', *Intellectual Origins of Islamic Resurgence in the Modern Arab World,* New York: State University of New York Press, 1996, p. 4.
23. Ibid., p. 37.
24. Samuel P. Huntington, "Will More Countries Become Democratic?", *Political Science Quarterly,* Vol. 99, 1984, p. 99.
25. Daniel Pipes, *In the Path of God: Islam and Political Power,* New York: Basic Books, 1983, p. 144.

26. Bernard Lewis, 'Islam and Liberal Democracy,' *The Atlantic Monthly,* 1993, pp. 54-55. See also Bernard Lewis, *What Went Wrong?,* op. cit. For Lewis' views, see Cemil Aydin, "The Politics of Conceptualizing Islam and the West", *Ethics and International Affairs*, Vol. 18, No. 3, 2004.
27. Francis Fukuyama, 'The West has Won: Radical Islam can't Beat Democracy and Capitalism', *The Guardian*, October 11, 2001.
28. See Yahya Sadowski, "The New Orientalism and the Democracy Debate", *Middle East Report,* No. 193, 1993, pp. 14-21.
29. See Aaron Wildavsky, "Choosing Preferences by Constructing Institutions: A Cultural Theory of Preference Formation", *American Political Science Review,* Vol/No. 81, 1987, pp. 3-21.
30. See John L. Esposito, *What Everyone Needs to Know about Islam*, Oxford: Oxford University Press, 2002, p. 39-58.
31. See Robert D. Lee, *Overcoming Tradition and Modernity: The Search for Islamic Authenticity*, Boulder, CO: Westview Press, 1997.
32. See Nikki K. Keddie, *An Islamic Response to Imperialism: Political and Religious Writings of Sayyid Jamal al-Din 'al-Afghani,* Berkeley: University of California Press, 1983.
33. See Yvonne Haddad, "Muhammad Abduh: Pioneer of Islamic Reform," in Ali Rahnema, (ed.), *Pioneers of Islamic Revival,* London: Zed Books, 1994, pp. 31-63.
34. Albert Hourani, *Arabic Thought in the Liberal Age 1798-1939,* Cambridge University Press, 1983, p. 138.
35. Ibid., p. 139.
36. N.R. Keddie, "An Islamic Response to Materialism: Political and Religious Writings of Sayyid Jamal al-Din al-Afhani", Berkeley: University of California Press, 1968, pp. 81-84.
37. Paul Brykczynski, "Radical Islam and the Nation: The Relationship between Religion and Nationalism in the Political Thought of Hassan al-Banna and Sayyid Qutb", *History of Political Culture,* Vol. 5, No. 1, 2005, p. 5. Accessed at http://www.ucalgary.ca/hic on 24 July, 2009.
38. A. Hourani, op. cit., p. 114.
39. John L. Esposito, op. cit., p. 61.
40. Albert Hourani, op. cit., pp.52-53.

41. Aziz Esmail, "Islam and Modernity: Intellectual Horizons", *The Muslim Almanac: The Reference Work on History, Faith and Culture, and Peoples of Islam*, Detroit: Gale Research Inc., 1995, pp. 453-457.
42. Şerif Mardin, *The Genesis of Young Ottoman Thought: A Study in the Modernization of Turkish Political Ideas*. Syracuse, NY: Syracuse University Press, 2000; and *Religion, Society and Modernity in Turkey*. Syracuse, NY: Syracuse University Press, 2002.
43. See John L. Esposito, *Voices of Resurgent Islam*, Oxford and New York: Oxford University Press, 1983; John L. Esposito, *Islam and Politics,* op. cit.; and John L. Esposito and John O. Voll, *Makers of Contemporary Islam*, New York: Oxford University Press, 2001.
44. Ali Mirsepassi, "Intellectual Discourse and the Politics of Modernisation: Negotiating Modernity in Iran", Cambridge: Cambridge University Press, 2000, p. 1.
45. Ali Mirsepassi, op. cit., p.1.
46. Said Amir Arjomand, "THE REFORM MOVEMENT AND THE DEBATE ON MODERNITY AND TRADITION IN CONTEMPORARY IRAN", *International Journal of Middle East Studies*, Vol. 34, 2002, p. 723.
47. Ibid., p. 724.
48. See Dieter Senghaas, *The Clash within Civilisations-Coming to terms with Cultural Conflicts*, London & New York: Routledge, 2002.
49. Moataz A. Fattah and Jim Butterfield, "Muslim Cultural Entrepreneurs and the Democracy Debate", *Critique: Critical Middle Eastern Studies*, Vol. 15, No. 1, 2006, pp. 49-78.
50. See Ibrahim M. Abu-Rabi, "Contemporary Islamic Intellectual History: A Theoritical Perspective", Muis Occasional Paper Series, No. 2, 2006.
51. See Nikki R. Keddie, *An Islamic Response to Imperialism: Political and Religious Writings of Sayyid Jamal ad-Din 'al-Afghani'*, Berkeley and Los Angeles: University of California Press, 1983.
52. See M. H. Kerr, *Islamic Reform-The Political and Legal Theories of Muhammad 'Abduh and Rashid Rida*, Berkeley: University of California Press, 1966.

53. A.-H. Hairi, *Shi'ism and Constitutionalism in Iran: A Study of the Role Played by the Persian Residents of Iraq in Iranian Politics*, Leiden: Lieden University Press, 1977.
54. See E. Browne, *The Persian Revolution, 1905-1909,* Cambridge: Cambridge University Press, 1910.
55. Lauren Langman & Douglas Morris, op. cit., pp. 69-70.
56. Yusuf al-Qaradawi, *Our Culture between Extroversion and Introversion,* Cairo: Dar al-Shorouq, 2000, p. 41.
57. Jamal al-Din al-Afghani (1838-1897) and Muhammad Abduh (1848-1905) argued that if Islam is understood properly and explained correctly, as was the case in the golden age of Islamic civilization, Muslims would not have been so easily defeated and dominated by European power. See Nikki R. Keddie, *Sayyid Jamāl ad-Dīn "al-Afghānī": A Political Biography.* Berkeley, CA: University of California Press, 1972; Nikki R. Keddie, *An Islamic Response to Imperialism: Political and religious Writings of Sayyid Jamal ad-Din 'al-Afghani'*, Berkeley and Los Angeles: University of California Press, 1983; R. Matthee, 'Jamal al-Din al-Afghani and the Egyptian National Debate' in: *International Journal of Middle East Studies,* Vol. 21, 1989, pp. 151-169; and E. Kedourie, *Afghani and Abduh. An Essay on Religious Unbelief and Political Activism Modern Islam,* London: Cass, 1966. The basic question that confronted these early modern Muslims reformers was Islam's compatibility with modernity. See Nasr Abu Zayd, *Reformation of Islamic Thought: A Critical Historical Analysis,* Amsterdam: Amsterdam University Press, 2006.
58. Mohamed al-Ghazali, *Constitution of Unity among Muslims,* Cairo: Dar al-Shorouq, 1997, p. 156.
59. Ali Shariati and Farhang Rajaee, *What Is to Be Done: The Enlightened Thinkers and an Islamic Renaissance,* Houston, Tex.: Institute for Research and Islamic Studies, 1986.
60. Yusuf al-Qaradawi, *Our Nation between Two Centuries,* Cairo: Dar al-Shorouq, 2000, p. 45.
61. Fazlur Rahman, *Islam and Modernity: Transformation of an Intellectual Tradition,* Chicago: University of Chicago Press, 1982, p. 34.
62. Hassan al-Turabi, *Politics and Governance,* London: Dar al-Saqqi, 2003, p. 41.

63. Nikki R. Keddie, "Intellectuals in the Modern Middle East: A Brief Historical Consideration," *Daedalus*, Vol/No. 44, 1972, p. 9.
64. Roumi and Yünüs Emre in Turkey, Ibn Sina and Sorawardi in Persia, or Ibn Rushd in Andalus.
65. A. Hourani, *A History of the Arab Peoples,* Cambridge, Mass.: The Belknap Press of the Harvard University Press, 1991, p. 168.
66. Ibrahim M. Abu-Rabi, *Contemporary Arab Thought: Studies in Post-1967 Arab Intellectual History*, London: Pluto, 2004.
67. See Richard P. Mitchell, *The Society of the Muslim Brothers*, London: Oxford University Press, 1969.
68. For important works of Seyyed Qutb see S. Qutb, Ma'alim fi al-Tariq (Signposts on the Road), (Cairo: dar al-Shuruq, 1988); S. Qutb, Al-'Adalah al-Ijtima'iyyah fi al-Islam (Social Justice in Islam), (Cairo: Dar al-Shuruq, 1980); See also L. Binder, *Islamic Liberalism: A Critique of Development Ideologies*, Chicago: University of Chicago Press, 1988.
69. A. Shari'ati, *On Sociology of Islam*, translated by H. Algar, Berkeley: Mirza Press, 1979.
70. R. Khomeini, *Islam and Revolution, Writings and Declararations of Imam Khomeini*, translated and annotated by H. Algar, Berkeley: Mizan Press, 1981.
71. See A.H.M Kirk-Greene, *On Crown Service: A History of HM Colonial and Overseas Civil services,* London: I.B. Tauris, 1999; Brian Bond, *British Military Policy Between the Two World Wars,* Oxford: Clarendon Press, 1980; and James Lunt, *Imperial Sunset: Frontier Soldiering in the 20th Century,* London: Macdonald, 1981.
72. Lauren Langman & Douglas Morris, op. cit., p. 71.
73. Karen Armstrong, *The Battle for God*, New York: Alfred A. Knopf, 2000, p. 221.
74. John L. Esposito, *Unholy War: Terror in the Name of Islam*, New York: Oxford University Press, 2002, p. 52.
75. Gilles Kepel, *Jihad: The Trail of Political Islam*, Cambridge: Harvard University Press, 2002, p. 26.
76. Sayyid Qutb and William E. Shepard, *Sayyid Qutb and Islamic Activism: A Translation and Critical Analysis of Social Justice in Islam*, Leiden: E.J. Brill, 1996, p. 2.
77. Karen Armstrong, op. cit., p. 243.

78. Charles E. Butterworth and I. William Zartman, ed., *Between the State and Islam*, Cambridge and New York: Woodrow Wilson Center Press and Cambridge University Press, 2001, p. 24. See also, Mushin Mehdi, "Modernity and Islam", in Joseph Kitagawa (ed.), *Modern Trends in World Religions*, La Salle, Ill: Open Court, 1959, pp. 1-30. See Charles E. Butterworth, "Prudence vs. Legitimacy: The Persistent Theme in Islamic Political Thought", in Ali E. Hillal Dessouki (ed.), *Islamic Resurgence in the Arab World*, New York: Praeger, 1982, pp. 84-114; and Charles E. Butterworth, "Political Islam: The Origins", in Charles E. Butterworth and I. William Zartman (ed.), *Political Islam*, a special issue of *The Annals of the American Academy of Political and Social Science*, 524, 1992, pp. 26-37.
79. Peter Gran, *Islamic Roots of Capitalism: Egypt, 1760-1840*, University of Texas Press, 1978.
80. See Reinhard Schulze 'Is There An Islamic Modernity', in *The Islamic World and the West: an Introduction to Political Cultures and International Relations*, edited by Kai Hafez, Brill, Leiden, Boston & Köln, 2000, pp. 21-32.
81. C.R. Wickham, *Mobilising Islam: Religion, Activism and Political Change in Egypt*, New York: Oxford University Press, 2003; and R.A. Euben, *Enemy in the Mirror: Islamic Fundamentalism and the Limtis of Modern Rationalism*, Princeton: Princeton University press, 1999.
82. See B. Tibi, *The Challenge of Fundamentalism,* Berkeley: University of California Press, 1998, pp. 33-118.
83. See Trish Madigan Op, op. cit.
84. Mohammad Iqbal, *The Reconstruction of Religious Thought in Islam*, Lahore: Oxford University Press, 1930/1934; J.L. Esposito, 'Muhammad Iqbal and the Islamic State', in: J.L. Esposito (ed.), *Voices of Resurgent Islam*, New York & Oxford: Oxford University Press, 1983.
85. John Cooper, "The Limits of the Sacred: The Epistemology of Abd al-Karim Soroush", in John Cooper, Ronald Nettler and Mohamed Mahmoud (eds), *Islam and Modernity: Muslim Intellectuals Respcnd*, London: I. B. Tauris, 1998, pp. 38-56.
86. See Muhammad Khalid Masud, "The Construction and Deconstruction of Secularism as an Ideology in Contemporary

Muslim Thought", *Asian Journal of Social Science,* Vol. 33, No. 3.

87. Fazlur Rahman, "The Impact of modernity on Islam", in Edward J. Jurji, (ed.), *Religious Pluralism and World Community, Interfaith and Intercultural Communication*, Leiden: Brill, 1969, p. 254.
88. For political Islam, see E. Tyan, 'Djihad', *EI2*, Vol. 2, pp. 538–40; See also James Turner Johnson and John Kelsay (eds.), *Cross, Crescent and Sword: The Justification and Limitation of War in Western and Islamic Tradition, Contributions to the Study of Religion*, No. 27, New York, Westport, CT and London: Greenwood Press, 1990; John Kelsay and James Turner Johnson (eds.), *Just War and Jihad: Historical and Theoretical Perspectives on War and Peace in Western and Islamic Traditions, Contributions to the Study of Religion*, No. 28, New York, Westport, CT and London: Greenwood Press, 1991; John L. Esposito, *The Islamic Threat* Oxford: Oxford University Press, 1999; John L. Esposito, *Unholy War: Terror in the Name of God,* Oxford: Oxford University Press, 2002; Gilles Kepel, *Jihad: The Trail of Political Islam,* Cambridge, MA: Harvard University Press, 2002; M. J. Akbar, *The Shade of Swords,* London: Routledge, 2003; Bernard Lewis, *What Went Wrong?,* op. cit.; and Jason Burke, *Al-Qaeda: Casting a Shadow of Terror,* London and New York: I. B. Tauris, 2003. For more interpretations, see John Gray, *Al-Qaeda and What It Means to be Modern,* London: Faber, 2003.
89. Albert Hourani, op. cit., p. 148.
90. See Ziya Onis and E. Fuat Keyman, "A New Path Emerges", *Journal Of Democracy*, Vol. 14, No. 2, 2003, pp. 95-107; Hakan M. Yavuz, *Islamic Political Identity in Turkey*, Oxford: Oxford University Press, 2003; and Hakan M. Yavuz, *Emergence of a New Turkey: Islam Democracy and the AK Parti*, Utah Series in Turkish and Islamic Studies, Utah: University of Utah Press, 2006.
91. See Reuel Marc Gerecht, *The Islamic Paradox: Shiite Clerics, Sunni Fundamentalists, and the Coming of Arab Democracy*, Washington, D.C.: AEI Press, 2004.
92. See Genieve Abdo, *Answering Only to God: Faith and Freedom in Twenty-First- Century Iran*, New York: Henry Holt, 2003; Stephen Fairbanks, "A New Era for Iran", *Middle East Policy*,

Vol. 5, No. 3, 1997; David Menashri, *Post-revolutionary Politics in Iran: Religion, Society, and Power*, London; Portland, OR: Frank Cass, 2001; Olivier Roy, "A Thermidor of Islamic Yuppies ? Conftict and Compromise in Iran's Politics" *Middle East Journal*, Vol. 52, No. 2, 1999, pp. 217:231; and Assef Bayat, "Islamism and Social Movement Theory", *Third World Quarterly*, Vol. 26, No. 6, 2005, pp. 891-906.

93. See Alev Cinar, *Modernity, Islam, and Secularism in Turkey : Bodies, Places, and Time*, Minneapolis: University of Minnesota Press, 2005; Gareth Jenkins, *Political Islam in Turkey,* London: Palgrave Macmillan, 2007; E. Ozdalga, *The Veiling Issue, Official Secularism and Popular Islam in Modern Turkey*, Nordic Institute of Asian Studies Nias Report Series, London: Routledge, 1997; Hakan M. Yavuz, *Islamic Political Identity in Turkey*, Oxford: Oxford University Press, 2003; Hakan M. Yavuz, *Emergence of a New Turkey : Islam Democracy and the AK Parti*, Utah Series in Turkish and Islamic Studies, Utah: University of Utah Press, 2006; Jenny B. White, *Islamist Mobilization in Turkey : A Study in Vernacular Politics,* Seattle : University of Washington Press, 2002; and Marvin Howe, *Turkey: A Nation Divided over Islam's Revival*, Boulder: Westview Press, 2004.
94. Khaled Abou El Fadl, 'Islam: Images, Politics and Paradox,' *Middle East Report,* 221, 2001.
95. J. al-'Azm Sadek, *Critique of Religious Thought,* Beirut, 1969, p.69; and Farag Fouda, *A Dialogue on Secularism,* Cairo: Dar Al-Fikr for Research and Studies, 1993, p. 6.
96. Murad Wahba, *The Virus of Retardation,* Cairo: Al-Haya'a al-Massreyya Lil-Ketab, 1998, p. 41.
97. Turki Al-Hamad, *Culture Facing the Challenges of Change,* London: Dar al-Saqi, 1993, p. 82.
98. Mohamed Arkoun, *Rethinking Islam: Common Questions, Uncommon Answers,* ed. And trans. by Robert D. Lee, Boulder: Westview, 1994, p. 3.
99. Lauren Langman & Douglas Morris, op. cit., pp. 63-65.
100. See Fawaz A Gerges, America *and Political Islam: Clash of Cultures or Clash of Interests?* Cambridge: Cambridge University Press, 1999.
101. See Ronald Inglehart, *Culture Shift in Advanced Industrial Society*, Princeton, N.J.: Princeton University Press, 1990; and

Ronald Inglehart, *Modernisation and Postmoderization: Cultural, Economic, and Political Change in 43 Societies*, Princeton, N.J.; Chichester: Princeton University Press, 1997.

102. Katerina Dalacoura, *Islam, Liberalism and Human Rights*, London: I.B. Tauris, 1998, P. 192. See also, Armando Salvatore, *Islam and the Political Discourse of Modernity*, Reading: Ithaca Press, 1997.

103. Francis Fukuyama, 'The End of History?', *The National Interest*, 16 (1981), p4. For a more recent exposition of the same theme, see Michael Mandelbaum, *The Ideas That Conquered the World: Peace, Democracy and Free Markets in the Twenty-first Century,* New York: Public Affairs, 2002.

104. Lauren Langman & Douglas Morris, op. cit., p. 63.

105. Brett Bowden, 'The "Standard of Civilization" and the Universalising Project', *Alternatives*, Vol. 29, No. 1, 2004, pp. 43-68. Even Saddam Hussein was reelected President by 100 percent of Iraqi voters shortly before his ouster, although few would consider this a genuine democratic process. Why did he bother with this curious act of mimicry?

106. See William Shepard, 'Islam and Ideology: Towards a Typology', *International Journal of Middle East Studies,* Vol. 19, No. 3, 1987, pp. 307-35. See also Iliya Harik, *Democratic Theory and Modernity: Western and Islamic Perspectives*, London and Beirut: Al Saqi Publishers, 2001.

107. See John Waterbury, 'Democracy without Democrats?,' in Ghassan Salama (ed.), *Democracy without Democrats? The Renewal of Politics in the Muslim World*, London: I.B. Tauris, 1994.

108. I. William Zartman, *Political Elites in Arab North Africa: Morocco, Algeria, Tunisia, Libya, and Egypt,* New York: Longman, 1982, p. 34.

109. Robert Fisk, *Pity the Nation: The Abduction of Lebanon*, New York: Thunder's Mouth Press/Nation Books, 2002, p. 19.

110. Hosni Mubarak, *Speeches, President Mubarak : G-15,* Cairo: Arab Republic of Egypt, Ministry of Information, State Information Service, 1992, p. 23.

111. James Schofield, *Silent over Africa: Stories of War and Genocide,* Sydney, Australia/New York: Harper Collins, 1996, p. 113.

112. Luis Martnez, *The Algerian Civil War, 1990-1998*, The Ceri Series in Comparative Politics and International Studies, New York: Columbia University Press in association with the Centre d'Etudes et de Recherches Internationales, 2000, p. 18.
113. Hafez Assad and Mustafa Talas, *That Is What Assad Said*, Dimashq: Talas, 1990, p. 82.
114. Ghassan Salamah, *Democracy without Democrats?: The Renewal of Politics in the Muslim World,* London & New York: I.B. Tauris Publishers, 1994, p. 9.
115. Bahgat Korany, 'Democracy, Islam, and the Study of Middle Eastern Politics, Arab Democratization: A Poor Cousin?,' *Political Science and Politics,* Vol. 27, No. 3, 1994, p. 512.
116. See John Voll, *Islam: Continuity and Change in the Modern World,* Syracuse: Syracuse University Press, 1995.
117. Bernard Lewis, "Islam and Liberal Democracy: A Historical Overview," *Journal of Democracy*, Vol. 7, 1996, p. 54.
118. See Jamal al-Din Afghani, Muhammad Abduh, and Jamiyat al-Urwah al-Wuthqa., *Al-Urwah Al-Wuthqa, Wa-Al-Thawrah Al-Tahririyah Al-Kubra*, 1st ed., Cairo: Dar al-Arab, 1957; Khaldun Sati Husry, *Three Reformers: A Study in Modern Arab Political Thought*, 1st ed., Beirut: Khayats, 1966; and Mohamed Omara, *The Legacy of Islam and the Scrutiny of Human Reasoning,* Cairo: Dar Al-Wehda, 1980.
119. See Mohamed. A. al-Gabri, *On the Future of Arab Culture,* (in Arabic), Beirut: Center for the Study of Arab Unity, 1987; Rachid al-Ghannouchi, *Rights of Citizenship: The Status of Non-Muslims in an Islamic State,* (in Arabic), Tunisia: Dar-Alsahwa, 1988; al-Ghazali, *Constitution of Unity among Muslims*; al-Qaradawi, *Our Culture between Extroversion and Introversion.*
120. Alan George, *Syria: Neither Bread nor Freedom,* New York: Zed Books, 2003, p. 14; A. B. S. Jafri, *The Political Parties of Pakistan,* Karachi: Royal Book Co., 2002, p.41; Ian Marsh, Jean Blondel, and Takashi Inoguchi, *Democracy, Governance, and Economic Performance: East and Southeast Asia, The Changing Nature of Democracy,* Tokyo and New York: United Nations University Press, 1999, p. 31; and A. A. Ujo, *Understanding Political Parties in Nigeria,* Kaduna, Nigeria: Klamidas Books, 2000), p. 79.
121. See Mohamed S. al-'Aawa, *On the Political System of the Islamic State,* Cairo: Dar-Alshorouk, 1989; Mohamed al-

Ghazali, *Islam and Political Dictatorship,* Cairo: Dar Al-Kotob al-Islamia, ND; M al-Khalidi, *Criticism of Democratic System (Naqdh Al-Nizzam Al-Democrratie),* Beriut: Dar Al-Jeel, 1984; Salman Bin Fahd al-'Oda, *The End of History*, Al-Salafyoon, 2000; Yusuf al-Qaradawi, *On the Fiqh of the Islamic State,* Cairo: Dar al-Shorouq, 2001; Fahmi Howaidi, *Citizens Not Dhimies: The Status of Non-Muslims in Muslims' Society,* Cairo: Dar Al-Shorouq, 1985; Mohamed Khatami, 'An Interview on CNN,' January 7, 1998; Mawdudi, *Islam Facing Modern Challenges,* Kuwait: Dar al-Qalam, 1980; Mohamed Said No'amani, 'The Feasability of Dialogue among Cultures,' (al-Jazeera.net, 2002); Sayyid Qutb, *The Future Is for This Religion,* Gary, Ind.: International Islamic Federalism of Student Organization, 1970.

122. Hisham Sharabi, *Arab Intellectuals and the West: The Formative Years, 1875-1914,* Baltimore: Johns Hopkins Press, 1970, p. 121.

123. See Mohamed S. al-Ashmawi, *Against Islamic Extremism : The Writings of Muhammad Sa`Id Al-`Ashmawy,* Gainesville: University Press of Florida, 1998; Ref'at al-Sa'eed, *Al-'Alamnya Bayyeen Al-Islam Wa Al-Ta'sloum (Secularism between Islam and Fake Islmization), Ketab Al-Ahali,* Cairo: Al-Tagou' Party in Egypt, 2001; Ahmad Baghdadi, *Renovation of the Religious Thought,* Damascus: Al Mada Publishing Company, 1999; Ahamad Abdelmo'eti Heggazi, 'From Real World to the Text and Not Vice Versa,' *Al-Ahram*, February 6, 2002; Mohamed Khalaf Allah, *The Qura'anic Foundations of Progress,* Cairo: Ketab al-Ahali, 1984; Fatima Mernissi, *Islam and Democracy: Fear of the Modern World,* Reading, Mass.: Addison-Wesley Pub. Co., 1992.

124. John O. Voll, "Islam and Democracy: Is Modernization a Barrier?", *Religion Compass,* Vol. 1, No. 1, 2007, p. 173. Quoted from Ahrar Ahmad,"Islam and Democracy: Text, Tradition, and History," *American Journal of Islamic Social Sciences*, Vol. 20, No. 1, 2003, pp. 35–36.

10

Changing Dynamics of Muslim Brotherhood in Egyptian Politics

Fazzur Rahman

Introduction

One cannot understand the various aspects of Political Islamic Movements or what is called 'Political Islam' unless one explores the *Al-Ikhwan al-Muslimeen* (the Muslim Brotherhood), founded in Egypt in 1928 by Hasan Al-Banna.

MBH was first of its kind which oriented Islamic philosophy towards politicization within the context of colonization. It asserts the fact that Islam and modernization were well-knit and intimately compatible with each other and in doing so, it needs not to compromise the generic validation of its philosophy.

One of the major objective of the MBH since its inception has been to fulfill the core objective of Islam by reshaping the society in the light of Quranic teaching and ushering into formation of true Muslim community by injecting Islamic moral values and self-righteousness.

Muslim Brotherhood's ideological foundation was based on the conviction that so-called Islamic modernist and Islamist secularist as well as *Ulema* had not been able to stem the tide of western colonization of mental and cultural make up of the masses and simultaneously have failed to contribute anything to the true development of the society. Islam of Brotherhood, was simultaneously a civilization, a way of life, an ideology and in final culmination a state in itself. [1]

MBH is considered to be the fountainhead of all Islamic movements around the world and its several outfits are operating in different parts of the Arab countries with variant names like in Kuwait, it is known as *Constitutional Movement*, in Jordan it caries the name of *Islamic Working Front*, in Palestine it is called *Hamas* and Yemeni branch carries the name of *Reform Movement* and in Algeria it is *Peace Movement*. [2]

Muslim Brotherhood during Kings Regime

The evolutionary phase of Muslim Brotherhood was well coincided with the liberation struggle against Imperialist forces in most part Asia and Africa. In the aftermath of liberation movements, a divided Muslim landscape began to assume different political shapes as a result of divergent background and variant nature of respective independent struggle. Some were aspiring to establish democracies, others were satisfied to embrace royal dynasty propped up by western powers while the rest looked to choose socialist model. [3]

British had governed Egypt since 1882 and despite being granted freedom in 1922; Egypt was forced to allow a de facto British commissioner who continued to dictate the policy to royal monarchy.

During the first decade of its existence, MBH members were mostly preoccupied with consolidating the organization and its entire energy was devoted to make it more of national character. Most of its members remained actives in promoting education and committed themselves in other domains of social services. MBH members were more interested in preaching those aspects of Islamic teaching which had its direct bearing on moral of society like prohibition of vices such as gambling, prostitution, usury, monopolies, book and song which were not in conformation with social ethics of Islam.

Since its inception, Muslim Brotherhood has passed through different shades, pattern and natures of its relation with the contemporary regimes from the kings to present day President Mubarak. The historical trajectory of its relation with the state establishment can be termed as a journey from war of attrition to that of cooperative contestation and this variation was subjected to existing political circumstances.

As noted earlier that MBH in its initial days had concentrated more and more on building the organization and shown no inclination towards playing substantial political role in national politics. When king Farouk was in power in 1940s, the role of MBH did not go beyond occasional suggestion to the king on mode of governance and on policy matter.

For example, in 1936 Al-Banna wrote a letter to President Farouk pursuing him to establish an Islamic order and advocated for more and more power to local political bodies.

Again in 1938, he is reported to have asked King Farouk to dissolve all the political parties since all had gone corrupt and proving very catalyst in dividing the society on ideological lines. [4] According to one member of executive committee of MBH, Hamid Abdul Majeed, earlier, Banna was more concerned with the religious reform within society and had hoped that at some later stage MBH would become the political voices as well. To prove the point, Banna, withdrew himself from political fray in the election of 1943 and chose to concentrate on religious and social reform. [5]

In late 1940s, MBH altered its tactical relationship with the regime and they, instead of working within the system so far, sought altogether different mechanism to facilitate the change in the regime.

This sudden change in MBH policy introduced a new era of relation between King and MBH when both were at path of confrontation. King Farouk sought its complete marginalization but full-fledged and well-organized involvement of MBH along with the Arab army in 1948 Arab-Israel war enhanced its base which had become a source of social legitimacy.

Muslim Brotherhood and Nasser

MBH was not unknown to Nassėr and way back in 1948 both Nasser and the head of MBH Banna in a meeting had agreed to support each other to create a wide and joint base of support among military free Officer and secular Muslims officer under the banner of Egyptian Self Rule. These joint efforts would be more constructive and lead to a quicker revolution than by going alone and carving an exclusive path for itself. Once librated, the Egypt could determine the best way to govern the country. [6] Later, Nasser succeeded in overthrowing the monarchy in July 1952 and with the help of Muslim Brotherhood hoped to steer the course towards the Islamic government.

But once Nasser consolidated himself into the new power bastion, he opted to distance himself from the MBH on the pretext that after Banna, he would not be bale to carry further with MBH. He had acquired power through his personal charisma since he was the first ever Egyptian to ever rule Egypt. He was being seen as a great rescuer of the masses who had history of suffering and plights and Nasser was the only hope for them. [7] He had captured the imagination of Egyptian masses and posed himself to be a single true embodiment of people's hope and aspirations. Nasser tried to silence all the voices of opposition in the name of its mission of making a modern, independent and progressive Egypt.

While MBH people had hoped that through the participation and cooperation with the new regime, the leftist, secularist, democratic and nationalist voices would be marginalizes and liquidated and thus it would pave the way for greater space for the MBH, which would culminate over the years in taking over the political reign of Egypt.

Showing his secular Pan-Arab nationalist posture, in no lesser time Nasser made it categorical that he had neither desire to introduce an Islamic order in Egypt nor was ready to tolerate the powerful dissent to his authoritarian rule. Now, first and foremost priority for Nasser and his Free Officers was to stifle permanently the voice of discontent.

MBH was rebuffed with Nasser's ensuing policy and felt deceived. Nasser's growing anti MBH stance was much to do with mounting pressure of Coptic Christina and other Muslim secular forces who had no fascination for promotion of any kind of exclusive Islamic and had no desire for an Islamic Egypt.

Perhaps this was the beginning of war of attrition between the Nasser and MBH when undermining the legitimacy of each other became main components of their political plank.

Now both were trying to carve out an independent political space for themselves apart from posing to be the true voices of the masses and real representative of people.

The shifting nature of relationship between two can be judged by the fact that one of the radical face and mentor of MBH in 1950s, Sayyed Qutb had once told "I was working with Free Officer till February 1953 but when my ideas and thought seemed to be clashing with them, I started maintaining distance from them". [8]

Gradually, Nasser had started ruling the country with the notion that it was army rather than masses that would protect his power. Slowly but steadily, he was able to eliminate all existing political parties and had become the sole master of political power in Egypt. [9]

According to one political analyst, Osama Ghazali, Nasser had skillfully exploited existing regional and global political situation in his favor and was bale to marginalize the other centers of power like MBH. [10] In the name of social and economic development, Nasser had appropriated all political power in his hand and justified the dictatorial style of leadership for sake of progress.

Nasser's reliance on his charisma and politics of sloganeering did not last longer since it not helped to deliver at social and economic front. His much hyped policy of land reform and comprehensive socialism was meant to benefit merely tiny section of society who later emerged as bourgeois enjoying bursting control over political and social institution like religious endowment, trade union, volunteer organizations, and student unions. There was no sign of convergence between his promise of national integration and social justice and performance.

Whereas MBH's notion of civil society was in complete contrast to political, social, religious and ideological forces that controlled the Egyptian society. But MBH point of departure was the welfare of the masses and their assimilation into the society that preserves their political, religious and cultural right and privileges. They did not perceive Nasserism as a radical departure from the conditions prevailing in pre-revolution period.

The post revolutionary social and economic plight of the common masses had provided a fertile ground for MBH to assert itself politically and helped as an outlet for expression of their grievances.

For first two years after the revolution, they made every attempt to have common working relation with Nasser and some of the MBH members even joined his party, *Liberation Rally* formed by Nasser. But later, they found that Nasser's policy was not only different but fundamentally antagonistic to Islam and annihilation of MBH constituted one of the major elements of his policy.

To sort out the matter, a meeting took place between MBH and Nasser on 30th of July 1954, where Nasser rejected all the previous demands of MBH and refused any further cooperation with MBH leadership. It was same Nasser who before the 1952 revolution used to extend his ear to very advice coming from MBH and one of its members is reported to have told him in a personal meeting: "That we consider yours as a reformist movement and if you do well you do it for the country and if you deviate from your mission, we will give you guidelines in the light of Quran". [11] Given this apathetic instance of Nasser vis-à-vis MBH, they were forced to review its relation with Nasser.

A conflict was nevertheless inevitable as Free Officer was in no mood to allow any voices for MBH and after a series of incidents of conspiracy and confrontation, relation between two broke down on 26 October 1954 and so the process of demolition of the single existing agency (MBH) between the masses and the state started.

This treachery and treason on the part of Nasser jolted the psychic of leadership and played a critical role in shaping the future political and intellectual outlook of MBH leadership towards Nasserism and the newly established political institutions. It was at this stage that several members of MBH resigned form the Liberation Rally of Nasser.

Nasser's growing antagonism toward MBH can be assessed from a fact that in 1953, he enacted a legislation authorizing Education Minster to transfer those faculty members merely on the suspicion of having any kind of affiliation with MBH or Communist group to non-teaching department and made every endeavors through series of legislation to deprive MBH from capturing political space in university campuses or and local bodies. [12]

In February, 1954, large number of members and followers of MBH were sent to jail following a huge protest and strike in campuses against Nasser anti-democratic policy. [13] Again in October 1954, large scale arrest took place when a member of MBH allegedly tried to assassinate Nasser in the city of Alexandria during a public speech. But the Brethren countered the charges claiming that it was a hatched conspiracy of itself to malign the Islamic forces and to exterminate this organization-a powerful civil society between the masses and the Nasserite autocratic state.

With the intension of according legitimacy to his regime, Nasser had established a legislative councils (Nationalist Union) in 1957, and later this experience was repeated in 1960, 64 and in 1969 again. In election of 1957, Executive Council of Nationalist Union (headed by Nasser himself) approved merely 1748 candidates out of total 2508 who had filed the nomination. The main objective of rejection of such a large number of nominations was to prevent MBH sympathizers form joining the fray and stop them from reaching to

Assembly. [14] The elected Assembly of 1957 had a total number of 342 members where 94 were from Army Officers group, 103 from Professional group and 124 from farmers and workers. No representation was given to group having religious leaning and more than that, all elected members had prior state blessing since it was not possible for them to reach at their own. [15] Not merely this, he had reigned in the entire professional unions where MBH could seek no membership and they were prohibited from contesting the election and not allowed to become the member of any decision making authority.

Between1954 and 1969, anyone suspected to have any kind of affiliation with MBH was not allowed to contest the election of any political body .According to a new legislation enacted by Nasser, it was obligatory for all those seeking the election of professional union to have advance membership of his Nationalist Union (later became Arab Socialist Union). He had dissolved Lawyers and Journalist Associations several times in past and was not prepared to accommodate voice of protest against him. [16]

But the defeat of Egypt led Arab world in 1967 war against Israel created a crisis of legitimacy for Nasser. This defeat resulted in a drastic failure of his nationalist and socialist project. This defeat made the encounter with the Self more painful than with the others which caused a different course of relationship between religion, state and the society. This defeat touched the most sensitive emotional and psychological foundation of people of Egypt and this particular moment was blessing in disguise for MBH. [17]

Return to religion was a natural outcome of this defeat causing an impulse towards new social and political action. Now MBH were well-situated to assert themselves both politically an ideologically. Nasser was no more an unchallenged autocrat and his oppressive policy was no more prized for him. Masses at large were looking for a alternate model of validation where MBH found itself well-placed to heal the mental trauma inflicted by the defeat and fulfill aspiration of the masses.

Autocratic policy of Nasser of 1950s and 60s was completely overhauled and replaced by gradual opening of political space for voices of opposition and particularly to MBH who were the strongest political voices after the state in Egypt.

Now MBH joined the mainstream street political movement demanding free and fair election in the campus and called for freedom of press. They also demanded withdrawal of Police forces from university premises. Nasser was forced to relax the laws regarding election of professional Unions. Through his famous March Declaration of 1968, he introduced some major changes in his policy aimed to provide political spaces for opposition which was not likely the case before the defeat of 1967. [18] Large numbers of MBH cadres were set free form jail and according to a contemporary repot, there were only 140 members left in jail in 1970 when Sadat came to power after departure of Nasser. [19]

The post 1967 period paved the way for a traditional religious legitimacy of state that MBH was seeking since Nasser came to power. By 1969, full-fledged political training camps run by MBH had become active and socio-cum-political activism re-witnessed in mosques and university campuses. [20] The post-defeat juncture of relationship between Nasser and MBH was no longer of loggerhead.

But it was rather transformed into placid and calm political battle, where former was battling for his survival and later was asserting to thrive in brewing environment of political frustration.

But during most of the tenure of Nasser, MBH could not capitalize on the existing poor economic situation and oppressive political system as they were unable to enhance its political and social base since most of its members were in jail while he was in power.

Anwar Sadat and Assertion of Muslim Brotherhood

Anwar Sadat had inherited a politically broken, ideologically defeated and economically grimed Egypt when he had succeeded Nasser in September 1970. In his key mission to pose himself a different patriot, he introduced a new political culture promising that he would seek legal legitimacy instated of traditional or charismatic one. Within few years after coming into power, he introduced some constitutional amendment declaring that no political discrimination would be made merely for one's political, religious and ideological affiliation. In 1976, he introduced a limited multi-party system (a major shift form earlier single party system in form of Arab Socialist Union introduced by Nasser), were introduced. [21]

In order to get rid of Nasserists within Egyptian political system Sadat adopted the policy of co-existence with MBH. Integration of MBH in his design of political system helped him to larger extent in elimination of influential Leftist power block in the country. [22] He adopted policy of accommodation vis-à-vis religious forces with the notion that his Islam-driven policy would accord him a political legitimacy that he required urgently to consolidate himself in power.

All MBH prisoners were set free and the exiled members of MBH were allowed to come back to Egypt. They were also allowed to resume the publication of their banned magazine and journals. They reopened their offices and headquarters in different parts of country which were put under ban during Nasser's regime. [23]

The priority for MBH after they had found in Sadat a future friend was to obtain official recognition from the state which they had been deprived of since 1954. However, Sadat had made his intention quite clear announcing that he would seek all cooperation and coordination of MBH but would not retreat from the policy of his predecessor as far as according official rank is concerned. According to a Journal, *Lawaaul-Islam*, sympathizer of MBH, only between 1977 and 1990, for more than forty times, the issue of revoking the ban against MBH was raised with several Egyptian courts but in vain. [24]

MBH had welcomed new party law of 1976 expressing its wishes to join the main stream national politics. But there were difference of opinions among decision makers within MBH where one section advocating that MBH's role in Egyptian society as an intellectual and Islamic movement was more cultural than political. The core philosophy and the true objective of the movement can't be forsaken for sake of official status. On the other hand, there were few who were strongly propagating in favor of seeking legal protection from the state either by working as a political block or as a true Islamic movement. [25]

At this stage MBH had the hope that President Sadat would allow MBH to enter in the Parliament on the ground of being a major socio-political forces in Egyptian, if not as a political party in its narrow literal sense. But Sadat showed no inclination of this sort hinting that law of the land does not allow political formation in the name of religion. Instead, he offered a suggestion asking them to merge with one of the existing three major political parties of the day.

MBH countered this argument of President Sadat claiming that organization did not represent a religious movement in its generic sense but rather, it worked with the mission of orienting the national polity towards Islam. They also pointed out that since Egypt in its 1971 constitution had categorically declared Islam to be religion of state, so it was not in keeping with the spirit of the constitutional to ban the party merely for its religious leaning. It also promised to seek the constitutional and democratic means to achieve power. [26]

In the first election of 1976 in Sadat's regime, some members of the MBH fought the election under the banner Arab Socialist Party, as suggested by Sadat earlier. Six of its members made to the Egyptian parliament but to preserve the distinct religious character of the movement, it refused the offer to join the advisory council of the Parliament and meanwhile refused third consecutive offer by President Sadat to accord MBH a status of charitable organization. [27]

Large number of students in and around the campus was highly impressed with the ideology of MBH and more with their charitable work like providing books to poor students, residential complexes at lesser prices, transport facility for the students and other financial assistance. Student Unions supported by MBH in different colleges were providing much better service in comparison to those Nasserists who had earlier command of the Unions. In late 70s, several members from other Islamic organizations left their respective organization and joined the MBH.

In later half of his presidency Sadat had given free hands to Islamist forces and even security forces were not allowed to intervene in their political activities. This lenient policy on the part of the state towards MBH at one point had caused a rift between Sadat and higher authorities within the security forces.

The new constitution put forward by him recognized Islam as a source of legislation. In this situation, MBH was well-posited to mobilize the masse in the name of Islam and their task became easier when constitutional amendment of 1980 declared Islamic Sharia, 'the' source of legislation.

Number of Islamic publications increased many-fold and its members had captured a considerable political space for themselves and exert further pressure on President for complete execution of Islamic laws in country. [28] They started bringing out daily and weekly leaflets highlighting the policies and program of MBH and pointing out its political and social achievements.

In continuation of his policy of leaving the legacy of Nasser behind, he introduced new open economic policy (*Infitah*). The opening of national economy to foreign investors and traders had created a new bourgeoisie like Nasser's socialist land reform had introduced a landed bourgeoisie in Egypt. Gradually, newly created economic class (*Fat Cats*) had become the political priority for Sadat.

The emergence of new financial bourgeoisie and weakening of Sadat's control over the state was going simultaneously. This new economic policy initiated by President Sadat proved very valuable for MBH on both short term and long term. According to one member of MBH, this organization benefited most from the new economic policy since it helped to accumulate large amount of remittance from Egyptian workers as donation. [29]

The new economic initiative had led to accumulation of wealth in few hands causing rise in illiteracy, inequality, unemployment and unrest and anxiety in Egyptian society. Large numbers of masses were struggling to have one time food or cloths, and houses while small beneficiary were reaping all the fruits. MBH emerged to be one of the vehement critics of the policy and were mobilizing the masses against the regime of Sadat. They alleged that slogan of Faithful President by Sadat had proved hollow and the policy, according to them, had created a class who were exploiting Islam without knowing its true spirit.

The famous economic riot of 1977 had created an explosive situation in Egypt when state had been completely taken over by the rioters. MBH were at the forefront to capitalize such a volatile situation in its favor and launched a full-fledged campaign against the state and blamed the failed economic policy for the present unrest and instability in the country. [30]

The most impulsive phase of relation between state and MBH came when President Sadat landed in Israeli Knesset leading to signing of the Camp David Agreement in 1979. Sadat took U turn in his policy that had angered all the Islamic forces who termed it an act of treachery and called it completely an un-Islamic act. The Islamist forces he had nurtured and harbored for last one decade turned against him and became the biggest threat to his political survival.

Sadat responded to the rejection of MBH of his new policy with the large scale crackdown when hundred of MBH members were arrested. At the same time, a new development in Iran in form of Islamic revolution had given new momentum to MBH when it had captured the political imagination of the masses.

When Sadat was still in the midst of evolving his new device to counter the voice of opposition, he was assassinated by a fanatic member of Islamic group known as Jamaat-al-Jihad in October, 1981 and succeeded by Husne Mubarak.

During Sadat's regime, MBH enjoyed a substantial degree of freedom and received a considerable amount of cooperation unlike in the regime of Nasser. The nature of cooperative contestation between two helped MBH rebuild the organization which helped to obtain, if not official legitimacy, social legitimacy. They were able to invoke its religious leaning, augment its base and register it presence felt in different universities and professional unions. This ascendancy and increasing popularity of MBH proved catalyst in weakening Sadat political bases following the signing of Camp David Agreement.

Muslim Brotherhood in Era of President Husne Mubarak

Unlike his predecessor Sadat, Husne Mubarak did not belong to the generation of Free Officer. When Mubarak was made Vice President, in 1975, the intimacy between Sadat and MBH was at its peak and in this friendly environment Mubarak also had the opportunity to interact with its member.

Mubarak first major objective was to bring the stability in the country which had slipped into turmoil following assassination of Sadat and he could have not achieved that without being tolerant to opposition forces. He developed intimate relation with Al-Azhar and MBH to keep away the more radical Islamic forces from political scene.

Mubarak's political initiative of 1981 had once again awakened the hope of MBH to obtain official recognition. But again MBH met with frustration when found that new regime had not changed its instance of previous one.

Mubarak had followed the policy of concession towards MBH like his previous by allowing resumption of publication of two of the MBH Journals, *Al-Itasam* and *Al-Mukhtar Al-Islami* . He set free thousands of Islamist thrown in prison during last days of Sadat with the intention of mobilizing these force behind him to contain the extremist Islamic forces. He also revoked the law imposed by Sadat banning Lawyer association. His lenient and liberal policy towards these political organizations was more to do with his attempt to deviate the people's attention from his policy of rapprochement with Israel and United States. [31]

The election law of 1983 introduced by Mubarak had emphasised for promotion of party culture but purely in existing political setting which compelled MBH leadership to rethink over its strategy. A small section of the MBH was in favor of achieving the status of political party with the intention of getting legal protection. [32] After accession of Mubarak, two major changes took place on policy front of MBH. Unlike 1970s, now they were strictly in favor of political participation as an independent organization in an alliance with one of the existing legal party.

MBH at this stage was representing different contours of Islamism that reflected the different aspiration of old and new generation. Dissention and differences over the establishment of the party and the route and procedure to be taken was quite obvious. [33] Those who advocated for participation in election argued that no longer can MBH work as a secret body and both political activities and organization building can go together. According to them, MBH needed more and more expertise and experience in national politics which could be acquired through political participation alone. They were of the view that MBH presence in parliament would help bring legal reform and would provide an opportunity to interact with government representative to explain the true aims and agenda of MBH. [34]

MBH again committed itself to rebuilding of the organization and laid down a comprehensive program and policy to enlarge its mass base availing the neutral policy of Mubarak. At this stage, they also brought about decentralization of power structure within organization where several other state and local units were enjoying some level of autonomy. Organizational election was also introduced to bring about internal democracy and official were no more appointed merely on the ground of their age and experiences.

The Islamisation of financial syndicates along with social services was new methods introduced to reach to the masses. MBH found these syndicates as an arena to expand among different segment of the society. [35] Several members of MBH started Islamic investment bank and other Islamic Estate enterprises which were sparing some share to help the organization.

Despite the fact that MBH had no official recognition, it was allowed by Mubarak to contest the election of 1984 in alliance with the Wafd Party. For the first time in its history, MBH entered into parliament as an opposition block with alliance of Wafd Party which had won total of 58 seats and the share of MBH was eight seats.

This time, MBH were more interested explaining its political position in parliament and according to one member of the MBH in parliament, "We are not worried about the size of our number here but what is important for us at this moment is to make our presence realized by both people and state". [36]

Unlike its past history, MBH was now had a different plan in national politics and had no apprehension in forging political alliance with its ideological and political adversaries extending all cooperation to communist and Nasserite as well.

The success of MBH had opened a new room for the debate among leadership to become a full-fledged political party. This was not an easy choice for MBH as they had always looked down upon the political culture based on party system. Some argued that all means were closed for MBH and if wanted to be heeded on the national issues, it would have to become a political party.

To discuss the matter further, a special committed was formed to look into and concerned committee proposed two possible names for the party, *Egypt Reform Party* and other *Shura Party*. Both had detailed political agenda for the MBH. At the same time there were some who strangely advocated for mergence of MBH with other parties. [37]

By late 1980s, MBH had emerged as a force which can't be any more pushed aside since it had established itself as major political voice, if not in national politics, at least among student unions and other professional trade unions through intense social engagement with different segment of the society. Their voice was no more confined to seek the recognition for itself alone but they were playing an important role in shaping the structure of the political field. [38]

The opposition forced Mubarak to amend the election laws in December 1986 allowing the independent candidates (10 percent of total seats were reserved for independent candidates) also to contest the election. Assembly was dissolved and fresh election took place in February, 1987. This time MBH made alliance with Labor party and Ahrar Party and enhanced its performance by gaining 36 seats in comparison to eight seats gained last time. [39] MBH accused the state machinery of election rigging and claimed that it would have got more than 150 seats if transparency would have been exercised by the state.

It was for the frost time in its history when MBH emerged as the single largest opposition party in Egyptian politics. With this startling performance, MBH had full belief that now it would be recognized as a political party (according to party law, any party getting more than twenty seats entitled to register itself as an independent party) .

This time MBH as an opposition was more vocal and most of its debate revolved around application of Islamic laws, violation of human rights and poor heath and educational condition in the country. At this stage of its political existence, they were well aware of the fact that any direct confrontation with the regime would spoil its political future. Extending supports to President Mubarak for his second term in 1987was also a part of the policy of not being at logger head with regime at a stage when they were still struggling to obtain official recognition.

End of 1980s had witnessed sudden rise of extremist activities in Egypt. These extremist forces were voicing anger against MBH's support to Mubarak and his policy of combating terrorism. Only in 1988, more than nine incident of fighting between member of extremist Jama-al-Islamiyah and Security Forces was recorded following the attack on two former Ministers and some journalists. [40]

In its attempt to counter the extremist voices, state itself adopted the policy of Islamisation of its institution. It started Islamic daily and weekly like *Lawau-al-Islam* and *Aqeedati* and extended the hours of TV and Radio program devoted to religious teaching. Erstwhile Information Minister himself used to give talk on TV on Islamic issues.

Earlier, state had anticipated MBH to extend its full cooperation in its fight against extremist forces but MBH was not prepared to lose its social base and always came with well-guarded reaction to state policy. MBH was trying to avail rising tide of extremism to exert additional pressure on the government to get legal status by conveying a message that they were true voice of Ism and as long as state did not recognize them, they would have to face these extremist forces. [41]

This strategy of MBH had infuriated the regime and decided to review its policy towards it. State apprehension was growing against MBH and was blamed for this distrust between government and Islamic forces. Despites growing political intervention of state institution, MBH continued to grow and expand its bases among different unions and political bodies.

The policy of Egyptian government during first Gulf war and rising inflation and foreign investment as a result of World Bank and IMF program of structural brought MBH to full confrontation with the government. Mubarak government under pressure of IMF and World Bank was particularly worried about the growing economic strength of MBH and special measures were adopted to check its funding by cracking down against several Islamic investment bank run by MBH members.

1990s witnessed a fundamental change in relation between MBH and President Mubarak which can be well described as a shift from cooperation and coexistence to struggle and contestation for political legitimacy. MBH in the first half of the last decade of 20th century was committed to capture the political space and was looking for the politicization of its social legitimacy acquired through its social services and it was working constantly to carve out its political space among different political and nonpolitical formation.

1990s was also the decade of major political development at domestic, regional and global level. It witnessed the end of Cold War and emergence of US as the single global power that was imposing a new world order and calling for normalization of relation with Israel. United State along with the regimes in the region was well aware of the fact that Islamic forces would be quite opposed to this new geo-strategic arrangement proposed by United States. At the regional level, government was alarmed by the victory of Islamist in the election in Algeria and growing popularity of Hamas which had organizational link with MBH.

1990s also witnessed a democratic wave in greater part of the globe. Arab regimes were also asked to bring democratic reform in respective country. It was the decades when a large number of Human Right Groups had become quite active and raising its voice for more political freedom and civil liberty. They were exerting constant pressure on all regimes not to suppress political dissent. Political globalization had its roots in freedom of press and freedom of expression and political mobilization serving as the cornerstone of civil society. Given this changing context of global polity, which had brought partial political liberalization in Egypt was well received by MBH to assert its religious and political identity to expand itself further.

In particular, the first *Intifadah* of 1987 in Palestine had come as a blessing in disguise for MBH. All Arab regime in general and Egypt in particular were facing all sort of criticism and were under intense social pressure to review its policy in the region. MBH did not allow this moment to go un-availed and it emerged as true platform for expression of masses anger.

MBH decided to boycott the election of 1990 on the ground of apathetic attitude of the government in last Parliament. They were more frustrated by introduction of new clause by which candidate was only allowed to fight as an independent and not under any party banner. But they did not leave its fight for legal recognition. During the absence of five years from Parliament (1990-1995), they concentrated on political activities and were able to secure majority in several unions like Lawyers, Doctors and Engineers unions.

Despite being absent from Parliament, they always took political stand and condemned Iraqi attack on Kuwait falling in line with the stand of Egyptian government. But they also opposed the attack of US led forces against Iraq which was supported by the government of Egypt.

MBH also exploited the frustration and plight of masses caused by new economic policy and partial withdrawal of the state form economic domain. It became more active in field of economic development where it extended all kind of social services through the chain of its chartable associates. Meanwhile, another fresh attempt was made in direction of forming a political party, *Hizbul Amal* but there was no consensus so far over nature of independent political party. [42]

MBH decision to participate in the election of 1995 was shocking for the regime. Apart from 180 MBH members who entered into fray, several others fought under different political banner. This was alarming for the government and it could not have allowed further consolidation of MBH as political forces.

Mubarak was also scared of the fact that major gain for MBH in this election would spoil his chance for his fourth term later in 1999. Security forces entered to prevent them from entering into political fray and as a result only one member could make it to parliament who himself later was ousted allegedly because of his association with some illegal party. [43] The second half of 1990s saw an open confrontation between MBH and the state and for the first time in era of Mubarak, hundred of MBH activists thrown in jail and several were tried in military court which had its only precedent during Nasser's regime. There was complete ban on its activities and all Islamic investment banks were put under scanner.

In the face of growing coercion of state against MBH, two stream of opinions emerged within; one called for open confrontation while other called for restrained policy and devote its activism to those space where state had no stake.

The parliamentary election of 2000 was unique in its sense that it was held under complete judicial administration. MBH also participated in the election without alliance with any party. It filed total 75 candidates and all were independent. This time their agenda was not radical and slogan, "Islam is the only solution", was completely absent form the campaign. This was partially because of fear of the state machinery they had experienced in 1995. [44] Despite the absent of free and friendly environment, MBH was able to secure 18 seats and had emerged once again as single largest opposition party.

The Parliamentary election of 2005 came at a time when President Mubarak was also planning to become the president for the fourth consecutive term which was rejected by all opposition parties including MBH. This was also an era when US under its policy of *Promotion of Democracy in the Middle East,* was calling for more and more transparency in the democratic election of the country and respect the voices of descent.

The election of 2005 proved to be a catalyst fro MBH when its 88 candidates won seats out of total 161 who had contested the election. The regime was unable to digest this major political victory of MBH. This election proved the level of social entrenchment and political popularity of it. Given this political ascendancy, changing environment in the region after Hamas victory in Palestine and retreat of US from its agenda of political reform in the Middle East. Egyptian government evolved a comprehensive plan to curtail the influence of MBH as a political force and contract its political space in the country. A comprehensive constitutional amendment was introduced in 2007 granting sweeping power to security forces and banning all political parties with religious or any particular ideological leaning. [45]

To counter this oppressive measures of state, MBH decided to form a political party in August 2007 and there was nothing innovative in its decision of forming a political party. In past twenty five years, they had decided at least five times to form a political party; first *Shura party* in 1987, *Al-Islah* in 1991, *Al-Amal* in 1994, *Al-Wast* in 1996.The constant decision of MBH in 1980s and 1990s to form political party was out of its will to translate its social authenticity into political legitimacy.

MBH distributed the first draft of policy and program of its new proposed party among some selected group of intellectuals. Major part of this document was devoted to explanation of nature of state stipulating that state would be civic state and people would be true source of sovereignty.

State will fully protect the interest of the minority and will provide complete religious freedom. The other prominent issue that surfaced in the draft was about nature of the relation between the MBH as a movement and as a party. Small section of MBH called for complete transformation of MBH into a political entity in which the head of the MBH organization would act like the head of MBH party as well.

The nature of MBH polity between 2000 and 2007 was more guided by the domestic, regional and global development. The augmenting role of Human Right Activist and call for Free Press was tactically exploited by Islamic forces. Deep rooted penetration of electronic media and growing level of consciousness of masses played very essential role in the process of mobilization. MBH was no more a force operating at the periphery and in isolation but had become active at several fronts. It also expanded its social network as a strategy to escape the state gaze and had become proactive in its interface with state institution as well.

Conclusion

In the preceding pages, I have analyzed the evolving journey of Muslim Brotherhood from an Islamic organization dedicated to task of creating a religious society to emerging as a national political force. An organization which was opposed to party culture in 40s and 50s took several initiatives later in 80s and 90s to have the party of its own. We have also noticed that for the last three decades it has carved out an independent and exclusive political space for its own and struggling very hard to capture the contested political zone of the state.

The basic means and ways sought by MBH to attain political power was to develop a well-spread network of social services organizations for all segments of the society ranging from students to working class to women to elite professional. These organization and syndicates worked as an outlet for expression of social grievances highlighting the weakness and failure of the government and meanwhile working as a pointer for the state.

As far as the nature of relation between MBH and state is concerned, it is well marked by uneven pattern and it has its own ups and downs depending upon the nature and policy of the contemporary regime. For example, President Nasser in first half of 1950s had chosen to have the policy of coexistence and tolerance towards MBH. But when he consolidated himself and become politically unchallenged, MBH became the first of his victim and abandoned all policy of accommodation.

Unlike Nasser, President Sadat was quite friendly with MBH and that was also a well-guarded political shift. Sadat wanted to leave the legacy of Nasser behind and was of the view that his political legitimacy resides in these Islamic groups.

The era of Mubarak witnessed the similar nature and pattern of relation between two. The first decade of Mubarak tenure as president is well characterized by policy of coexistence and cooperation while nearly next two decade can be termed as a period of cooperative contestation and confrontation. In particular, the era of Mubarak is an era of constant struggle between the two in order to acquire political legitimacy where the former is seeking the legitimacy from the state and the later through its social services.

MBH since its participation in Egyptian politics in 1970s had adopted a strategy of adaptation with the existing circumstances and has always worked within the limit of the state institutional and never opted for unconstitutional means to capture the state apparatus.

Throughout its existence, it has worked as counterbalance force against the radical segment of Islamic groups in Egypt like *Jamaat Islami* and served to maintain the political balance and neutralization of tension caused by these radical forces. [46]

Notes

1. Ibrahim Abu M. *Contemporary Arab Thought Rabi*. (London : Pluto Press, 2004), p. 65.
2. Dr. Hisham Al-Auzi, *Siraa ala-Al-Shariah Al-Ikhwanul-Muslimun wa Mubarak 1984-2007* (Beirut: Mrkaz-Dirasatyl Wahdatul Wataniyah), p. 52-53.
3. Akbar.S. Ahmad, *A Journey into Islam*, Viking India, 2007, p. 12.
4. Mir Zohair Hussain, *Global Islamic Politics* (New York: Harper Collins Publisher, 1995, p. 53-54.
5. Al-Auzi, op. cit. p. 82.
6. Abdullah Imam, *Abd-al Nasser wa al-ikwan-al Muslimoon: al-Unf-al-Din Fi Misr* (Abdul Nasser and Muslim Brotherhood: Islamic Violence in Egypt) (Cairo: Dar-al-khiyal Printer, 1997(83-90).
7. Al-Auzi, op. cit., p. 68.
8. Fattah, 310.
9. Ninette. S. Fahmy *The Politics of Egypt: State- Society Relationship* (London: Routledge, 2002), p. 33.
10. Al-Auzi, op. cit., p. 69.
11. Salah Abdul Fattah Khalidi, *Sayyed Qutb: Min-al-milaad –ilal-Istishhad* (Syria: Daral-Qalam, 1991), p. 294.
12. Al-Auzi, , op. cit., p. 71.
13. Kirk J. Beattie, *Egypt during Nasser Years: Ideology, Politics and Civil Society* (Boulder, CO; west View Press , 1994), p. 139.
14. Al-Auzi, op. cit., p. 71.
15. Ali Din Halal, *tatawur-al-Nizam-al-Siyasi Fi Misr* 1803-1998 (Cairo: Mrkaz-al-Buhoos wa-al-Dirasat-al-Siyasiyah, 1997), p.182-183.
16. Kirk J. Beattie, *Egypt during Nasser Years: Ideology, Politics and Civil Society* (Boulder, CO; West View Press, 1994), p. 139.
17. Ibrahim Abu Rabi, op. cit., p. 61.
18. Al-Auzi, op. cit., p. 73.
19. Sami Sharf, *Abdul Nasser: Kaifa Hakama Misr* (Cairo: MAdbuli-al-Saghir, 1996).
20. Dr. Zohurul Bari, *Re-emergence of Muslim Brotherhood in Egypt* (New Delhi: Lancer Books, 1995), pp. 82-83.
21. Al-Auzi, op. cit., pp. 75-76.
22. Al-Auzi, op. cit., p. 75.

23. Mahmood Jami, *Aaraftu Sadat* (Cairo: Al-Maktab-al-Misri-al-Hadith, 1999), p. 189.
24. Al-Auzi, op. cit., p. 79.
25. Al-Auzi, op. cit., p. 80.
26. Al-Auzi, op. cit., p. 81.
27. Al-Auzi, op. cit., p. 83.
28. Al-Auzi, op. cit., p. 77.
29. Yvonne Haddad, *Islamic Awakening in Egypt*, Arab Studies Quarterly. Vol. 9, no.3 1987), p. 255.
30. Saad Eddin Ibrahim, *An Islamic Alternative in Egypt*: *The Muslim Brotherhood and Sadat*, in Saad Eddin Ibrahim , *Egypt, Islam and Democracy - Critical Essay with a new Postscript* (Cairo: New York: American University in Cairo Press, 2000), pp. 35-40.
31. Al-Auzi, op. cit., p. 103.
32. Al-Auzi, op. cit., p. 99.
33. Salwa Ismail, *Rethinking Islamic Politics: Culture, the State and Islam* (London: I.B. Tauris, 2003), p. 29.
34. Al-Auzi, op. cit., p. 101.
35. Salwa Ismail, op. cit. p. 29.
36. Al-Auzi, op. cit., p. 125.
37. Al-Auzi, op. cit., pp. 134-135.
38. Salwa Ismail, op. cit., p. 33.
39. Al-Auzi, op. cit., p. 168.
40. Al-Auzi, op. cit., p. 174.
41. Mustafa Mashhoor, *At-tiyarul-al-Islami wa Daurahul-Fil-Bana* (Cairo: Darul-al-Tauzee wa-al-Nashr-al-Islamiyah, 1987), p. 45-46.
42. Al-Auzi, op. cit., p. 208.
43. Al-Auzi, op. cit., p. 239.
44. Al-Auzi, op. cit., p. 267.
45. Al-Auzi, op. cit., p. 272.
46. Salwa Ismail, op. cit., p. 33.

11

Islamic Resurgence in the Age of Globalization and Democracy: Hamas' Changing Strategies in Palestinian National Movement

Rajeesh Kumar P. P.

Introduction

The entering of Islamic Political Movements into the realm of mainstream electoral politics has intensified the debate between Islam and democracy. The practical experience of these movements with liberal democracy inevitably raises the question of compatibility of Islamic values with modern democracy. The phenomenon of globalization and the Western led process of democratization have also contributed immensely to this debate. Against this backdrop, it is worth to examine the socio-political relevance of Islamic movements in West Asia, their strategies and ideals in managing the challenges brought by the twin process; globalization and democratization.

The participation of Islamic Political Movements in the electoral democracy has created a new space to debate over the 'incompatibility thesis' between Islam and Democracy. In a peripheral view, it would be seen as triumph of liberal democracy over the Islamic values. But, these developments also shed lights on the flexibility of Islamic movements to accommodate the values of Western liberal democracy. It proves that the democratic values are inherent in the Islamic principles and demonstrates the popular legitimacy of the movements in the region. Moreover, it help us to counter the 'incompatibility thesis' developed by orthodox West and authoritative Islamic rulers [1]. It was a great setback on Huntington's prophecy of 'clash of civilization and the constructed 'Islamic threat' in the minds of West. It also challenges the perception supported by a sizable academic literature that speaks about the radical, undemocratic character of contemporary Islamic ideology. (Kedourie, 1992; Kramer, 1993; Huntington, 1996; Tibi, 1998)

This paper seeks to place the changing ideologies and strategies of Hamas towards Palestinian national movement. The central argument of this study is that the Islamic movements are genuinely receptive in nature for accepting and accommodating the values of the liberal democracy. The paper has four parts. The first two section will focuses on the Islam and Democracy debate and the Islamic resurgence in the twentieth century West Asia. The next part deals with a case study of Hamas; its origin, strategies in the Palestinian national struggle and its Islamic credentials. Finally the paper examines the democratic experiences of the movement and its changing strategies.

Linking Islam, Democracy and Globalization

In the wake of September 11 attack there has been a heightened focus on Islam in general and resurgent Islam in particular. The incident put forth a quest to interpret and reinterpret Islam in different ways. Islam inevitably becomes a new centre of attention, both in positive and in negative terms. Some scholars even begin to see September 11 as an evidence for the 'clash of civilization' between Islam and the West. Such a feeling and the suspicion was not developed in a vacuum. It emerged out of a constructed but an inherent and embedded belief in the incompatibility between Islam and the West. It highlights the emergence of a new reciprocity rooted in anguish and hatred.

Islam's compatibility with democracy is much discussed and contested one. It became one of the main features of today's Islamic political thought, media and political circles worldwide. An attempt to answer the question of compatibility of Islam and democracy necessitates a thorough examination of the inherent religious aspects of Islamic thought, and their relationship with modern democratic values. Though, it is not the aim of the paper to provide argument and counterargument regarding Islam and democracy debate, it is worthwhile to explore the existing debate. While discussing the debate on Islam and democracy, we must keep in mind the ambiguity and interpretations of the term democracy. [2]

Prevailing media and intellectual circles in the West (acknowledging there are few exceptions) view Islam as being at the root of authoritarian polity in the Muslim world. For them, since, Islam believes in god's sovereignty, popular power has diminished. (Lewis 1994: 54) Huntington (1996) sees Islam as a menace to the Western culture and even predicted the possibility of a civilizational conflict in the future between Islam and the West. He points out that the Islamic world has been largely unaffected by the political revolution called the "Third Wave" of democratization. (Huntington 1991)

Choueiri (1996:22) observes the Islamic belief in God's sovereignty goes hand in hand with the doctrine of *jihad* and that ultimately leads Islam to be identified with totalitarian state. Fauzi M. Najjar (1958:175) argues Islam has very little in common with modem democracy and there is no scope for democratic change in Islamic world without undergoing a serious reformation of its basic principles. He says that for adopting a democratic form of government Islam must realize that they are essentially incompatible with modem democracy. Some Western scholars often quote Abu-l Ala' Mawdudi's political views for supporting their argument that Islam is the very antithesis of democracy. Mawdudi's examination of the 'theory of the caliphate and the nature of democracy in Islam' explicitly reveals the democratic principles that rooted in Islamic teachings. Mawdudi opines "Islam is a society in which everyone is a caliph of God, and an equal participation in the Caliphate. It cannot tolerate any class divisions". (Donohue and Esposito, 2007: 268)

Azam Tamimi (2007) traces the history of intellectual debate on Islam and democracy through analyzing the views of Rifa'ah al-Tahtawi, Khyar al-din Tunisi, Jamal al-din Afgani, Abdurrahman al-Kawakibi, Malik Bennabi and Raschid al-Ghannouchi. These thinkers are unambiguous about the inherency of democratic principles in Islam. Rashid Ghannouchi, one among them advocates an Islamic system that features majority rule, free elections, a free press, protection of minorities, equality of all secular and religious parties, and full women's rights in everything from polling booths, dress codes, and divorce courts to the top job at the presidential palace. According to him believers are guaranteed the right of *ijtihad* (independent reasoning) in interpreting the Qur'anic texts. The democratic values of political pluralism and tolerance are rightly compatible with Islam. (Donohue and Esposito, 2007)

Omar Caha (2003) has made a brilliant study about the possibility of the reconciliation of Islam with democratic values. He notes by nature Islam does not oppose to human contribution. Islam begin with an appeal to human reason. Before assigning one of his companions for governorship, the Prophet wanted to know as to how he planned to resolve possible problems, which he would encounter in his place of tenure. The answer was "I will try to resolve them on the basis of the Quran, Sunnah and my own opinion". This suggests that, in Islam, there is ample scope for freedom of action as far as Muslim rulers are concerned. According to Caha '*the Medina Agreement*'[3] was determined by historical condition rather than religion. He compares the values of Islam and liberal democracy in a historical way.

Advocates of incompatibility thesis observe individual and religious freedom are absent in Islam. But, a more correct interpretation, based on the sacred text and valid traditions, finds Islam highly supportive of freedom of thought and religion. There are a number of Qur'anic verses that support the notion of freedom of religion and belief. For instance, "there is no compulsion in religion", "O unbelievers, I serve not what you serve and you are not serving what I serve….. To you your religion, and to me my religion". (Kamrava, 2006) There is no inherent incompatibility between democracy and Islam. Like all scriptures, the Qur'an can be interpreted to support many different types of political behavior and systems of government. (Zartman, 1992)

Abdul Karim Soroush, an eminent Islamic scholar in the contemporary era argues there is no contradiction between Islam and freedoms inherent in democracy. Islam and democracy are not only compatible, their association is inevitable also. Soroush says Islamic religion is evolving one. Sacred texts do not change, but interpretation of them is always in flux because understanding is influenced by the age and the changing conditions in which believers live. (Wright, 1996) Eckelman and Piscotari (1996) also recognize the possibility of the compatibility of Islam and democracy. According to them the diversity of ideological interpretations and actual political practices are there in Muslim societies. Esposito and Voll (1993) notes Islamic concepts like *shura* (consultation), *ijma* (consensus) and *ijtihad* (independent judgement) seems to be compatible with democratic principles and ideals. The Islamic law has made off with four sources, namely Qur'an, *Sunnah*, *ijma* (consensus of the Muslims), and *kıyas* (analogy). Three of these sources are human constructs and have a cultural character. In other words, sources other than the Qur'an are not revelations from God, but are human-oriented. Consensus of the learned and analogy are surely human activities since they are products of an alliance among Muslims and their individual opinions.

It is true that the phenomenon of globalization promotes the value of democracy at ideational level. It highlights the success of liberal democracy in managing the field of globalization through the controls over the media, economy, trade routes and also the international institutions. One of the major objectives of contemporary globalization is to create a global citizen with same magnitude and mind settings. It would promote the expansion of western market and liberal democracy into the other parts of the world. One can hypothetically argue that if the field of globalization managed by the East, eastern ideas and values will be promoted globally. The concept of 'oriental globalization' describes a world system existed in the past that was dominated by the Eastern ideas and goods. (see Frank, 2002; Hobson, 2004) Hence, the challenges brought by globalization to Islam are a matter of competitive legitimacy rather than absolute legitimacy.

Asef Bayat (2007) observe the failure and contradictions of Islamist project that entailed a rethinking of Islamism from within the global context of globalization of languages of civil society, pluralism and democracy. As stated above, globalization of the languages of civil society and democracy is a question of competitive legitimacy. The adoption of this globalized language by Islamic political movement is not a matter of failure and success. It is only a matter of accommodation, reconciliation and changing strategies.

Islamic Resurgence in Twentieth Century West Asia

Islamic resurgence was one of the significant phenomenon in the Twentieth century. There are two dominant views in resurgent literatures. The first set of scholars argue that it was Islam's instinct political nature that leads to the resurgence of political Islam. They see Islam as a religion prone to politicization. Islam's link with politics is a question predominantly important in modern times. The political system of Islam is based on three principles of '*tawheedd*' [3] (Oneness of God) '*risala*'(Prophethood) and *Khilafa* (Caliphate). *Risala* is the medium through which Islam receive the laws of Allah, Qur'an and its authoritative interpretation (*Sharia*). An analysis of the political face of Islam would inevitably be helpful to understand the fact that from the very beginning itself Islam has a close nexus with the political affairs. The social and religious teachings of Islam gave birth to Islamic resurgence and Muslim politics.

Yet another view is that the radical Islamic movements have arisen in reaction to the attempts of rapid modernization and developments, the process which could not fulfill the expectations of the majority of the population in Muslim countries. (Esposito, 2000) In the second half of the 20th Century national state failed to handle the tasks of development. The result has been the rise of radical Islam which promises an alternative to the secular institution of the national state. Simon W. Murden (2002) argues that the Islamic revival was a consequence of social failure of Muslim societies. To a large extent militant Islamic groups is the result of disillusioned youth revolt in many countries of West Asia. In the 1950s, and 1960s the hopes of people in the Arab world was based on socialism and pan-Arabism. When these ideologies failed there was a strong 'return to Islam'. "The reaction to the fading dream of modernization was tempered by the ideological appeal of nationalism and by the absence of plausible alternative". (Tibi, 2001)

In 1950 and 60's Islam was sidelined by Nationalist Secularist states, but the political and economic failure of these states opened the way for return of Islam. The Islamic revival from 1970's manifested itself in many ways. Ordinary Muslims reaffirmed Islamic rituals and social practices. Muslim intellectuals turned away from Western thoughts and bend towards Islamic references. (Murden, 2002) Akhbar S. Ahmed (1991: 12) points out "Modernism in Muslim society is engendered by European colonialism. The modern period had led the Muslims into a cul-de-sac. Muslims, as most people who beliefs in God asked "if God had abandoned them". The other Muslims turned the question round, they had abandoned God. The answer turns to the direction of Islam, and that ultimately turn to God". (Ahmad, 1991) The increase in

Muslim activism in recent decades is driven by many factors, first, influential radical thinkers have insisted that Muslim must go beyond the spiritual *jihad* (the struggle to be a good Muslim) second, growth in literary and global communication has made Muslims more conscious of being part of a broader Islamic community, third much of the Muslim world, is afflicted with failed states and corrupt regimes. (Norton, 2002)

The decline of Arab nationalism and Arab socialism also promoted the rise of Islamic resistance movements in various parts of the Muslim world. The branches of Muslim Brotherhood established in Egypt in 1928 by Hasan al Banna was the principal transnational network in the Arab world. The popular Islamic political movements in Algeria, Syria, Jordan, Egypt, Tunisia and the Israeli occupied territories claimed connections to the Muslim Brotherhood. In the 1970s and 1980s a wave of Islamic inspired instability swept across the Muslim world. *Gama-al Islamiya in Egypt and al jihadi in Saudi Arabia, Hizb- al Tahir al islami* (Islamic Liberation Party) and Muhammad's army in Jordan, *Hezbollah* in Lebanon and Hamas in occupied territory were emerged as an encounter with the failed nationalist rulers and western modernity. Ayubi (1981) summarizes the consequences of rapid economic development in West Asia. Across the Muslim world fundamentalists mobilized Muslims for political ends. Universities and Mosque became the centers of new politics. The Islamic movements sought to create a parallel society at the local level but it also organized across national and the international spaces.

Hamas: The Islamic Heir of Palestinian National Movement

Hamas–Islamic Resistance Movement (Harkat al-muqauwama al-Islamiya) emerged out of the Palestinian branch of the Muslim brotherhood (*Ikhwan)* in 1987 during the first intifada. Since then the organization is one of the active parties in the Israeli-Palestinian conflict. Hamas emerged as an

Islamic alternative to the secular PLO and made endeavor to Islamize the Palestine question and the Palestinian polity. A close study of Hamas' strategies reveals a similarity to other Islamic movements in the Arab world concerning political participations. The religious idiom has always played an important role in the evolution of Palestinian nationalism and in the Palestinian Israeli conflict. At the heart of Hamas' ideology is the emphasis on the 'Islamic essence' of the Palestinian cause. Hamas therefore criticizes the PLO for portraying the conflict as one between Palestinian nationalism and Zionism. The religious essence of the conflict means that it is first and foremost a 'war of religion and faith.

To clearly understand the attitude of Hamas towards Palestinian nationalism, we should examine its Islamic identity through the affiliation with Muslim Brotherhood. Muslim brotherhood is a group founded in Egypt in 1928 by Hasan al-Banna aiming at working towards the establishment of an Islamic state in the Muslims countries. In the occupied territories the Brotherhood adopted charity and educational works and avoiding direct confrontation with Israel. Sheik Ahmed Yazin (later became Hamas' leader) was the Brotherhood's main representative in occupied territories.

On December 8, 1987 a motor accident between an Israeli truck and vehicles transporting Palestinian workers triggered riots that grew to a wider popular uprising later known as *intifada.* But there are many other factors stood behind the formation of Hamas. The traditional governments of West Asia and other organizations used Islam for their political legitimacy. Islamic revolution in Iran, armed struggle in Algeria and Lebanon accelerated the formation of Hamas. Hamas formed in the shadow of great distress which rooted in the minds of Palestinian minds. The birth of Hamas represented the Palestinian embodiment of resurgent (political) Islam in the Middle East. (Roy, 2003)

In the initial stages of its growth Hamas followed a negative response towards the Palestinian peace process. They were not ready to recognize Israel as a state and its right to exist for a long time. In September 1989, Israel declared Hamas an illegal organization and Hamas, therefore, started its military operations in 1994 with a suicide bombing on Israeli city. Israel retaliated with targeted killing of Hamas leaders and activists. Yehiyeh Ayyash, a top leader of *al Qassem brigade* –Hamas' armed wing, Saleh Shehada, Ismail Shanab, Sheik Ahmd Yazin and Abdul Aziz Rantizi were killed by Israeli attack. The charter of the Islamic Resistance Movement which codifies the ideology, beliefs and aims of the movement stated that 'Israel is a new crusader state'. Hamas' ultimate proclaimed goal is the liberation of Palestine and the establishment of an Islamic state in the liberated land. It includes the Islamization of society, the process of making Islam more central to public and private life. (Gunning, 2004)

Hamas—Changing Strategies

Since the emergence in the late 1980s, perhaps the most significant turning point in Hamas's political life has been its victory in the January 2006 Palestinian Council (PC) elections in the West Bank and the Gaza Strip. Overnight, it was transformed from an opposition movement that had no part in the "national" governing structure to a party called upon to govern. (Hourb, 2006) Hamas transition from a so called terrorist outfit to a political party of national standing is very significant one not only in the context of Palestinian national movement but in the context of ideological transformation of Islamic resurgence movements also. Its attitudes towards elections and peace process and even towards Israel's right to existence are transforming. In 1993 Hamas publicly rejected Oslo Accord and in 1992, the organization published an internal bulletin which presented its position on elections. Hamas had been a strong critic of Declaration of Principles and elections. The explanation was the movement ruled out participation because elections were bound to be a part of humiliating and shameful agreement and because it was assumed that they would be held under Israeli dominations. (Mishal and Sela, 2002:13)

The transformation process in Hamas did not, however, start with its entrance into parliamentary politics in 2006, but can be traced back to the mid-1990s when Hamas started searching for political accommodation within the status quo of Palestinian society. (Roy, 2005) The substantial changes that the movement has undergone since that time can be understood at the ideological as well as at the behavioural level. At the ideological level, the evolution in the movement's main documents is illuminating. By the beginning of 2005 it became apparent that Hamas had followed a change in strategies. Hamas ready to talk with Palestinian Authority and PLO, and Cairo meeting paved the way for Hamas to concentrate its energies on challenges to share power in Palestinian legislature. Hamas was seen to be redefined its strategy of proposed power sharing in the Palestine Authority and Fatah. (Edwards, 2005:318) In the first round elections Hamas won enough votes to secure a majority in the Gaza strip. May 2005 elections Hamas won over 2, 70,000 votes than the Fatah rivals. By the end of second round local elections Hamas won 48 seats. Hamas' victory in the legislative elections of January 25, 2006 appeared to be a surprise for the local and global community. Hamas enjoyed a resounding victory in Palestinian Legislative Council elections and secured 74 seats out of 132.

Since its victory, the entire debate was focused on Hamas' lack of political experiences. Does the Hamas victory advance peace in the Middle East? Is democracy served by the electoral gains of Islamists and why Islamism is so appealing to the electorate? To answer these question one should examine the evolving thoughts and strategies of Hamas. A scrutiny of Hamas' new documents namely; 2005 Electoral Platform, Draft of National Unity Government and the Cabinet Platform of 2006 will be helpful. The movements widening perspective is explicit in these documents. Unfortunately, these remarkable documents are excluded from the discussions of western media and policy makers.

The Electoral Platform for Change and Reform begins with political justifications for the Hamas changed position, "compelled by our conviction that we are defending one of the greatest ports of Islam; and by our duty to reform the Palestinian reality and alleviate the suffering of our people and shielding them from corruption, as well as by our hope to strengthen national unity and Palestinian internal affairs, we have decided to take part in the Palestinian legislative elections". (Quoted in Hourb, 2006) The fourteen page document comprises broadest visions concerning all aspects of Palestinian life and guarantees a political action based on political freedoms and pluralism.

The draft of National Unity Government Program comprises thirty-nine articles reveals the external pressure on Hamas to recognize international conventions and agreements on Palestine. It emphasizes the rebuilding of democratic institutions and civil society (ibid). The Cabinet Platform delivered by Ismail Haniyeh on 27 March 2006 before the newly elected parliament is remarkable in the context of changing strategies. The document renounces the factional, tribal and clan chauvinisms and reinforcing the *shura* (consultancy) and democracy. It asserted that " we stress the need to reinforce the spirit of tolerance, cooperation, coexistence among the Muslims, the Christians and the Samaritans in the framework of citizenship that does not discriminate against any on the basis of religion"(Hourb). These documents symbolize an evolution of Hamas' political thinking toward pragmatism by denouncing the radical positions.

Besides these documents, the opinions of Hamas second generation leaders will be helpful to find the democratic concern developing into the movement. New leaders and spokesman of Hamas are confident in their Islamic and democratic credentials. Mashhour Abdel Halim, Hamas's leader in the Bourj el-Barajneh Camp in Beirut, referred to the *shura* (assembly) system as described in the Quran to illustrate that the idea of a people's assembly is not foreign to Islam. It is crystal clear according to a verse in the Holy Quran that within the system of *shura* Islamic decision makers must respect the view of the majority. (Hovdenak, 2009) Further, he explained that Hamas belongs to a tradition within the Islamic movement that accepts that there is room for *ijtihad,* that is, interpretation of the Holy Scripture, which is important for Hamas's appearance as a politically flexible movement with high capabilities to adapt to rapidly changing circumstances and conditions.

Hamas' leader Mesh'al' words, clearly represents the movements changing strategies and adherence to political pluralism. "Be with us, and don't abandon political partnership. Our hearts are open for you; our hands are extended to you. Let us turn a new page, and work together for the best of our people based on mutual respect and cooperation. We are one people, united in the resistance, and must unite in the political arena as well"(PIC website). Dr. Salah Bardawil leader of Hamas in southern Gaza said in the Arabic language edition of Ashasrq al-Awsat, January 30, 2006 "Hamas has absolutely never and is absolutely not thinking of the enactment of any laws that impose Islamic teachings and force upon the society." He said religious teachings are followed when they are accepted by the people "not when they are imposed by terrorizing and frightening". (Chandan, 2009) Sheikh Yassin once stated that "I want a multi-party democratic state, and I want whosoever wins those elections to assume power." When asked by the interviewer if this would still be the case if the Communist Party were to win the elections Sheikh Yassin replied "I would respect the wishes of the Palestinian people even if the Communist Party won" (ibid).

Hence, one can conclude that Hamas' political ideology and practice is one that shares many principles with Western democratic and progressive ideas. Instead of being inspired by the secular democratic traditions of the Western milieu, the movement is enthused by similar principles in the cultural context and traditions of Arab and Islamic history. Hamas eventual moderation was driven in part by strategic calculation and political learning and a product of changes in international context. We have come across some major departures from the founding principles of the Hamas over the course of its political evolution. The final and perhaps most important accommodation made by the Hamas was their newfound willingness to work with political parties like Fatah, Popular Front for the Liberation of Palestinian (PLFP) and Democratic Front for the Liberation of Palestinian (DLFP). Hamas has essentially made the choice to work within given political systems.

Conclusion

The changing strategies and visions of Hamas help us to reformulate the Islam and democracy debate in a fruitful manner. Rather than failure and contradictions of Islamic movement it shows their strategies of reconciliation and accommodation in changing local and global context. It also shows the adaptability by Islamic political system and the democratic values. The landslide victory of Hamas was a realization for the entire Islamic movements that they can approach people with their changing strategies and goals. It also proves that their public support that was much higher than they expect.

On the one hand it denotes the success of Islamic political movements by engaging with the changing context and needs of the society where they are slot. On the other it implicitly and explicitly shows the failure of liberal democracy and the entire democratization project in the Arab world. The project of democratization aims to replace Islam from the socio-political realm of the Arab world and to delegitimize its principles and teachings. The project intends to defeat and sideline the Islamic movements from people. But the Islamic movement cleverly utilizes the same ideology for their benefit. Through participating in electoral politics, the movements not only overcome the western led democratization project in the Arab World. These democratic experience also help us to counter the incompatibility thesis about Islam and democracy.

Notes

1. Both the orthodox West and authoritative rulers in the Muslim world have a significant role in promoting the *compatibility thesis*. The former developed and popularized the compatibility thesis for legitimizing the values of Western liberal ideology an the later has utilized the thesis for legitimizing their despotic rule.
2. Democracy is, generally, accepted as a mode of governance, which came to the fore and evolved as an alternative to despotic regimes prevailing in both traditional and modern societies. The most fundamental values of democracy are human rights and liberties. Various scholars defined and interpret democracy in different ways. (See Giovanni Sartori's The Theory of Democracy Revisited, 1987).
3. There are three categories of *tawheed* commonly referred; *Tawheed al-Ruboobeeyah (*Unity of Lordship*), Tawheed al-Asmaa was-sifaat (*Unity of Allah's Names and Attributes) and *Tawheed al-Ebaadah* (Unity of Allah's Worship).

References

Ahmad, Akbar S. (1991), *Post Modernism and Islam*, London: Routledge.

Akbarzadeh, Shahram (2006), "Does the Hamas Victory Advance Peace in the Middle East", *Australian Journal of International Affairs*, 60(2):201-206.

Ayubi, Nazih M. (1991), Political Islam: Religion and Politics in the Arab World, London: Routledge.

Bayat, Asef (2007), Making Islam Democratic: Social Movements and Post-Islamist Turn, Stanford: Stanford University Press.

Caha, Omar (2003), "Islam and Democracy: A Theoretical Discussion on the Compatibility of Islam and Democracy", *Alternatives,* 2(3&4):106-134.

Chandan, Sukant (2009), http://www.recogniseresistance.net.

Choueiri, Youssef M. (1990), *Islamic Fundamentalism*, London: Pinter.

Donohue, John J. and John L Esposito (2006), *Islam in Transition: Muslim Perspectives*, New York: Oxford University Press.

Eickleman Dale F. and James Piscatori (1990), *Muslim Politics*, Princeton: Princeton University Press.

Esposito John L. and John O. Voll (1996), *Islam and Democracy,* Oxford: Oxford University Press.

Frank, A. G. (2002), *Reorient: Global Economy in Asian Ag,* California: University of California Press.

Gunning, Jeroin (2004), "Peace with Hamas? The Transforming Potential of Political Participations", *International Affairs,* 80(2): 233-55.

Hobson, John M. (2004), *Eastern Origin of Western Civilization,* Cambridge: Cambridge University Press.

Hovdenak, Are (2009), "Hamas in Transition: The Failure of Sanctions', *Democratization* 16(1):59- 80.

Hroub, Khaled (2006), "A "New Hamas" Through its New Documents", *Journal of Palestine Studies,* 35(4):6-27.

Huntington, Samuel P. (1996), "Clash of Civilizations and the Remaking of World Order", New York: Simon& Schuster.

Huntington, Samuel P. (1991), *The Third Wave*, Norman: University of Oklahoma Press.

Kamrava, Marvan Ed. (2006), New Voices of Islam: Rethinking Politics and Modernity- A Reader, London: I. B. Tauris.

Kedourie, Elie (1992), *Politics in the Middle East,* Oxford: Oxford University Press.

Kramer, Martin (1996), "Fundamentalist Islam at Large: The Drive for Power", *Middle East Quarterly*, 3(2):37-49.

Lewis, Bernard (1994), *Islam and the West*, Oxford: Oxford University Press.

Midlarsky, Manus I. (1998), "Democracy and Islam: Implications for Civilizational Conflict and the Democratic Peace", *International Studies Quarterly*, 42(3): 485-511.

Milton-Edwards, Beverley (2007), "Hamas: Victory with Ballots and Bullets", *Global Change Peace & Security*, 19(3):301-316.

Milton-Edwards, Beverly, (2005), "Prepared for Power: Hamas Governance and Conflict", *Civil War* 7(4): 311- 329.

Mishal, Shaul and Avraham Sela (2002), "Participation without Presence: Hamas, the Palestinian Authority and Politics of Negotiated Coexistence", *Middle Eastern Studies*, 38(3).

Murden, W. Simon (2002), *Islam Middle East and New Global Hegemony*, London: Lyhne Rienner Publications.

Najjar, Fauzi M. (1958), "Islam and Modern Democracy" *The Review of Politics,* 20(2):164-180.

Norton, R. A. (2002), "Activism and Reform in Islam", *Current History,* 101(658).

Roy, Sara (2003), "Hamas and the Political Islam in Palestine", *Current History,* 102(660).

Roy, Sara (2008), Failing Peace. Gaza and the Palestinian-Israeli Conflict, London: Pluto Press.

Sartori, Giovanni (1987), *The Theory of Democracy Revisited,* New Jersey: Chatham House Publishers.

Tamimi, Azaam (2007), *Hamas: Unwritten Chapters,* London: Hurst and Company.

Tamimi, Aazam (2007), "Islam and Democracy from Tahtawi to Ghannouchi", *Theory, Culture and Society,* 24: 39-58.

Tibi, Basam (2005), *Islam Between Culture and Politics,* New York: MacMillan.

Wright, Robin (1996), "Islam and Liberal Democracy: Two Visions of Reformation," *Journal of Democracy,* 7.2: 64-75.

Zartman I. William (1992), "Democracy and Islam: The Cultural Dialectic", *Annals of the American Academy of Political and Social Science,* 524:181-191.

Index

Index